Living in an Environmentally Traumatized World

Living in an Environmentally Traumatized World

Healing Ourselves and Our Planet

Darlyne G. Nemeth, Robert B. Hamilton, and Judy Kuriansky, Editors

Practical and Applied Psychology
Judy Kuriansky, Series Editor

 PRAEGER

AN IMPRINT OF ABC-CLIO, LLC
Santa Barbara, California • Denver, Colorado • Oxford, England

Library of Congress Cataloging-in-Publication Data

Living in an environmentally traumatized world : healing ourselves and our planet / Darlyne G. Nemeth, Robert B. Hamilton, and Judy Kuriansky, editors.
    p. cm. — (Practical and applied psychology)
    Includes bibliographical references and index.
    ISBN 978–0–313–39731–8 (hbk. : alk. paper) — ISBN 978–0–313–39732–5 (e-book)
1. Environmental psychology. 2. Climatic changes—Psychological aspects. 3. Human ecology—Psychological aspects. 4. Global environmental change—Psychological aspects. I. Nemeth, Darlyne Gaynor. II. Hamilton, Robert B. III. Kuriansky, Judith.
BF353.5.C55L58   2012
155.9—dc23   2012022710

ISBN: 978–0–313–39731–8
EISBN: 978–0–313–39732–5

16 15 14 13 12   1 2 3 4 5

This book is also available on the World Wide Web as an eBook.
Visit www.abc-clio.com for details.

Praeger
An Imprint of ABC-CLIO, LLC

ABC-CLIO, LLC
130 Cremona Drive, P.O. Box 1911
Santa Barbara, California 93116-1911

This book is printed on acid-free paper ∞

Manufactured in the United States of America

To all of the world's peoples and living things,
To those who have experienced environmental trauma,
and
To the world's biosphere
that is critically in need of our protection,
we dedicate this book.
Darlyne G. Nemeth
Robert B. Hamilton
Judy Kuriansky

Contents

Series Foreword

A terrifying tidal wave washes away thousands of precious lives. The earth moves under our feet, leaving thousands lifeless and homeless. With so many earthquakes, tsunamis, fires, floods, tornados, and other environmental tragedies in our present day, nature is wreaking havoc on our personal and global world. Given so many natural disasters, many say this is the worst of all times. So, how can we cope—and heal? This book offers hope.

So many times, I have been with survivors after such tragedies who ask, "Why did this happen?"; "Will it recur?"; "How can I go on?" Having been a mental health volunteer after so many natural disasters all over the world, I know how important it is to understand such events intellectually and to rebuild emotionally. The work presented in these pages helps on both those fronts. For that reason, I am proud to have this book, *Living in an Environmentally Traumatized World: Healing Ourselves and Our Planet*, in my Practical and Applied Psychology series, to be part of the editing team, and to present it to you as readers.

This book is pioneering in bringing together experts in the fields of psychology and ecoscience, weaving the two disciplines together. Thanks to the brilliant team of my co-editors, Dr. Darlyne Nemeth and Bob Hamilton, eminent themselves in the two fields respectively, we are treated to a holistic view of our world. Even with decades of experience in the field of disaster recovery, in working on this book, I have learned so much. I now understand about ecosystems and the biosphere, and how these important concepts relate to psychological issues—leading to feelings of being more in control, prepared, resilient, and empowered.

At a United Nations Department of Public Information/Non Governmental Organization (DPI/NGO) conference in Bonn, Germany, called "Sustainable Societies: Responsible Citizens," attendees at the opening event were greeted by characters on stilts dancing around us, fancifully dressed to represent the four elements: air, water, earth, and fire. Dancing with them was delightful, but the message implicit in the celebration, and in this book, is profound: we are an intimate part of our environment. We must know as much as we can about our planet and about ourselves to cope and heal, to survive and thrive.

Dr. Judy Kuriansky, PhD
Series Editor, Practical and Applied Psychology

Preface

Darlyne G. Nemeth, Robert B. Hamilton, and
Judy Kuriansky

Living is a matter of experiencing life to the fullest. It is the essence of being, in contrast to existing, which can be defined as a matter of surviving in difficult times. No matter what circumstances we face, the challenge is to live—not to merely exist—in our world. Indeed, our world can be defined as about us, our family, our neighborhood, our community, our country or our universe. I can be defined as one of these, some combination, or all of them. In this book, we propose that our world is defined by the microcosm of ourselves but also by the macrocosm of our collective selves that comprise our world. How we define our world and ourselves at every moment in time determines our future. All definitions, of course, are a product of our unique past; but they must also include an acute awareness of the present and a hopeful anticipation of the future.

Living life to the fullest also requires being fully aware of ourselves and whether we are acutely aware of this precious moment in time or are merely passively accepting the passage of time. It also requires using gifts we possess as humans, namely, the abilities to think, reason, plan and solve problems. These skills are essential in order to cope with our currently environmentally challenged world. Living life to the fullest also involves being fully aware of ourselves in our environment. That is what this book addresses. We live in a context of our environment, which sadly is all too often subjected to trauma. Assuredly, every generation has had to face unique tragic circumstances, but the aggregate of such traumas has been daunting in our times. Some tragic large-scale circumstances we have been facing are human-made, including mass violence, wars and terrorism. Others are caused by natural disasters such as floods, tornadoes, tsunamis, earthquakes, and hurricanes. History is replete with these occurrences, but the number and variety of these are extensive in our lifetime. As a result, this book was created to serve is a valuable resource to cope with the current environmental traumas.

This book takes a holistic view of our environment that is necessary for coping with these traumas. Chapters address an understanding of natural science as well as psychological science, as an integrative way to cope with our environmentally challenged world and to heal ourselves and our planet. Our holistic view makes valuable connections between the disciplines of natural science and psychology, given the perspective that we have to understand our world from various integrated dimensions in order to cope effectively. The importance of such connection was documented by the American Psychological Association Task Force on Psychology and Global Climate Change (American Psychological Association, 2010). The co-editors of this book recognized the importance of this holistic approach when presenting a workshop about healing ourselves and our planet from environmental traumas, at the 2007 United Nations Department of Public Information/NGO Conference on Climate Change held in New York City (Nemeth et al., 2007). At our workshop, as in this book, we brought together experts from the fields of psychology and natural science to present approaches to the problems of climate change that are contributing to the occurrence of natural disasters. We emphasized the importance of understanding the natural science of disasters and climate change as well as the psychological ramifications, and then applying these perspectives to real-world situations in order to take practical action. Along with this multi-disciplinary view, we recommended a problem-solving model based on four steps: (1) Identify the problem, (2) Conduct analysis, (3) Define approaches, and (4) Devise Action Ideas and Plans (Fisher, Ury, and Patton, 1991).

The holistic model presented in this book is further grounded in sound psychological principles derived mainly from Gestalt psychology. Originated in Germany over a century ago by three important theorists, Kurt Koffka, Wolfgang Kohler, and Max Wertheimer, the gestalt perspective reminds us that "parts derive their nature and functions from the wholes in which they exist and cannot be understood apart from their wholes" (Wolman, 1989). Our current age of specialization has taken us too far a field from the valuable Gestalt view that the whole is greater than the sum of its parts; that every aspect of our living world contributes to the occurrences of, and coping with, environmental changes and disasters. Thus, the chapters in this book are meant to provide a view of the forest, as well as the trees.

Humankind has certainly survived many environmental changes in the past. We now face increasing challenges and are sure to face more challenges ahead. For this, we need to understand the nature of our holistic world, from the perspectives of natural science and psychology, in order to deal with changes and to be prepared to minimize further traumas. To help us cope and prepare, this book presents valuable explanations of our environment and invaluable ways to minimize damage to human health and well-being in the face of environmental challenges. Both future natural catastrophes and the unexpected consequence of human-made changes are assessed and addressed. Throughout, we emphasize that change is inevitable; we must plan for it and manage it as well as possible, to greatly reduce future disruptions. Overriding principles throughout these chapters are that accurate information must be available for all in order to cope and that working together is essential to live in harmony with our ever-changing, environmentally-challenged world.

Over time, our relationship to the environment becomes increasingly different and more complex than in earlier times. Fortunately, we are beginning to pay more attention to our relationship to our planet and our resources. On one hand, as humans we affect our environment; as the population increases, we have more demand for more resources and put more strain on or planet. On the other hand, natural and unexpected forces greatly impact us, forcing change. While humankind has survived environmental challenges throughout the past, can we survive the traumas of the present and those of the future? This book explores ways we can do that.

In the face of environmental traumas, we cannot afford to be passive. The earth needs help. Our land, waters, and air are changing. Populations of plants and animals are disappearing, and entire species are becoming extinct as their habitats are altered or eliminated. Accompanying these changes, people are getting sick and suffering with disease, famine, abuse, and hunger. Will we ignore all of this or choose to be aware, and do something about it? All too often in history and present times, people sit back and think, "It cannot happen to me" and "It cannot happen now." But what we do now is crucial for our survival. Now is the time that our lives and our planet are in danger because of changes that have happened or that we have made. Now is the time to wake up and do something to stem the tide of potential destruction.

Opening our eyes and choosing to see the present and impending problems of our environment is challenging. The world is not static, but constantly changing. Many changes occur naturally and can be devastating. According to the United Nations's Hyogo Framework, natural hazards such as earthquakes, hurricanes, tsunamis, and floods are defined as "natural phenomena." While most natural phenomena may be inevitable, "disasters" are not. A disaster results from the combination of the naturally occurring hazards, combined with conditions of vulnerability (such as inadequate housing or settlements located in disaster-prone areas) and insufficient capacity to cope with this situation.

Given this distinction, a multilevel disaster risk-reduction strategy must be developed to minimize a society's vulnerability to disaster and avoid or limit the impact of natural hazards. We must do what we can to ensure that earthquakes, hurricanes, volcanic eruptions, tsunamis, and floods are only hazards and do not become disasters. We must plan to minimize human mortality, injuries, illnesses, and psychological and social stress. We must also rebuild the environment to be conducive to our future well-being. Devastating disasters like fires, floods, and mudslides in nature are caused or greatly aggravated by activities of humans. Therefore, even in the case of events we think we cannot control, we are responsible to prevent as much disaster as possible by our actions.

Knowledge is power, and from that knowledge comes appropriate actions. Once we are armed with knowledge and options to act, we are energized and can make a difference. We can prepare for anticipated as well as unexpected changes—including dramatic ones that will inevitably befall our environment, whether we like it or not.

The time for passivity is over. Change is inevitable; in fact, our very existence causes change. As the number of humans on this planet increases, environmental changes accelerate, resources become depleted, contamination and pollution accumulate and energy use increases. This induces even more change. This book reviews the nature of our environment in all its aspects, from flora and fauna to the natural elements of air and water, to the actions that humankind takes, and can take, in dealing with changes. We discuss past changes and how they have influenced the present and foreshadow the future; we review how localized change affects unanticipated places and discuss how uncertainty increases as changes modify our biosphere.

The warning bells have already sounded, as evidenced from the extent of traumatic events that have already beset our environment and our lives. All living things, lands, peoples and resources are important. The air, the planet, and the biosphere must be valued and protected so that we may have a safe and healthy present and tomorrow.

This book examines the status of our environment, from the oceans to the mountains, from the birds that fly in the air to the fish and mammals that live in the sea, from the mysteries of the forests to the vastness of the deserts. All aspects are considered in perspective to how humans cope with their environment. Survival depends on knowing what is happening at every level of our biosphere. This information allows us to develop integrated management systems that not only answer today's problems but also ensure sustainability in the foreseeable future. Environmental tragedies have shown us that shortsighted solutions can lead to unintended consequences, with devastating results, evidenced by the faulty protection plan for the levees in New Orleans, the city in the United States that suffered from the breaks in the barriers that led to massive flooding and devastation.

To survive, and prevent, environmental tragedies in our current world, humans must solve issues like "How do we preserve our forests?" "Are we endangering other species that may ultimately endanger our own survival?" and "How do we emotionally cope with the tragedies that leaves us bereft of loved ones, home, and livelihood?" Regarding our resources, it is time to understand, and evaluate, use of our lands, waters, and air we breathe. Energy and natural resources are necessary for life, but how we use them can further endanger our existence. While natural phenomena may lead to a tragedy, we can also exacerbate the problem, as happened in northern Japan in the case of the 2011 tsunami/earthquake that led to the explosion in the Fukushima nuclear power plants. Mankind could not control the waters but flaws in the power plant design prevented operation of essential pumps.

Chapters in this book importantly address recent environmental changes, as well as our own actions that have greatly impacted our lives. For example, cutting down the cypress swamps south of New Orleans and building more canals through the wetlands have greatly reduced the natural barriers to hurricane devastation. All natural disasters cause devastation and are thus similar in all cases, yet, resulting damages and disruptions of some disasters can also differ, depending on human behavior. In the case of the earthquakes in Haiti and Chile in 2010, differences in the infrastructure and human institutions of these two countries led to different outcomes. Stricter building codes in Chile resulted in less damage than the much more lenient ones in Haiti. Many valuable lessons can be learned from analyzing such differences and evaluating the results of different practices. The British Petroleum oil spill in the Gulf of Mexico—the explosion of the oil rig that led to 11 deaths and dumped tons of toxic waste in the waters—and our reactions to it are instructive on many levels and illustrate many points made in this book. The after-effects of that crisis continues to affect the habitat, animal and plant life, and health and welfare of people. Similarly, the nuclear power plant explosion in Japan continues to endanger our waters and food supply, spreading toxicity across the oceans years later. The environmental disaster in Japan represents a multilevel environmental disaster, as a combination of natural and human-induced problems stemming from the earthquake, tsunami and nuclear power plant deficiencies. These disasters, their causes and consequences are examined in these chapters, so that we can minimize and, better yet, eliminate future problems, both expected and unexpected.

The overriding theme of this book is that we must prepare, preserve, and protect our selves and our world from environmental changes and disasters. Armed with the information for these chapters, we can do this.

REFERENCES

American Psychological Association. (2010). *Psychology and global climate change: Addressing a multi-faceted phenomenon and set of challenges.* Report of the American Psychological Association Task Force on the Interface between Psychology and Global Climate Change.

Fisher, R., Ury, W. L., & Patton, B. M. (1991). *Getting to yes: Negotiating agreement without giving in*. New York: Penguin Books.

Nemeth, D. G., Garrido, G., Onishi, Y., Hamilton, B., Nemeth, D., & Albuquerque, J. (2007, September). *Strategies to facilitate biosphere management and lifestyle change: Measures to protect the environment and prevent drastic sequelae of current and future climate changes*. Symposium presented at the 60th Annual United Nations DPI/NGO Conference Midday Workshops, New York.

Wolman, B. B. (Ed.) (1989). *Dictionary of behavioral science* (2nd ed.). San Diego, CA: Academic Press, Inc.

Acknowledgments

DARLYNE NEMETH

I am so blessed to have Judy Kuriansky and Bob Hamilton as my dear friends and Don Nemeth as my wonderful and supportive husband. Your proactive thinking and prosocial behaviors have been an inspiration.

To "Dr. Judy" Kuriansky, thank you for all you have done to help the peoples of the world, for your gifted teaching and mentoring of future psychologists, for your organizational development work at the United Nations on behalf of the World Council for Psychotherapy and other nongovernmental organizations (NGOs), and for your media expertise. You have enriched and enhanced psychology and the world from all of your dedicated efforts for the good of humankind.

To Bob Hamilton, who is truly a visionary scientist. You see the world as it was, as it is, and as it could be. You understand that a multitiered level and scale approach is needed to address the world's problems. You see how all people and living things must be holistically evaluated to protect and preserve the earth, humankind, and all living things. For your wisdom and vision, I am deeply in awe.

To my wonderful husband, Don Nemeth, whose knowledge of and love for the earth is unrivaled. Over the last 40-plus years, I have learned so much from you about the land and people's abuse of it. You have sensitized me to the beauty and nature of all living things.

To our renowned scientific contributors, Yasuo Onishi, Bob Muller, Joao Albuquerque, as well as Bob Hamilton and Don Nemeth, thank you for your unique perspectives and contributions to this book.

To our human resource contributors, Gloria Alvernaz Mulcahy, Taighlor Whittington, Sue Zelinski, Anna Onishi, and Alex Steger, as well as Judy Kuriansky, thank you for your insight and expertise. From Gloria's perspective on indigenous peoples to Anna and Alex's perspective on the technology of the new media, much can be learned about how to be in concert and in contact with one another and Mother Earth.

To my family, Madeline, David, and Colin Simmons, and Drs. Sue Jensen and Richard Gaynor, thank you for your understanding and support of this very important project.

To my clinical and research staff, Amber Gremillion, Ashton Smith, and Chelsie Songy who have assisted in the technical preparation of this manuscript—from the e-mail contacts with the contributors, to the APA formatting of all chapter references, to the preparation of a multidisciplinary glossary, I am most appreciative.

But none of this would have been possible without my excellent research coordinator, coauthor, and clinical assistant, L. Taighlor Whittington. For your dedication, perseverance, computer and editing skills, and pleasant personality, I am profoundly grateful. Your constant support and encouragement will never be forgotten.

ROBERT B. HAMILTON

I especially want to thank Darlyne Nemeth for presenting a vision of a unification of psychology with background information on biology so that psychologists could understand the impacts of biology on people. Why she chose me, I do not know, but it gave me an excuse to think more deeply about environmental decision-making. Darlyne and her husband, Don, encouraged me and gave me a platform from which to bounce ideas. When presenting some of these ideas at the United Nations, I met other contributors of this book, and we exchanged ideas. Yasuo Onishi seemed to be a kindred spirit.

I especially want to thank my wife, Jean, for putting up with my long hours and sometimes grouchy ways when the book was being written and edited. She even prepared special meals for me and the Nemeths on days we worked late on the book. That was the perfect situation for us to unwind.

Darlyne's staff was wonderful and helpful. They even seemed to tolerate and reasonably interpret my illegible squiggles on various manuscripts.

Dr. Judy is a whirlwind of energy and enthusiasm. I don't know how she can do so much so quickly. I could hardly keep up with her e-mails. Her enthusiasm and insights were especially useful as we finished the book.

JUDY KURIANSKY

Appreciation goes to all my friends and colleagues who have made me aware of the peril of our planet and inspired me to take action to preserve and conserve. Extend my sincerest thanks to my cherished good friend, Darlyne, the first editor of this book, who has been an inspiration to me and enriched my life in so many ways. I have been fortunate to share many intense and important helping and healing experiences that she initiated, including her wellness workshops after

Hurricane Katrina, when she rose to help her state after that tragedy; trainings in China after the earthquake there for an overflow room of compassionate Chinese people eager to learn about ways to help their suffering people; and panels and workshops for the World Council of Psychotherapy for which we both serve as nongovernmental organization (NGO) representatives at the United Nations. It was at a panel for this organization at the Department of Public Information (DPI)/NGO conference that she gathered a group of top experts devoted to saving the planet, and then had the vision—and persistence—to produce this book. She is truly a pioneer, creating those innovative projects, as well as a credentialing process for disaster mental health workers. On top of all that, I have the utmost respect for her becoming a neuropsychologist devoted to helping people suffering with brain disorders and being a forerunner in securing prescription rights for psychologists. I am blessed that she has brought me into sharing all these experiences with her. Her friendship and colleagueship to me is immeasurable, as is her compassion and devotion to those in need, and to the larger cosmos. All that is truly admirable and a gift to me and the world. I also acknowledge our co-editor, Bob Hamilton, who like Darlyne, is a pioneer. Years before anyone else, Bob predicted dire straits for our universe unless we pay attention. He has been impressively devoted to this project and to the planet's survival, revealed in all his hard work and intelligent contributions throughout our working together. In that regard, I am similarly grateful to all the chapter authors in this book, who have opened my eyes to the importance and precarious situation of our natural resources, with the resulting imperative to protect our environment, out of respect, and necessity to preserve our own lives. The chapters about our air, water and forest, and about change, are captivating and motivating to read.

Many events and people have contributed to my expanded awareness of the nature of the world, and the current crises that we face. In this regard, I acknowledge President Clinton and his Clinton Global Initiative, which I have attended for the past few years, where I have been exposed to experts talking about global problems and solutions. In the same vein, I appreciate my role over many years as an NGO representative to the United Nations for the International Association of Applied Psychology and the World Council of Psychotherapy, where I am constantly stimulated to be aware of global issues, and better yet, able to participate in international commissions and humanitarian projects and to advocate for global solutions, many of which address what's called the United Nations Millennium Development Goals and upcoming Sustainable Development Goals. These include alleviating poverty, empowering women and combating disease. Many other experiences have added to my education and expanded my awareness about our environment, all of which fuel my enthusiasm about the importance of this book. These experiences include moderating many workshops at annual United Nations DPI/NGO conferences, held around the world, about topics like sustainable societies, disarmament, and trauma recovery.

While I have spent many years as a relationship counselor and been well known for giving advice in public forums, on the radio, on TV, in magazines, and in newspapers worldwide, I have long been involved in projects of psychological first aid after human-induced traumas. These include the September 11 terrorist attacks and violence in the Middle East, and natural disasters like Hurricanes Hugo and Katrina; floods and tornadoes in my own country, the United States; as well as natural disasters abroad, including the tsunami in Southeast Asia and earthquakes in Australia, China, Haiti, and Japan. I value the experiences in my Global Kids Connect Project that have connected children suffering from such traumas across borders, like Haiti and Japan, and in my Stand Up for Peace Project where my co-founder, Russell Daisey, and I have participated in Global Harmony concerts and symposia around the world. Russell has been the most amazingly talented, supportive, and loyal friend and colleague throughout so many recovery missions in trauma zones, lifting the spirits of everyone around us. Throughout these experiences, I have also met so many beautiful people, and survivors of disaster, who inspire me with their courage and resilience, remind me of the love and joy that heals us all, and intensify my commitment to the messages inherent in the title and chapter contents of this book.

My deep love goes to my mother, a true angel on this planet, who has been my cheerleader all through my life, showing me the true meaning of love and appreciation. I honor her as the model for goodness and caring for others and the universe that makes me devoted to make a difference and make this world a better place. I also profoundly honor my beloved father as the source of the curiosity and commitment that inspires me and the boundless awe that drives me. When my dad took the family on a trip to Niagara Falls, he insisted we go over the falls, under the falls, around the falls, and through the falls, to see and appreciate the phenomenon from all perspectives. That spirit, I realize, is the source of the holistic approach to this book. His zestful approach to life is the explanation for those who ask where I get the enthusiasm and energy to stay up for nights at a time, committed to projects like this book. With a respectful nod to Gloria Mulcahy, a friend and chapter author in this book, I further honor all my ancestors who have greatly contributed to my growth, and all the beings that enrich my journey on this earth.

Part I

Our Natural Resources: Gaining Intellectual and Psychological Perspective

Essential and basic needs for life depend on our environment, including the elements of our water, air, forests, and earth. We must drink water to live, breathe air to exist, and allow the earth to sustain us. Although our biosphere provides our basic needs, we seldom protect or replenish it. Further, we rarely understand these elements as well as the changes they go through naturally and changes that we impose upon them. Yet when disaster that involves these elements strikes, like floods, fires, tornadoes, tsunamis, and earthquakes, we become frighteningly aware of the importance of these elements in our lives. Confusion about these events compounds the resulting emotional trauma as we wonder "How could this have happened?" and as we feel "When will it happen again?"

The chapters in this part of the book help us to better understand the elements in our environment and how we need to adapt to them and protect them for survival. This understanding is absolutely critical to help us deal with the emotional aftermath of natural disasters.

1

Our Basic Needs: Challenges in an Ever-Changing World

Robert B. Hamilton, Darlyne G. Nemeth, and Judy Kuriansky

Natural laws of the universe determine that change is inevitable and will continue to occur indefinitely when conditions are appropriate. There are many dimensions of change to be considered. Certainly, change affects us all, no matter what the source or cause, although it may not affect all of us in the same way. For example, the change may have positive or negative consequences, and from a psychological point of view, change may be perceived as positive or negative and experienced as welcome or dreaded. The effects of change occur at all levels of our social and political organizations, extending from the individual to the family, clan, city, state, country, and biosphere. Changes can also occur rapidly or slowly. Further, the effects of sudden changes on us can be immediate, may persist, or may become more obvious over time. The details of change can also vary in time and space.

As this book addresses environmental traumas we are facing in our current times, and how to heal, this chapter sets the stage by addressing the nature of change. We approach this subject of change from the perspective of both the natural sciences and psychology.

In this chapter, we explain why change is inevitable. We discuss changes that have occurred in the past and that will likely occur in the future. Although it is possible to anticipate the general nature of future changes, a precise description of the nature of the changes, along with their location and timing, is impossible. The more distant future changes are, the more inaccurate our predictions will be.

We may have difficulty coping with some violent and undesirable changes. But when we understand physical laws, we can use this knowledge to cause, direct, or modify changes to obtain specific goals and to manage them. Through such management, we can reduce the occurrence and impact of disruptive changes in the future and institute more positive outcomes. Methods of coping with change as individuals and groups will be investigated and discussed throughout this book.

This chapter—and the very contents of this book—is an outgrowth of presentations made by some of the present editors and authors at the sixtieth annual DPI/NGO conference held at the United Nations headquarters in New York in 2007 (Nemeth et al., 2007). The theme of the conference was "Climate Change: How It Impacts Us All." The presentations, which highlighted the problem-solving strategies of Fisher, Ury, and Patton (1991), focused on proactive strategies to manage climate change. Our purpose here, however, is to generalize and include all changes caused by environmental events, including those that are natural and those that are exacerbated by human actions. In other words, many environmental tragedies occur naturally and are beyond our control, but in some cases, human beings make errors in an effort to mange the environment and contribute to disaster when, unfortunately, some of their behaviors do not produce the intended positive results.

BACKGROUND

Change is a natural part of life and evolution. It has occurred since the dawn of the universe and will continue as long as there is something to change. Physical laws are the causes of changes on this earth and throughout the universe. Since the time when life evolved, living things have been a major cause of change. Once humans evolved, we began trying to manage our environment for our perceived benefit. Much of the variation in time and space that we notice in our environment has been caused by cumulative actions of people in the near and distant past or in the present. The wisdom of some of these changes seems doubtful in hindsight, but we will likely continue to make changes that we believe will benefit some, if not all, of us. Hopefully we can ensure that future human-induced changes will result in planned consequences with a minimum of negative unexpected results. For example, multi-age forest management would produce less damage than even-age forest management; but changes would still occur. Because of the complexity of our environment and the resulting likelihood of unexpected consequences, known outcomes may not always be possible. This complexity is explained well by Pulitzer Prize–winning author James Gleick (1987), who explores the cultural ramifications of science and technology in his book about chaos theory and the Butterfly Effect, where very small differences in conditions can result in drastically different consequences. For example, deforestation can result in weather change because solar reflectivity patterns control wind direction and intensity, and reflectivity is affected by forest cover.

The world is changing more than it would without human beings because as humans, we encourage change that we perceive to be beneficial. The likely results of our management actions in many cases may not be only unknown but also unknowable. Likely outcomes are even more uncertain because we are making decisions about environments that have been rare or absent in the past (e.g., fracking the earth to recover natural gas), and thus are new to us, rather than dealing with environments we formerly occupied that were clearly more familiar and better known. As a result, we should be especially cautious when we deliberately choose to alter familiar environments, which may lead to unanticipated outcomes. It would be best to have a way to return to known and familiar conditions of the past when undesirable results occur.

Many factors affect our ability to adapt to altered situations. These include demands on our resources, which are strained by individual use of necessary resources and compounded by increasing numbers of people who use the available resources. Further, planning related to the use of resources is even more difficult now than it was in the past. This is complicated by the fact that constituencies involved in the use of resources are constantly changing and often have noncompatible goals. As a result, our leaders must balance the needs of these constituencies while simultaneously resisting the temptation to profit as individuals or groups from the anticipated results of the decisions they make. They must not be selfish, acting in self-interest, but instead be prosocial—acting in the interests of the whole—to benefit humankind at all levels. This may be an almost impossible task at times.

As the number of people on the planet increases, so does our collective impact on the environment. Because of lack of foresight and planning as well as lack of consideration of possible impacts at all possible locations and all possible times, many past changes have been detrimental and continue to make our lives on this earth more challenging. An example of this is the destruction of the rainforest in the Amazon for commercial profit, which produces carbon dioxide and increases greenhouse gas into the atmosphere. Individual changes may have been more minor than clearing an entire forest, like clearing a small wood lot, but the cumulative effect of a series of these minor changes can be detrimental, that is, it may lead to what amounts to the loss of a forest. This type of escalating situation shows how we must begin to look at the whole as well as the parts. In fact, we must extend our analyses of the likely results of any small action to include broader spatial and temporal scales as well as to evaluate the effects of our actions on all levels, from individuals to the biosphere (the entire earth).

We are now living in an environment suffering from significant problems that are the result of natural and human-made changes, including pollution, resource scarcity, waste accumulation, and overcrowding. Many of these results are complicated by our mismanagement that may not even be intentional or expected. Since these unanticipated results of our management often negatively affect our present and our future, we should learn from our past actions and minimize mistakes so that we do not repeat them. We should plan in such a way as to be able to reverse our actions and return as close as possible to the premanagement condition when our management produced anticipated and more positive results.

Our management of our environment is often designed to benefit certain segments of our society. These actions, however, can cause problems for other segments. For example, when we clear the forest, in an act of what can be called planned management, we benefit from the harvest of the timber in the short term, but long-term negative effects can include reducing the supply of timber in the future, burning debris that may pollute the air, and reduced forest cover that can affect the water table and increase runoff. A short-term effect can be that we establish new opportunities to produce crops or livestock, but negative long-term effects include habitat for forest species being replaced by habitat for species that occupy the forest edges or clearings, and the size of the habitat patches being reduced. In such a process, some people and systems benefit directly, but others do not.

This mix of positive and negative outcomes may change over time, as management continues. Psychologists and politicians must be prepared to deal with the anticipated and unanticipated, positive and negative, aspects of such planned management. The situation becomes even more complicated when unanticipated changes occur. The people negatively affected may be different and more numerous than anticipated. Others who have benefited may already have profited from the situation and may not be interested in being prosocial to find solutions that benefit others.

In planning for the future, we are working to accomplish specific goals. In these situations, important questions arise. Who established these goals? What factors are important? Where and when do we want to accomplish the goals? Are the goals accepted by all the affected parties at all levels of organization? Are the goals compatible with long-term material and energy supplies? Are they equitable? Are undesirable side effects absent? Can the goals be sustained at all spatial and temporal scales and at all levels of organization? These are important questions we should ask.

TYPES OF CHANGE

There are various types of change we must consider, including temporal and spatial changes that are discussed in the following sections.

Temporal Change

The earth is approximately 4.5 billion years old. Originally, it was a lifeless sphere. It took about 800 million years for life to first appear, which was about 3.7 billion years ago. It was not until about 500 million years ago that the first vertebrates—fish—appeared. Originally there were no continents, the atmosphere contained no oxygen, and conditions could not have supported life as we know it now. Through a series of natural changes that took millions of years, precursors of living things finally evolved. As time went by, these entities eventually became living things. Over millions of years, these entities interacted with the environment to create conditions that were conducive to the evolution of more complex life forms. As these living things survived and evolved, they helped create conditions that have resulted in the world that we now know.

Some changes are cyclic and occur at regular intervals, for example, every day or throughout the year. These occur because of changes in our environment caused by the daily rotation of the earth on its axis or the year it takes to complete an orbit around the sun. The orbit of our moon causes changes in moon phase and corresponding changes in tides. Winter precipitation and spring thawing result in yearly flooding. Ocean currents off of the coast of South America shift as we shift from El Niño to La Niña every three years or so to greatly affect the earth's climate. Longer cycles such as the sun-spot cycle cause changes in our climate or transmission of electronic signals in space. Longer cycles exist such as the climatic changes that caused the ice ages. Many other long-term changes are not cyclic and seem to result from nonperiodic changes in our environment.

We know the consequences of cyclic changes. We know what to expect as seasons change. We have a good idea when to plant and when to harvest. We anticipate biyearly migrations of birds, fish, and whales. Every year we not only anticipate the coming tropical storm season, we even have models that we use to predict the number of storms and their likely location and severity. We anticipate the weather and climate consequences as we shift from El Niño to La Niña (Philander, 1990).

The changes that most negatively affect humans occur suddenly with little or no warning. Often, we do not have time to move out of danger. We cannot stop the actions of earthquakes, tornados, or volcanoes, but we have developed the ability in some cases to predict the occurrence, allowing time for people to move to safe places. This may not always be possible. If warning is insufficient, much death and damage can occur. Those who are not killed can be wounded or traumatized. At that point, psychologists can help the survivors recover and return to some semblance of their normal life.

This process of change will continue indefinitely. Our environment has slowly changed until we have reached our current condition, and it will continue to change. As rational beings, we will consciously attempt to optimize conditions for our benefit. Unfortunately, any change in the environment benefits some species and damages others. Our requirements as humans are somewhat unique, and the environment that is optimum for us is not optimal for most other species. That is why species extinction rates are high, diversity is decreasing, and we have endangered species. Given that human beings influence the environment much more than other species, the environment continues to change to benefit people rather than other species (including species that are not formally identified as endangered). To save those endangered species, we must manage to benefit them in habitats suitable for them—even if those habitats are not particularly suitable for providing the resources we as humans prefer or require.

Unfortunately, the surface area of the earth will not change, and we are running out of space for ourselves and all other species. As we change the environment to provide for our needs, we simultaneously negatively change the environments of other less-adaptable species. We are running out of space to provide habitats for all. Every year the problem gets worse, and it will continue to get worse as our numbers and resource use increase. Species that can survive in human-altered habitats are the ones most likely to survive along with humans. For example, species such as roaches, rats, and mice will persist, despite our efforts to eliminate them, because their habitats are like our habitats, and they have lived in proximity to people for a long time. On the other hand, some species will become increasingly rare, and others will become extinct. This trend will continue as long as our numbers and use of resources continue to expand. Over time, as humans, we will have outcompeted many other species and will have changed the world in ways that today we cannot imagine. Thus, sustainability is uncertain.

Spatial Change

Effects of change vary not only over time but also in space. This is why the earth is not homogeneous. Land and water occur in known patterns that are the result of physical laws and past changes. Subsurface earth is not homogeneous and varies greatly from the surface to the core. Continents sit atop tectonic plates that occasionally move and cause earthquakes. Underground water is pumped to the surface for our use. Areas of volcanism and other geothermal activity are scattered. Geologists study their variations and causes. We prepare maps to show the locations of features of interest. The atmosphere varies greatly vertically and horizontally. The oceans vary greatly by region and are influenced by strong currents. The types of animals and plants vary in predictable ways and are influenced by climate that is associated with latitude and longitude as well as physical factors on the surface. These variations are all important and will be discussed thoroughly in separate chapters in this book.

The world is not homogeneous. Therefore, many resources we require are not distributed homogeneously. Historically, people have settled where necessary resources are available and abundant, for example, near rivers and mineral-rich lands. Some resources that at one time were not considered essential became essential when uses for them were discovered as civilization evolved. Examples are oil and other fossil fuels, which are considered essential now as energy sources. But their availability is scattered, resulting in their becoming central in much of contemporary world politics. Another example is gold. When this commodity was deemed valuable and was discovered only in certain locales, including California and Alaska, people hastened to obtain it and settled in suitable places to find it and get rich (Brands, 2003).

When change occurs at particular locations, the effects vary with distance from the epicenter of that change. For example, as we track hurricanes, the effects are different at varying distances from the eye of the storm and within different quadrants of the storm (Schwartz, 2007). The effects are also different given the type of natural hazard. For example, hurricanes affect much more space than tornadoes. The effects of a volcanic eruption vary in space and are affected by the slopes associated with the volcano, the wind speed and direction, and the force of the eruption. Similarly, when we manage an environment, the effects of our actions frequently extend past the boundary of the area where that action was applied. Sometimes the actions do not affect the property of those who promulgated the action. Acid rain is an example of unexpected results from the release of sulfur dioxide and other gases from smoke stacks (Likens, Driscoll, & Buso, 1996). The effect sulfur dioxide release can extend downwind to different states or even countries. The same is true for ash from volcanic explosions. In 2011, airports in Europe were closed by a volcanic eruption in Iceland. Many disruptions at specific locations, like sites of earthquakes and volcanic eruptions, are large and greatly affect environments and their occupants.

Living Things Cause Change

Additional causes of change are the activities of people and other living things. Living itself requires change, but the effects caused by the lives of individual organisms are usually small in comparison to the evolution of the universe. More change is caused by social beings as they acquire and use energy in groups. All living things modify their habitat as a consequence of acquiring resources, growing, and moving. To increase their survival, they also develop behaviors that extensively modify the environment. Most of us are aware of the ability of beavers to build dams and change water availability in ways that are beneficial to themselves. Similarly, the success of humans in dominating our planet is due to our ability to modify our environments. Unlike other species, many of the changes that humans make are planned and often are conducted in diverse and dramatic ways. Our highly developed brains and behaviors facilitate this. Some examples are tool making, cutting and clearing forests, developing croplands, mechanizing farming, and flooding for impoundment of ponds and lakes. Some outcomes from changes resulting from these actions have been unintended, like polluted air and water, shortages of water and energy, and desertification. The changes are unintended and thus not anticipated. Some negative outcomes are unavoidable and are simply the price for conducting some of our activities, but others can possibly be avoided with more forethought. For example, if the management companies and government agencies had been more diligent in developing and enforcing deep water drilling regulations, the BP oil spill may have been avoided.

Responses to Change

As human beings, we do our best to adapt to our environment or manipulate the environment to adapt to us. We try to allow for anticipated changes. That is why we have maps of long-term flooding probabilities. But because floods could occur in consecutive years, efforts such as establishing where flooding might occur only once per 100 years reflects only an average. Because environments are changing, flood maps may not be as accurate as they were designed to be and must often be revised (Dinicola, 2005). The fact that massive floods occur, in theory, every 100 years or so and are unlikely in no way minimizes the damage they cause when they do occur. For example, in an effort to control floods and minimize potential damages from flooding along the Mississippi River, levees were constructed to keep the river in its banks and prevent annual flooding. But in 2011, winter snow and spring rainfall were unusually high, and the levees did not prevent extensive flooding along the lower Mississippi River. This example of attempting to manage a natural phenomenon shows anticipated and unanticipated results, some of which were positive and some of which were negative. For example, the levees in most years kept the river within its banks. This reduced inconvenience to those living in the flood plain but deprived agricultural land of nutrients from the river. Consequently, fertilizer must now be applied to supply needed nutrients. This causes its own problems. In addition, the lack of flooding along the lower part of the river has eliminated the annual deposition of silt from the floodwaters. Louisiana depended on these silt-laden waters to maintain land lost through compaction and erosion. Land loss is extensive because there is no input of silt to replace natural land loss (Britsch & Dunbar, 1993). Lack of upstream flooding causes water within the levees to flow faster and the volume to be much higher. In high water years, such as 2011, floodways are opened and much change occurs on land that is only occasionally flooded. The initial decision to build the levees and maintain them has greatly changed our environment along the river, some changes were anticipated and others were not. Another unintended consequence is a large dead zone, which is a periodically occurring area of water that cannot support the majority of sea life. It is located in the Gulf of Mexico and is caused by runoff of fertilizer and nutrients from upstream farms (Diaz & Rosenberg, 2008).

Some disruptive changes occur regularly, but not at precisely predetermined times or locations. An example is hurricanes. We know the general seasons and locations where they may occur, but we need more precise knowledge to minimize the disruptions they cause. With sufficient warning, we can act to minimize property damage and human suffering. Even when we have a good idea of potential danger areas and are warned with seemingly sufficient time to act, human suffering, death, and property damage often occur. We can minimize the problems but not eliminate them. We tolerate some danger because many of the potentially affected areas are otherwise attractive and productive. There is even flood property insurance for those who choose to live in hurricane-prone areas.

Other dangers are less precisely predicted in time and space than hurricanes. Earthquakes, for example, can be devastating. We know they occur along earthquake faults at unpredictable times. Still, we build over and near these fault lines. We accept some danger but have attempted to minimize damage by establishing construction standards that will eliminate or minimize structural damage. As in the case of floods being unpredictable despite an anticipation of a 100-year flood, there is also great variation in earthquake intensity and standards. The Richter scale reading from the Chilean earthquake in 2010 was 8.8, and that from the 2010 earthquake in Haiti was 6. The reading was over 9 for the 2011 earthquake in Japan. The Richter scale is logarithmic, so the earthquakes in Chile and in Japan were many times more powerful than the earthquake in Haiti. The Chilean and Japanese governments have adopted earthquake-tolerant construction standards, but the Haitian community was too poor and unorganized as a country to develop and enforce such standards. All three earthquakes occurred in areas of high population density. Infrastructure damage in Chile and Japan was less and physical recovery was quicker than in Haiti, where to this day, a large number of survivors are still homeless and live in refugee camps. The above examples illustrate that to efficiently deal with change, infrastructure, government stability, and adopting construction standards in earthquake-prone areas are all important.

We can also aggravate problems by lack of caution in how we live and work, which can make us more vulnerable. Earthquakes, mudslides, and hurricanes are relatively rare, but they are accompanied by known dangers that we often underestimate. We build on top of the San Andreas and other faults, and we settle and build in flood plains and below sea level (as in the case of areas affected by Hurricane Katrina), yet we assume we can avoid damage (e.g., by levees not breeching). The result is that we are not as cautious or safe as we should be. Nor are we as wise since we expend resources to protect or compensate those who choose to live in particularly dangerous places, when building elsewhere may have alleviated the problem and allowed us to use resources more wisely. Choosing to live in areas with high population density also makes us more vulnerable to devastating and costly tragedies, as illustrated by the September 11, 2001 attack on the World Trade Center towers in New York City. In locations where the population density is lower and crowds do not create chaos, people can sometimes more easily flee from scenes of devastation. As population density increases throughout the world, there are fewer safe places to seek refuge. Adding to this situation, unpopulated habitats are now concentrated in places that are unfavorable for human life.

The impact of environmental disaster is escalated when the occurrences are a surprise and there is no time for people to prepare. Scientists are attempting to find a means to predict the location and timing of future events like earthquakes. There has been some success in designing such technology, but the warning time is often only seconds. That may not be enough time for people to escape buildings and avoid being buried in rubble caused by the event, even if people respond immediately.

On some occasions, one environmental disaster can lead to others—a domino effect. For example, the energy released from earthquakes can be transferred to water and result in tsunamis that can cause further immense devastation. This multiplicity of events occurred in northern Japan in March 2011. Those who saw images of the tsunami that struck Japan as a result of the earthquakes could view the enormous energy involved as the rising water lifted vehicles and structures, and moved them like toys. The devastation from the earthquake and tsunami was compounded by damage to nuclear power plants that were disabled because of loss of power and inability to apply necessary cooling water. These plants were supposed to be able to resist earthquakes and tsunamis, but these natural events were more powerful than anticipated.

The triple disruption in Japan could have been minimized by prior planning. If there had been early warning, and time had been available to flee, people could have reached higher ground to avoid the impact of the tsunamis. Lives could have been saved, even if structural and property damage were still extensive. Devoting energy to sufficient planning and infrastructure, as well as sufficient funds to cover such preparedness, can counteract the enormous destructive energy involved in such disasters.

After such cataclysms have occurred, we must deal with the results on many levels. Damage is devastating on multiple levels related to a society's infrastructure, as well as on the institutions established to manage our lives. Damage is also devastating to human life and health, both physical and mental. With regard to the latter, psychologists are essential to help restore the mental health of individuals and communities, an issue that is discussed in other chapters of this book.

Minimizing Future Problems

As we emphasize in this chapter, change is inevitable. We may perceive it as positive, negative, or neutral. Our initial perceptions may not persist as time goes by and as we gather more information. Also, not all people perceive change in the same way. We are grateful for changes we perceive as positive and wish to continue them. Conversely, we usually want to eliminate or reverse perceived negative changes. While we have no control over many environmental changes, like hurricanes, tornadoes, and earthquakes, we may be able to avoid or minimize dire consequences by avoiding situations where these cataclysmic changes are likely to occur. For example, we should not build on flood plains or hurricane-prone areas, or near earthquake faults. If there are good reasons for being in these susceptible areas, we can establish construction codes that can minimize or eliminate future damage. We can also attempt to predict the occurrences of these catastrophes in time and space, and evacuate when danger is imminent. Unfortunately, this has not been possible in some dramatic recent cases of hurricanes, tsunamis, and earthquakes. However, in other cases, usable warnings have been possible for tornados, avalanches, and mudslides, as recent developments in weather radar provided enough time to warn those in danger to seek shelter in basements, safe rooms or other cover.

More than any species, human beings can exert control over their environment. This control has been facilitated by living in families and clans, and with the establishment of villages, cities, states, countries, and groups of countries. An individual may be a member of each of these groups. Collective action is more effective than individual action to ensure our survival from diverse environmental challenges that face our existence in current times. Fortunately, peoples from different nations are coming together more readily to work on solutions to common environmental problems that face countries and our biosphere. This is evident, for example, in activities at the United Nations, where commissions like the Commission on Social Development and the Commission on Sustainable Development, take place regularly, where delegates from members states meet together to make resolutions for the common good, taking the needs of civil society into account. Despite common efforts, members on all these levels of organization have their own interests and may be affected by changes in different ways. Each group attempts to maximize their particular benefits, which may be at the expense of other groups, leading to potential conflicts.

Individuals and groups from these different levels of society attempt to maximize the environment of their group and its members. Each group has its own needs, history, religion, and traditions. Conflicts among communities, cultures, or countries can occur because of many factors, which include competition for resources; past differences with neighbors; and religious and philosophical differences about the proper ways to govern, interact with the environment, or deal with neighbors. Within each level, there are groups that have their own philosophies and agendas. They organize and attempt to get their agendas adopted. A good example is political parties. Even when there is agreement on a plan, results often do not manifest as planned because of the complexity of the world (see Gleick, 1987, "Butterfly Effect"). Questions arise: Do we have good strategies to deal with the changes we plan and carry out? What is a good strategy? In cases where we are not sure that a desired result can be accomplished, it is best to choose a plan that is easily reversed if unanticipated problems occur. It is also best not to deviate greatly from what is known to have worked in the past.

We can more easily manage changes that we choose than those that are imposed upon us. Small changes are obviously easier to manage and to maintain more safely, than bigger ones. But we need to be aware, as was pointed out previously, that by changing the environment, we cause change that can be detrimental to other life forms by eliminating or modifying their habitats and causing them to become extinct or in danger of extinction. But there are other potentially detrimental effects. Our water supplies are decreasing, land is turning to desert, trash is accumulating, and air and water are becoming polluted. Many of these changes have resulted from efforts to increase our standard of living and allow more people to achieve "progress." These efforts, however, may have severe negative future impacts on not only other species and environmental elements, but also on humans. When negative effects occur, one solution, as has been mentioned previously, is to revert to procedures that have been less deleterious in the past. This possibility should always be considered.

There is currently dispute among environmental experts and the public as to the likelihood of change that is detrimental to society, the consequences of future changes, and the urgency of taking immediate action to avert dangers. Some constituencies also desire to modify changes that already have occurred. Many proposed ideas are controversial. Questions arise: How do we evaluate solutions? What criteria should we use? An important criterion should be the evaluation of how a change would affect the survival of humankind. Another criterion should be to evaluate how the change would affect the way that we live or want to live and the effect on other life. With regard to the latter, we must become better predictors of the consequences when we contemplate change—past, present, and future. This point is emphasized in this chapter: consideration of the past is always useful since we know past conditions in which humans have survived. Maintaining those conditions—rather than trying to manage new, untested environments—would be more likely to ensure our survival. Alteration from past suitable conditions may be risky. If we are to engage in risktaking, we must ensure that there will be a path to return to a proven set of conditions.

Humans will not survive forever if the earth becomes inhospitable. Fortunately, many changes that would cause the earth to become inhospitable may take millions of years. If and when that day comes, for humans to survive forever as a species, some solution, like moving to other hospitable planets, must become feasible. A far preferred solution to prevent this future event would be for people today to limit their resource use. In other words, we must change our ways if we are to continue indefinitely to live on this planet.

Traumatic Changes

Traumatic changes are rapid changes in conditions that almost immediately threaten the survival or welfare of humankind. These are due to unexpected or unpredicted environmental changes brought about by natural hazardous events such as floods, hurricanes, fires, and tsunamis. The damages these events cause can be immediate and tragic.

Responses to Traumatic Changes

When natural disasters occurs in the physical world, damage can occur to the physical and psychological health of the affected population. Therefore, assistance is necessary on both the physical and emotional levels. Medical conditions after a disaster are complicated. Medical personnel who can attend to the many who are wounded are invariably in dire short supply. Hospitals, clinics and health services may have been damaged or destroyed. With electricity lines disabled, power may be limited to generators, and fuel for generators may be scarce or difficult to obtain. Medicine and other medical supplies are invariably also in short supply because of greater than anticipated number of wounded people or breaks in the supply chain because of infrastructure damage, such as destruction of roads or buildings. Water supplies may be contaminated. Each of these problems may in turn cause additional problems.

Similar to the physical effects, emotional aftereffects can be equally devastating, as people are traumatized by the experience and their losses. Mental health professionals and psychotherapists can be invaluable in helping people deal with the effects of traumatic events that affect their psychological and physical state as well as the destruction of their homes and other infrastructure that support their lives. The tragedy of Hurricane Katrina is an example of devastation that can occur as a result of a traumatic event (Nemeth, 2007) (See Chapter 7).

To complicate these problems, safety may be greatly compromised because some people may try to take advantage of the chaos and loot or rob law-abiding citizens and their property. Lack of sufficient police and safety measures exacerbates these problems.

THE EARTH

Although technically a part of a solar system, earth is seemingly an isolated planet, but it is not perfectly isolated. It is bombarded by constant but variable energy from the sun. The presence of the sun and moon causes gravitational attraction that results in tides. Tidal water can be utilized to produce electricity. It increases availability of nutrients and thus affects productivity. There has been little other input besides an occasional meteorite and some cosmic radiation. Although large meteorites impacting earth are extremely rare, some have greatly impacted our planet's history (Chapman & Morrison, 1994) and future impacts could be devastating. The only significant and constant output is reflected and radiant energy, but we have succeeded in sending spaceships to the moon and beyond, and we have the ability to continue to do so with sufficient utilization of human effort and sufficient energy expenditure.

Matter

The earth consists of a finite supply of matter. In chemistry, we learn that matter is made of elements, which—except for radioactive ones—cannot be changed to other elements. All of the materials we use are comprised of these elements. Knowledge of the properties of these elements and their combinations as well as the ability to produce new desirable combinations has greatly facilitated changes we have made and are making to the planet. Because the supply of each element is finite and constant, shortages can occur. Many of these combinations occur naturally and were present before the influence of humans. We humans are unique in our ability to understand elemental properties, to visualize and produce new combinations, and to utilize them. The distribution of the elements and their naturally occurring combinations is not uniform. At any one location, most are absent, but there may be combinations of particular elements or compounds that can be mined or harvested to benefit people. As we learn more, elements that we thought had no use have become invaluable in many ways.

Much of human commerce depends on obtaining valuable materials, processing them, and shipping them to locations where they are utilized for various purposes. Trade is the backbone of modern local and world economies. Shortages of particularly valuable materials can result in hardship that may lead to conflicts and even war. For example, oil has been utilized in various ways to provide energy and as raw material in the manufacture of many goods that are now utilized extensively throughout the world. These goods are then shipped to the site of their eventual use. The energy derived from processed fossil fuels (hydrocarbons) provides most of the energy for the processing and transportation of other products. Areas of abundant oil supply and the infrastructure to extract it are localized. Supply of the amount extracted is close to the amount desired at any time, and extreme swings in prices that occur when the supply chain is disrupted are severe. Most modern economies require large supplies of oil and other hydrocarbons, or even carbon itself. Our existing resources are finite. The foreign policy of many countries is greatly affected by the availability of oil through extraction or obtaining of a reliable supply from other countries. As suggested previously, most of modern history is greatly influenced by the availability and procurement of oil.

The important point here is that our supplies of basic materials are finite. As the influence of humans over the earth increases, shortages of materials inevitably develop. In many cases, the shortages can negatively affect the way we live and may cause conflict. Attempting to increase the use of our limited resources will inevitably lead to conflict. We cannot continue to expand forever.

Energy

Energy is essential for all natural processes. Earth does have a constant input of energy as well as a built-in supply stored in its mantle and core and within elements and compounds. There continuous input of radiant energy from the sun and some radiant energy from the rest of the universe. Some of the energy from the sun that struck the earth in the past has been converted to chemical energy in biomass and has become stored underground as fossil energy in natural gas, oil, coal and other compounds. We also receive gravitational energy from the sun and the moon. This energy continuously causes tidal changes, which in turn can increase productivity in marshes and other tidal-effected areas (Steever, Warren, & Niering, 1976). There are efforts underway to produce electricity from the energy in the tides (Hammons, 2009). Gravitational energy is important through the use of turbines that harvest energy from water that is flowing downstream and impounded by dams. This water comes from rain or snow that forms in clouds as water vapor evaporates from the earth's surface.

A major difference between energy supply on earth and supply of materials is that there is a continuous input of new energy but no new input of materials. There is another important difference between energy and materials. Energy does work. When it does, some of it is lost. Accompanying the inevitable loss when energy is used are subtle changes in temperature and the system itself. Because of the constant loss of energy, we need a dependable supply of new energy. From a global view, we have a dependable supply of energy we receive from the sun. The energy available from the earth is gradually being lost, and the rate of loss will increase as we use more and more of it for our needs; but fortunately, the external energy from solar radiation and gravity is constantly available. The energy stored in fossil fuels such as petroleum, natural gas, and coal came from the sun millions of years ago when it was converted to vegetation through photosynthesis. When earth is looked at holistically, the input from the sun replenishes sun-related energy that is used now as well as the energy from the past that is stored in fossil fuels. As our energy requirements continue to increase, those supplied through use of fossil fuels and biomass production can become problematic. In addition, there is concern that the carbon dioxide (CO_2) and water vapor produced in the production process may have a detrimental effect on the world's climate (Lean & Rind, 2008).

Malthus Revisited

Our materials are finite. There is a limit to their supply. In 1798, the Reverend Thomas Malthus (1994) postulated that because food availability increases relatively slowly and population increases relatively fast, eventually the population will be limited because of lack of food. The ecologist Ehrlich (1968) argued that a food crisis was coming because of rapid population growth. Fortunately, that did not happen, due to changes in food production methods, such as mechanized farming, increased irrigation and fertilization, genetically improved crops and now genetic engineering, which resulted in food production growth. But there still is a distribution problem, and many people worldwide are starving. Another problem is that modern methods of food distribution require extensive use of fossil fuels, the use of which may eventually be limited by their availability (a situation that may be salvageable when alternate energy sources become available). Many critics have denounced Malthus's idea, especially as championed by environmentalist Paul Ehrlich. Economists have also refuted a food shortage, for example, J. L. Simon (1994), who asserted that the growing population constitutes a resource; therefore, productivity will increase as the population increases, and there will always be enough food. This debate largely ignores spatial and temporal scales. For example, in the Irish Potato Famine between 1845 and 1852, the Irish population was maintained only through emigration. There is no doubt that eventually our resource requirements will exceed the supply, and Malthus's theory will be vindicated unless we limit our growth and use our resources wisely.

The basic structure of the world's economies with continued exponential population growth cannot be maintained forever. Those peoples and cultures that live in harmony with their present environments should endure longer if others do not force a growth economy on them. That harmonious approach should be more easily sustainable than the continuous developmental approach that most of us are pursuing now.

Life

Life requires materials and energy. Almost all of our current energy comes directly or indirectly from the sun. Living organisms utilize energy to modify their environments in ways that will likely increase individual and species survival. They grow, search out and obtain food; build cocoons; digg holes; and build dams. Humans are unique in the quantity of energy we use beyond our basic needs to survive and alter environments, the complexity of the modifications we make, and the degree to which the modifications themselves can further modify environments. Many of humankind's modifications of the environment have been made possible by revolutionary discoveries like the use of fire; toolmaking; making materials that can be used to improve toolmaking and use; learning to grow, process, and harvest food; development of the internal combustion engine; the industrial revolution; and the development of transistors and computers to manage and store information to facilitate increased management of the environment and communications.

Humans' ability to alter environments has had many unanticipated results, many of which have negatively affected our species. Experts and other individuals have debated whether changes have been beneficial. Regardless of which side of the debate one takes, the world is much different now than it would have been without human activities, alterations, and interference. In addition, the effects of the energy we use are increasing exponentially, and often greedily, to the point where people can be said to be "energy hogs."

Currently, there are approximately 6.3 billion people on earth. This number is growing and is expected to be about 9 billion by 2050. In response to the question of what was greatest invention in human history, the great scientist Albert Einstein supposedly replied, "compound interest" (Blau, 1983). That means that as the number of humans increases, energy required by humans for basic needs increases proportional to our numbers. In addition, modern humans utilize energy to augment the basic necessities and to raise their standard of living. People with higher standards of living are presumed by many to be happier and more fulfilled. To equalize the standard of living of all, increased energy will be needed for those with low standards of living. Energy needs are thus expected to increase continually until the world's population stabilizes and the standard of living of all is equitable. Problems associated with energy supply will thus continue to increase into the foreseeable future. Other problems such as resource availability and distribution, pollution, and political and cultural changes will increase because of increasing population density.

Energy Sources

Much of the energy we use comes directly or indirectly from the sun. Some of this is captured by green plants through photosynthesis and is used directly or stored as carbohydrates to be used later or to provide energy for growth and necessary functions like movement, reproduction, and respiration. Much of this energy is used by animals, and some is stored as wood and other products. We plant crops, harvest them, and allow some to be consumed by livestock that are in turn harvested. We transport and use the harvest to provide for food needs throughout the world. In nature, photosynthesis is the basis for the energy needs of wild plants and animals that occupy them. When carbohydrates are used as a source of energy, oxygen is consumed and carbon dioxide and water are produced.

Carbohydrates present in the past have been fossilized and stored as oil, gas, coal, and peat through geological and geochemical processes. Some other sources of energy, for example, hydroelectric, which is fueled by evaporation of surface water and redeposited upstream as rainwater, are also powered by the sun.

Nuclear power plants; geothermal energy, which is heat from the earth; wind (powered by thermal differences caused by the sun); tides; and fuel cells are available as well. There is hope that more powerful sources can be developed. At one time, the potential of fusion was being explored, but we still have not been able to contain the potential power in a safe way. Some of these sources are being extensively utilized, and others are being developed. Despite all of these actual and potential energy resources, providing for anticipated demand will be difficult because of the time required to develop them, increased need, and depletion of fossil sources. In addition, energy sources that require land (e.g., wind farms) will be competing for other uses of the area such as food production and the maintenance of biodiversity. The side effects of energy production and use are becoming more obvious and stimulate debate regarding the wisdom of the use of each. For example, there is great concern among some experts and other groups of people about the potential negative effects of carbon dioxide that is released when we use fossil fuels.

Considering these issues outlined earlier in the chapter, more concern is needed about efficient and safe ways to conserve our resources, to apportion them wisely, and to provide alternate energy supplies for our future sustainability. Concern for our earth and our resources is essential, especially if our population continues to increase. We need increasingly more energy per person to satisfy our current needs, and for the world's economies to grow, which governments continue to believe is desirable. The concern is over whether all of this can be done.

THE CHALLENGE THAT LIES AHEAD

Given all the issues addressed in this chapter, it becomes clear that to survive—and to thrive—today, we need to be more conscious of our resources, our use of resources, and the way we interact with our environment. As the ensuing chapters reveal, we live in a holistic environment; that is, we are constantly affected by our external natural resources—air, water, earth—as well as our internal emotional state. Natural sciences and psychology merge. Our status is constantly affected by change, often by environmental events that are not in our control, or that we exacerbate by our actions. By being conscious, aware, and educated, we can adapt to these changes, and when they become traumatic, we can heal.

REFERENCES

Blau, E. (1983, May 27). Einstein revisited. New York Times (p. C1).

Brands, H. W. (2003). The age of gold: The California gold rush and the new American dream. New York: Anchor Books.

Britsch, L. D., & Dunbar, J. B. (1993). Land loss rates: Louisiana Coastal Plain. Journal of Coastal Research, 9(2), 324–338.

Chapman, C. R., & Morrison, D. (1994). Impacts on the earth by asteroids and comets: Assessing the hazard. *Nature, 367*(6458), 33–40. doi:10.1038/367033a0.

Diaz, R. J., & Rosenberg, R. (2008, August 15). Spreading dead zones and consequences for marine ecosystems. *Science, 321*(5891), 926–929.

Dinicola, K. (2005, August 22). The *"100-year flood"* [U.S. Geological Survey Fact Sheet 229-96]. (August 10, 2011) Retrieved from USGS science for a changing world Web site: http://pubs.usgs.gov/fs/FS-229-96.

Ehrlich, P. R. (1968). *The population bomb.* New York: Ballantine Books.

Gleick, J. (1987). *Chaos: Making a new science.* New York: Penguin Books.

Hammons, T. J. (2009). Tidal Energy Technologies: Currents, Wave an Offshore Wind Power in the United Kingdom, Europe, and North America, Renewable Energy, T. J. Hammons (Ed.), ISBN: 978-953-7619-52-7, InTech, Available from http://www.intechopen.com/books/renewable-energy/tidal-energy-technologies-currents-wave-and-offshore-wind-power-in-th-United-Kingdom-Europe-and-nov.

Lean, J. L., & Rind, D. H. (2008). How natural and anthropogenic influences alter global and regional surface temperatures: 1889–2006. *Geophysical Research Letters, 35*: 10.1029/20088GL034864.

Likens, G. E., Driscoll, C. T., & Buso, D. C. (1996, April 12). Long-term effects of acid rain: Response and recovery of a forest ecosystem. *Science, 272*(5259), 244–246. doi:10.1126/science.272.5259.244.

Malthus, T. R. (1994). *An essay on the principle of population* (G. Gilbert, Ed.). New York: Oxford University Press. (Original work published 1798.)

Nemeth, D. G., Albuquerque, J., Garrido, G., Hamilton, R., Nemeth, D. F., & Onishi, Y. (2007, September). Strategies to facilitate biosphere management and lifestyle change: Measures to protect the environment and prevent drastic sequelae of current and future climate changes. Symposium presented at the 60th Annual United Nations DPI/NGO Conference Midday Workshops, New York, NY.

Philander, S. G. H. (1990). *El niño, la niña, and the southern oscillation.* San Diego, CA: Academic Press.

Schwartz, R. (2007). *Hurricanes and the middle Atlantic states.* Alexandria, VA: Blue Diamond Books.

Simon, J. L. (1994). More people, greater wealth, more resources, healthier environment. *Economic Affairs, 14*(3), 22–29.

Steever, E. Z., Warren, R. S., & Niering, W. A. (1976). Tidal energy subsidy and standing crop production of Spartina alterniflora. *Estuarine and Coastal Marine Sciences, 4*(4), 473–478.

World population. (2011, July 27). Retrieved from Wikipedia Web site: http://en.wikipedia.org/wiki/World_population.

2

Our Living Waters: Polluting or Cleansing?

Yasuo Onishi

Many of us have heard that the human body is made up of mostly water. But so is our planet. Water is a powerful force of life but also of destruction. For that reason, an understanding of water is crucial in this exploration of our traumatized world and how to heal ourselves and our planet.

Water is a life-supporting substance that changes in time and space. It constantly moves around, through, and above the earth as water vapor, liquid water, or ice. Its changes in form reflect its interactions with the earth's air, land, humans, and other living beings as well as the moon and solar energy.

The earth neither loses nor gains water from space. It circulates around the globe and nourishes all living things. It is possible that the water you drink today contains water dinosaurs swam in (USGS, 2009). However, the quantity and quality of available liquid water are rapidly changing because we have treated water as an unlimited resource and overutilized it; we have also used it as a dumping ground for our wastes. Water has self-cleansing and self-healing capacities to absorb moderate modification without significant changes in its properties. However, if assaults are extreme, the aquatic environment can change itself in unanticipated and traumatic ways that can be too much for us humans to restore. Water in many developing countries becomes contaminated because of population growth, industrial and agricultural development, lack of resources to clean it, and lack of will to keep it clean.

Because our world is ever-changing, future changes in water availability and quality are inevitable. Many of these can be anticipated and corrected. The increasing human population and accompanying demand along with changes brought about by environmental factors can make adjustments difficult. We still have time before the full impact of long-term changes will become apparent. By understanding the causes and extent of changes, we can proactively implement needed actions to minimize damage.

WATER: A LIFE-SUPPORTING SUBSTANCE

Water covers 70 percent of the earth's surface and is part of a delicate, inter-active, 20-mile-high earth biosphere system consisting of air, water, land, and living beings. The first living organisms appeared in the ocean 3.5 billion years ago. Bacteria and other primitive organisms originally appeared in water and generated oxygen essential for energy production in most living things. Some people regard the earth as a self-regulating, living organism called Gaia that maintains conditions optimal for living things (Lovelock, 1979). To have water available, most people live along or near water bodies; Asian countries and U.S. western states heavily depend on glacier- and snowmelt river water.

Water circulates throughout the environment; this is called the hydrologic cycle. Water, mostly from the ocean's surface, evaporates into the atmosphere. It forms clouds and comes back to earth as rain and snow. Rainwater and melted snow drain over the land surface or go into groundwater and supply water to rivers and lakes. The water eventually returns to an ocean. Some water from the ocean and other surface sources then evaporates back into the air, thus continuing this endless circle. The hydrologic cycle acts as a pump to return water that flows downhill to higher elevations so that it can flow downhill again.

The amount, quality, and phase (ice, liquid water, or water vapor) of water affect how people and other living things survive. As we have seen, the earth has been constantly changing since its formation. Among these changes have been a series of ice ages and interglacier periods. Some of these changes resulted in mass extinction of living things. For example, over the last 520 million years, five mass extinctions have occurred. Three of these occurred when the ocean's surface water had the three highest water temperatures over those 520 million years. Another mass extinction occurred when the ocean's water was very cold, although not the coldest (Mayhew, Jenkins, & Benton, 2007). Another mass extinction killed dinosaurs about 65 million years ago when a meteorite crushed into the earth. The worst mass extinction event, the Permian-Triassic Extinction, occurred about 250 million years ago when the ocean had its highest water temperature, which was likely due to greenhouse gas effects. Ninety percent of marine species and 70 percent of terrestrial ones were killed at that time. Earth's air temperature has been relatively stable since the last ice age (about 10,000 years ago when humans evolved and became dominant).

Historically, we have considered water to be an unlimited resource to use and abundant enough that we do not worry about our actions with respect to it. Different cultures have different attitudes toward water.

Western civilizations strongly focus on technologies and using various natural resources to benefit humans. For example, water is used for hydroelectric power generation and irrigation.

Christianity places humans as a ruler of all living things (Genesis Chapter 1, Verses 28 of NIV Bible) "... God blessed them (man and female) and God said to them. Be fruitful and increase in number; fill the earth and subdue it. Rule over the fish of the sea and the birds of the air and over every living creature that moves on the ground" (New York International Bible Society, 1978). I hope that "Rule over the fish ..." is interpreted by people today as "steward the fish" or "administer the fish" to be more environmentally friendly. Some indigenous people and Asian religions regard humans and other living beings as equal; some of them respect nature to the point of worshipping mountains, seas, trees, and waterfalls as gods.

For many of us, economics have higher priority than environmental concerns until environmental changes adversely affect profit or the government regulates water uses. Too often, long-term effects are not reflected in economic decisions.

These perspectives may have led us to disregard the environment we live in and to underestimate the changes we may cause. As nature can absorb some human actions and change can be slow to occur, short-term changes are not noticed. This is why we should evaluate potential changes at all time scales. Because long-term changes are occurring, we are beginning to recognize problems and are beginning to act to correct them. Short-term changers are often local, but they can accumulate and eventually cause larger-scale problems.

Water: Short-Term, Local and Regional Changes

People require water, as do modern agricultural and industrial activities. But we regard water as a dumping place for industrial, agricultural, and municipal wastes; we often say, "the solution to pollution is dilution." The lack of understanding of how contaminated water affects the aquatic environment has resulted in adverse impacts that affect us all, as illustrated by the recent BP oil spill.

Once we realize what we have done to water resources, we can act to correct our mismanagement. Many attempts are being made to correct problems and restore the damaged aquatic environment, or at least eliminate new water contamination problems. These efforts include environmental cleanup, tighter environmental regulations, safer plant operations, and more efficient water use. Because we realize that human actions affect both people and our environment, the concept of environmental sustainability is taking hold. A sustainable lifestyle is accomplished by conservation, recycling, and use of biodegradable materials.

Accidents

An accident causes sudden dramatic damages to the environment. Three accidents demonstrate this: The 2011 Fukushima, Japan, Nuclear Power Plant accident; the 2010 BP oil spill in the Gulf of Mexico; and the 1986 Chernobyl Nuclear Power Plant accident.

Fukushima Nuclear Power Plant Accident in 2011

On March 11, 2011, the magnitude 9.0 East Japan Great Earthquake occurred in the Pacific Ocean, 43 miles off northeastern Japan. This earthquake was one of the five most powerful earthquakes on record. It triggered a 133-foot tsunami, which caused the deaths of 23,000 people and approximately $300 billion in damages. It also caused an electricity blackout at Fukushima Daiichi Nuclear Power Plant. Without electricity, the plant lost its ability to cool nuclear fuels in its reactor Units 1, 2, and 3, resulting in nuclear core meltdowns. The lack of cooling of these nuclear fuels at Units 1, 2, and 3 also caused three hydrogen explosions at Units 1, 3 and 4. Unit 4 had no nuclear fuels in its reactor core at that time, but still had a hydrogen explosion. These explosions, together with venting of air from Unit 2 reactor building resulted in radioactive materials (radionuclides, mostly iodine-131, cesium-134, and cesium-137) being spewed into the air. The resulting radioactivity (roughly 3×10^{17} Becquerel or 7 million curies) was almost that of the Hiroshima atomic bomb during World War II.

These radioactive materials that were spewed into the atmosphere were subsequently deposited on land and in the Pacific Ocean, thereby contaminating soil, water, plants, and fish. Domestic animals and some people were exposed to contaminated air and water, and consumed contaminated water, plants, milk, and meat. Due to damages to the reactor cores and structural damage caused by the hydrogen explosions, some water used to cool nuclear fuels in the reactor vessels became contaminated and leaked into the groundwater and the Pacific Ocean. Tokyo Electric Power Company, an operator of the nuclear plant, also released about 420,000 cubic feet of slightly radioactive water from the plant's buildings into the ocean to make room to store the more highly radioactively-contaminated water at the plant. This environmental contamination was said to be regional in scale, although the radionuclides released into the Pacific Ocean could be carried across ocean to the west coast of the United States. While these radionuclides crossing the ocean sound drastic, the ocean water would greatly dilute the materials by the time they reached the United States.

To reduce radiation damage, the Japanese government evacuated approximately 70,000 to 80,000 people from the vicinity of the Fukushima plant, and restricted the consumption of contaminated foods. Because iodine-131 decays and reduces its concentration to half its original concentration in 8 days, its contamination is reduced and disappears quickly. But cesium-134 and cesium-137 take 2 and 30 years, respectively, to reduce their concentrations by half, and their environmental contamination, especially cesium-137, will last much longer. The contaminated soil may become a long-term pollution source.

The plant was not built to withstand the conditions created by the East Japan Great Earthquake and subsequent tsunami. It is important to select appropriate design condition levels by considering consequences when beyond-the-design conditions occur. All Japanese nuclear plants except the Fukushima Daiichi plant, which will most likely not restart, are now required to install systems to avoid plantwide electric blackouts in the event of beyond-design tsunamis or other unexpected long-term electrical failure.

I have been working in Japan on the Fukushima accident response as well as at Chernobyl for over 25 years, and I have been impressed by the hard work and dedication of many of the workers at both locations. They have been dedicated to reducing the danger to the public and sometimes ignore danger to themselves.

Gulf of Mexico Oil Spill in 2010

On April 20, 2010, an explosion at the Deepwater Horizon drilling well in the Gulf of Mexico occurred, killing 11 people working on a platform at the water surface. Deepwater Horizon was drilled to BP's deep undersea oil reservoir located about 2.5 miles below the sea bottom. Gas that coexisted with oil in the deep reservoir escaped into the drilling well pipe and rose toward the surface. It expanded and exploded in the well.

A blowout preventer is a safety device that sits at the top of the well at the bottom of the gulf. It is designed to deal with extreme pressure and to control the flow of oil and gas. It did not function properly to stop the flow of oil and gas. Therefore, oil and gas gushed from the well at the blowout preventer, which was about a mile deep. The oil that escaped containment quickly spread to contaminate the water of the gulf and coastal beaches, bays, and marshes.

For the subsequent three months, oil and gas continuously gushed into the gulf until the well was capped. To reduce the oil that reached the surface and eventually the beaches and shores of states along the gulf, an oil dispersant was injected near the oil leaking point to break the oil up into small droplets, to reduce the amount of oil that reached the water surface. Instead of allowing the oil to float to the shore at the surface, this dispersant injection kept more oil within the water. The oil affected by the dispersants mostly was not seen and its effects are not well known. Some of it was consumed by bacteria called *Oceanospirillales* (ScienceDaily, 2010). The decision to use dispersants reduced the quantity of oil that reached the surface, where it was more visible and the effects more easily seen. From a spatial perspective, the problem expanded to include the water column and the bottom of the gulf. The temporal ramifications were not thoroughly analyzed. We do not know how long the released oil will affect the environments that it reached. Much of the oil in the gulf was transported by the warm Loop Current toward Louisiana and Mississippi and then toward Florida. The Loop Current becomes the Gulf Stream along the east coast of the United States and crosses the Atlantic Ocean to Europe as the North Atlantic Drift.

The long-term impacts to the aquatic environmental of this oil spill depend on many factors, including:

- Toxicity of oil and the dispersant to fish, shrimp, and other aquatic biota
- Ability of oil-eating microorganisms in the Gulf of Mexico to consume the dispersed oil
- Oil degradation and evaporation to air
- Breaking down of oil on the shore by forces of weather
- Oil transport out of the Gulf of Mexico by the Loop Current

The environmental contamination would most likely be regional in scale. But if fisheries are affected, food supplies could be affected in extended regions.

Chernobyl Nuclear Power Plant Accident in 1986

Unsafe technology and human error are a dangerous combination. The 1986 core meltdown of the Chernobyl Nuclear Plant, Unit 4 in the Ukraine released into the atmosphere six times the radioactive materials of the Hiroshima atomic bomb that was detonated during World War II (IAEA, 1991). The nuclear plant is approximately 70 miles north of Kiev, Ukraine, along the Pripyat River, a tributary of the Dnieper River that discharges its water to the Black Sea. The radioactive cloud produced from the Chernobyl accident fell mostly on the Dnieper River Basin in Ukraine, Belarus, and Russia.

Eight million Ukrainians drink water from the Dnieper River, and up to 20 million people consume agricultural produce irrigated by the water and fish caught in the river (Chernobyl Forum, 2005). Thus, migration of radionuclides into and within the rivers is important for determining potential health impacts, and most remediation activities have been aimed at protecting the public from contaminated water (Onishi et al., 2007a). This 1986 accident is the most devastating nuclear accident in history, while the Fukushima nuclear accident discussed previously is the second worst.

Many protective actions were implemented to reduce radionuclide influxes to these rivers and to retard radionuclide transport downstream. Some were successful, for example, construction of earthen dikes along the most contaminated Pripyat River floodplain in the vicinity of the Chernobyl Nuclear Plant, but many were ineffective or even harmful (Onishi, Voitsekhovich, & Zheleznyak, 2007b). Still, about 4,000 emergency workers, residents of the most contaminated areas, and people consuming radioactively contaminated foods and water are estimated will die as a result of the Chernobyl nuclear accident (Chernobyl Forum, 2005). Besides these expected deaths, the greatest public health problem caused by the accident may be psychological stresses, for example, helplessness and anxiety.

The root cause of this nuclear accident was lack of concern about potential dangers to the environment and human lives. To prevent future nuclear accidents and improve safety, Chernobyl-style reactors have been shut down, and many others have been modified. At the Chernobyl site, the Chernobyl Shelter, formally called the Sarcophagus, was constructed over Unit 4 of the Chernobyl plant immediately after the April 26, 1986, accident. However, it is only a temporary structure. To prevent future radionuclide releases into the atmosphere from possible collapse of the Chernobyl Shelter, a dome-shaped, movable, new safe confinement (NSC) is being constructed over the shelter (Onishi, Voitsekhovich, and Zheleznyak, 2007b). The NSC should reduce radionuclide contamination even further in the groundwater in the Chernobyl area and in the Pripyat and Dnieper Rivers.

Comparison of the Events

These three accidents—in Japan, the United States, and Ukraine—all were tragic to individuals and society. But some aspects of the consequences differ. In Japan, devastation caused by the natural disaster—the March 11, 2011 earthquake and tsunami—was obvious, certainly in the affected humans and the destruction to property. People cannot see and smell radiation that comes from a nuclear disaster. As a result, imagined as well as real radiation fears can grip people as they consider possible damages.

Natural disasters such as the one in Japan cannot directly be prevented from happening, though warning systems can alert people to an occurrence, and long-range attention to climate change may have some impact. But accidents in nuclear power plants and other industrial centers can be prevented by designing plants and facilities to function safely in any conditions that can be conceived. Even so, unexpected factors may interfere with safety. The longer something exists, the greater the likelihood that a rare and unexpected event will occur.

With respect to the oil spill, the demand for dependable energy supplies and concern for possible negative consequences at other sites led to drilling for oil under very challenging conditions, deep under the water surface in the Gulf of Mexico. Although the drilling was at one specific point, the ramifications of the spill extended to a large portion of the gulf, its shores, and nearby land and water. The resulting damage may persist for some time, with potential deleterious long-term effects. If we are going to modify our environments for what we consider useful purposes, we must ensure that our actions are safe and workable.

Outright Disregard for the Environment

Russia disclosed in 1993 that it had disposed of significant amounts of nuclear materials in 13 locations of the Kara and Barents Seas of the Arctic Ocean, and 10 locations in the Japan and the Okhotsk Seas and the Pacific Ocean off Russia's Kamchatka Peninsula. Ocean disposals of radioactive materials were a clear violation of the international London Treaty and shocked the world (Ishihara, 1993). Russia has since indicated that it no longer conducts ocean dumping.

The Kara and Barents Seas are shallow parts of the Arctic Ocean. These two seas are separated by the Island, Novaya Zemlya, which has been a sensitive military area. Soviet underground nuclear bomb testing was performed in this island's Chernaya Bay of the Kara Sea (Forman et al. 1995). Reactors of 17 nuclear submarines and Lenin ice breaker ships were disposed of in the Kara and the Barents Seas around the Novaya Zemlya Island between 1957 and 1991. Six submarine reactors and an ice breaker ship's reactor were sunk with nuclear fuels still in them. These two Arctic seas also received the radioactive reactor cooling water of nuclear submarines, and radioactively contaminated equipment was also dumped to these two seas. The total radioactivity from this dumping may have reached about 10 percent of the amount released in the Fukushima nuclear accident. This is in addition to over 3.7×10^{16} Becquerel (1 million curies) of radioactivity carried to the Kara Sea through the Ob and Yenisei Rivers, which received liquid radionuclides from nuclear fuel reprocessing plants at the Mayak, Tomsk, and Krasnoyarsk defense nuclear sites. Some estimate that the total amount disposed of in the oceans may have as high as to 9.3×10^{16} Becquerel (2.5 million curies).

Interestingly, plutonium found in the Kara Sea is not from the submarine reactors dumped in the sea; rather, it comes from the Mayak nuclear site and the global fallout from it (Beasley, 1995). In addition, the majority of the plutonium in the Canadian basis of the Arctic Ocean (North Polar, opposite from the Kara Sea) came from the Mayak defense nuclear site. However, the majority of cesium-137 in the Kara Sea is from England's Sellafield nuclear site along the Irish Sea. Iodain-129 that has been found in the Laptiv Sea (immediately east of Kara Sea) also came from the Sellafield Site (Beasley, 1995).

The Environment Regarded as Not Important

We sometimes consider adverse changes in the environment an acceptable price to pay in light of the benefit that the use of water resources can generate. And we often underestimate the damages we cause. This is usually because we do not look at all appropriate temporal and spatial scales. This happened in the Aral Sea when the large amount of water of two major rivers, the Amu Darya and the Syr Darya, flowing into the sea was diverted for irrigation.

The Aral Sea, an inland saltwater lake, is located in central Asia along Tajikistan, Uzbekistan, Turkmenistan, Kyrgyzstan, and Kazakhstan and before 1960 was the fourth largest inland sea in the world after the Caspian Sea, Lake Superior, and Lake Victoria. It is a relatively shallow, saline-water lake.

The Aral Sea has expanded and shrunk many times over the past several million years. Even within the last 10,000 years, it has repeatedly expanded and recessed with water level changes of over 60 feet due to natural climate changes and natural diversion of the Amu Darya away from it. Because it is located in the desert, its water has always been the foundation of local people's lives. There are now more than 50 million people living in this area. In the last 150 years, the water level change has only been around 13 to 16 feet. In 1960, the average water depth was 53 feet. The water surface area and volume were 26,000 square miles and 260 cubic miles, respectively. Its salinity was about 10 grams per liter, a little less than one-third of ocean salinity.

When referring to this southern part of the then Soviet Union, Russian revolutionary Vladimir Ilyich Lenin stated in 1918 that "Irrigation will do more than anything else to revive the area and regenerate it, bury the past and make the transition to socialism more certain" (New Scientist, 1989). Following this pronouncement, the former Soviet Union built many irrigation canals, including the 800-mile-long Karakum Canal that was developed from the 1940s to the 1960s to divert the river waters to the Kara Kum Desert before they get to the Aral Sea so that cotton and some rice could be grown. Consequently, the sea has a drastically reduced its depth. Its volume shrunk by 90 percent. Consequently, the Aral Sea split into two small lakes: the North Aral Sea (a northern part of the original Aral Sea) and the South Aral Sea (a thin strip of a southwestern edge of the original sea). This split exposed a large part of the salty sea bed to air. Salinity increased from 10 grams per liter to more than 40 grams per liter (which is saltier than sea water). This lake's reduction has been the most rapid and largest in the last 1,300 years.

The then Soviet government was aware that the Aral Sea would drastically shrink, but the agricultural products grown with the irrigation water were more valuable than the sea. But the consequences were worse than expected (Micklin, 1988). The Aral Sea shore moved 60 to 90 miles away from the original shore, decimating fishing and sea transportation. The smaller, shallower, and more salty Aral Sea had significantly reduced biological productivity, including waterfowl. Wind blew salt and contaminated dust from the exposed dried sea bed and deposited up to 100 million tons of salt annually over an area of roughly 300,000 square miles, producing a salty desert. Poorer health (e.g., asthma and other lung diseases) developed due to more frequent, salty, and toxic dust storms. The weather became more continental, with much colder winters, and much hotter and drier summers. The resulting continental weather reduced the growing season, causing significant economic losses.

Responding to this human-made disaster, Kazakhstan built the $86 million, 0.8-mile-long Kok-Aral Dam in the North Aral Sea in 2005 to separate the North Aral Sea from the bigger, saltier, and more polluted South Aral Sea and to maintain inflow from the Syr Darya into the North Aral Sea. This solution is working. Called the Kazakh Miracle, the North Aral Sea has regained

30 percent of its size since 2003, the average water depth increased from 100 feet in 2003 to 140 feet in 2008, and the seashore is extending toward the desert.

The number of fish species has increased from 1 to 15, and the fishery is now recovering. The local industry is growing. The winter has become milder, the summer cooler. There are more rains and less frequent sandstorms. To revegetate the dry, salty seabed, the native shrub, saxaul, has been planted. This shrub is appropriate for salty desert soil and grows 10 to 30 feet high. It reduces wind erosion and provides more suitable conditions for other plants and animals. The recovery of the North Aral Sea indicates that human-made disasters can sometimes be partly reversed with well-conceived mitigation.

Cleaning and Restoring the Water Environment

We are finally realizing damages we have caused to water and to humankind, and are taking the responsibility to clean up the mess and to undertake large-scale water restoration. The Gulf of Mexico's oil contamination is being evaluated, and some monetary compensation to victims is being given. The most expensive and complex remediation of water and soil environments in the world is being performed at the Hanford Nuclear Site in eastern Washington state. This is one of the sites the federal government established in 1943 under the Manhattan Project to produce nuclear bombs (Gephart, 2003). It was the first plutonium production site in the world. It had nine nuclear reactor plants and five reprocessing plants in a 586-square-mile area along the Columbia River.

These plants are no longer operational. From the 1940s to the 1970s, the reactors discharged radioactive liquid, including reactor cooling waters, into the Columbia River. Fortunately, the radionuclides, mostly zinc-65 have decayed (Washington State Office of Health, 2004). Within the Hanford Site, 177 large underground radioactive waste storage tanks stored 53 million gallons of high-level radioactive waste with 7×10^{18} Becquerel (190 million curies, or about 25 times the radioactivity released to the environment from the Fukushima nuclear accident and 25 times that of the Hiroshima atomic bomb). At least 67 of these storage tanks as well as nuclear fuel storage pools have or suspected to have leaked about a million gallons of radioactive and toxic chemicals, contaminating the underlying groundwater that is moving into the Columbia River (Hanf et al., 2004). Some of them, for example, strountium-90, tritium, hexavalent chromium, and nitrate (NO_3) have already reached the river.

To protect the groundwater and the Columbia River, the U.S. Department of Energy has been working (i) to remove the radioactive wastes stored in the storage tanks and the deteriorated spent nuclear fuels from the storage pools, (ii) cleansing the contaminated groundwater to stop the migration of radionuclides into the Columbia River, (iii) dismantling contaminated reactors and other nuclear facilities, (iv) removing contaminated soils, and (v) building a radioactive waste treatment plant. Cleansing the groundwater involves a process called the pump and treat which includes pumping out the contaminated groundwater, removing some contaminants, and pumping the cleaned water back into the groundwater.

The intensive remediation at the Hanford Site has been proceeding for more than two decades and has produced some good results, such as removing all liquid waste from 149 leak-prone, radioactive-waste-storage tanks. However, it is technically challenging, is expensive, and takes a long time to achieve the goal of restoring an acceptable aquatic environment. These remediation efforts cost about $2 billion per year and are expected to continue for several more decades at an estimated cost of $42 to $56 billion (Alvarez, 2005). It is good that we are taking the responsibility to remedy the damage we caused.

We cannot live without water. However, as illustrated in the preceding examples, we have mistreated water and have misunderstood how the aquatic environment responds to our actions. Our technologies are so vast that our actions become tragic at larger temporal and spatial scales. Our actions have produced many adverse impacts on aquatic environments and have affected the biosphere, including humans. We are now more aware of impacts of our actions at larger scales and have learned to be more responsible for our environment. After all, we live in this interactive environment—earth.

Water: Long-Term Global Changes

The earth has undergone many changes over its 4.6-billion-year history, with associated water changes. However, these changes were generally slow in human terms. The earth's recent atmospheric conditions are changing at a much faster rate. Global air temperature is rising, glaciers in the northern hemisphere are melting faster than they are forming, and the global average sea level has been rising over at least the last 100 years (IPCC, 2007). Precipitation rates are also changing. These changes are affecting the global aquatic environment. In the Pacific Northwest, climate models generally predict a 5 to 10 percent increase of precipitation (Hamlet et al., 2005). We pay much closer attention to local short-term changes than global long-term changes, even though the latter may affect us more than the former. Many adverse impacts of long-term, global scale changes are in addition to normal natural and human-induced disasters occurring now. Mitigating and adapting to climate change problems would also address many current problems, including water pollution, water security, extinction of many species, and population increase.

Long-term global changes are also expected to occur on rivers and oceans. The aquatic changes affect water resources we use, requiring us to adjust to these aquatic changes and promote sustainability. We are now realizing that we are powerful enough to affect the environment, whether we intend to or not.

We need to see facts as they are, evaluate them and form a rational consensus on required action plans, and proactively implement these actions to promote the betterment of humanity and the living things we share the earth with. It is as much a psychological challenge to break away from our old ways of thinking as a scientific and engineering challenge.

Changes on Water

Location, frequency, quantity, intensity, and timing of precipitation (rain and snow) along with snow and glacier accumulation and melting are changing. These changes are due to rapid climate change over the last 150 years (IPCC, 2007). These changes, as well as increased carbon dioxide influx into water bodies, alter river and oceans.

As global air temperature rises, there will be more precipitation globally because the higher air temperature evaporates more water and makes more clouds. At any given location, this may not necessarily be true. Some areas will get more precipitation, while others will get less. Higher latitude regions of the northern hemisphere are predicted to get more rain, not snow, due to higher air temperature. Deserts in tropical and subtropical zones will expand, making peripheral zones of the deserts drier. Global climate change models are in general agreement and predict higher air temperature in the future. Predictions of precipitation vary significantly and even forecast the opposite direction of precipitation change at some locations (Polonsky, 2009). Whether precipitation comes as rain or snow affects rivers' water conditions. Thus, there is uncertainty when estimating future river water conditions.

Globally, we have less glacial accumulation and more glacial melting. This is mainly because we have less snow and more rain in winter. Spring comes earlier, and summer lasts longer than before to melt more snow and glaciers. This may drastically impact people and biota using river water.

Almost two billion people live in glacier-snowmelt-fed river basins. The northern hemisphere glaciers may be reduced by up to 60 percent by 2050 (IPCC, 2007). Shrinking glacial snow coverage is happening in major east and south Asian rivers that originate from the Himalayas and Tibetan plateaus. In the western United States, 70 percent of river water is snowmelt, particularly in the Colombia, Snake, Colorado, Sacramento and San Joaquin Rivers. In the Pacific Northwest, less snow is accumulating in the Cascade Mountains, and each year snow melting is about three weeks earlier than a few decades ago (Hamlet et al., 2005). By 2050, the Columbia River discharge is predicted to be up to 50 percent more in winter but up to 50 percent less in summer (University of Washington, 2004). The future decline in river-water availability in summer will produce severe hardships to people who use the water of glacier-fed rivers. Climate change may also make the weather more unpredictable.

More severe storms and prolonged droughts could occur (IPCC, 2007), resulting in more unpredictable river flow rates and flooding levels. These uncertainties make water resources planning much more difficult.

The water levels of oceans are rising due to increased glacial melt. Levels also increase because water expands as water temperatures increase. Until around 1925, the global average sea level was rising at the rate of 0.7 millimeters per year. It is now rising about 2.5 millimeters per year. Evaporation increases as temperature increases, and more clouds form. This results in more precipitation and an increasing number and intensity of storms. Although we tend to focus on carbon dioxide as a greenhouse gas, water vapor is also a greenhouse gas that heats the atmosphere. Moreover, when water vapor cools in the air and condenses to form water droplets (which is the beginning of cloud formation), it releases 80 calories per gram of liquid water latent heat. This latent hear further increases the air temperature.

There are other changes. The seawater near the ocean surface becomes lighter due to the warmer sea-surface water and lighter freshwater influx from melted glaciers. Because deeper water is colder and heavier, it becomes more difficult for the lighter ocean-surface water to mix with the heavier, deeper water. That means the deeper water does not get as much oxygen from the sea surface as it was getting before.

Moreover, because the deeper water is rich with nutrients, the sea surface water does not get as many nutrients from the deep water as before. This condition is not good for aquatic biota. Plants and fish near the surface get fewer nutrients, while fish living in deeper water get less oxygen. This same phenomenon is also occurring in many lakes, reducing seasonal lake-water turnover that vertically mixes the lake water. This also leads to deterioration of lake water quality.

The global ocean current circulation, called the thermohaline circulation, may be weakened or disrupted if the current global warming trend continues for a long time. This circulation is a gigantic conveyer belt for the world ocean water, transferring tropical heat to the North and South Poles. The warm Gulf Stream moving north along the eastern coast of the United States from Florida is part of this circulation. By the time it reaches Greenland, cooled ocean surface water sinks to the ocean bottom, affecting the global weather.

Over roughly 700,000 years, the carbon dioxide level in the atmosphere has been around 180 parts per million during glacial periods and 280 parts per million during the interglacial periods such as the last 10,000 years (IPCC, 2007). It has increased since the 1850s and is currently 380 parts per million. The ocean absorbs a large amount of carbon dioxide from the atmosphere, about 30 percent of the anthropogenic carbon dioxide produced by human activities. The large carbon dioxide influx has the potential to increase ocean acidity, making it difficult for shelled organisms and corals to produce skeletons and shells.

TROUBLED WATER RESOURCES AND ADAPTATION TO THEM

Changing conditions of rivers and oceans impact the vital water resources we use. They affect municipal and industrial water supplies, irrigation for agriculture, hydroelectric power generation, recreation, and so on. Most of these water usages require fresh liquid water, mainly river water. All the world rivers combined have only 509 cubic miles of water. This is only 0.00015 percent of the world's water. This tiny fraction is our vital water. We need to watch our rivers and be careful to take care of them. Instream water usages are mainly for hydroelectric power generation, fisheries, ship and barge transportation, and recreation. Outstream water usages are mostly municipal and industrial water supplies, and agricultural irrigation. As available water resources change, competition and conflicts among various water users intensify.

Water Supply

The world's population is project to grow from 6.8 billion today to 9.1 billion in the next several decades. The more people on earth, the more water we use. Today, snowmelt and glacier-fed rivers have higher flow rates in winter and lower flow rates in summer (University of Washington, 2004). When the climate is changing, it is more difficult to predict future precipitation, and the amount and timing of available water. To secure future water availability, the Metropolitan Water District of Southern California, which serves 18 million Californians, made a 35-year water trade with the Palo Verde Irrigation District, which has the rights to use Colorado River water.

Irrigation Agriculture

Irrigation for agriculture removes by far the largest amount of river water. It accounts for 70 percent of global river water withdrawal and 90 percent of global consumptive (nonreusable) water use. Developing countries account for 75 percent of global irrigation use. China and India have the world's largest irrigation areas, and the Yellow (Huang He) River has seen significant reduction of its discharge. Due to increased irrigation and industrial water use, along with less precipitation, the Yellow River water does not reach the sea at times. Reckless river-water withdrawal for irrigation can have devastating impacts, as evidenced in the Aral Sea case. Eighty percent of California water usage is for irrigation. Some of these irrigation waters can be traded for municipal water usage, as the southern California water district has done.

The impact of climate change varies depending on many factors, including the nature of the change, crop types, water availability, adaptive measures to be taken, and agricultural production elsewhere in the world. As previously discussed, increased global temperature makes water less available in summer in the western United States. Higher temperature makes soil drier in summer when rivers have less available irrigation water (University of Idaho, 2005). Competition for scarce water resources among various water users will intensify. For example, 1,600 California farmers did not get irrigation water from the Klamath River in 2001, and their crops died. In 2002, they received Klamath River water, but about 34,000 salmon died in the river on the way to spawning that year.

Response

Any climate change can affect water resources. Because of changes occurring in water conditions, conflicts will intensify among various water-resource users. To resolve these conflicts, we need to find common goals. We must coordinate, collaborate, and compromise on our water uses. We individually and collectively need to consider various factors, including:

- Control population growth
- Diversify water supply sources, including surface and aquifer water storage and seawater desalinization
- Conserve and increase efficiency of water and electricity usage
- Build more renewable energy production capacity

These responses are technically and financially challenging. To implement these actions, we need to change how we see ourselves and the world surrounding us.

SUMMARY

Water is a part of a delicate, interactive, balancing biosphere system. It is the lifeblood of people and all living things. Our life-supporting water is changing on a global scale. Change will continue and may be accelerated by the increasing effects of people's activities on our world. Our activities have damaged our aquatic environments and thus our biosphere because we have treated water as an unlimited resource and have disregarded the impact of our actions. The speed and direction of the changes preclude us from maintaining our current lifestyle, which is adapted to current conditions. Fortunately, we are starting to realize that our actions impact the aquatic environment and are beginning to become better stewards of the earth's environment. Some expensive and long-term attempts that have been made to clean up locally and regionally contaminated waters have met with some success. Through our painful experiences, we now know that it is more economical and beneficial to take care of the environment from the beginning.

As our environment changes, we must become more flexible in response to new situations. Longer-term changes must be accounted for when planning for the future. Spatial effects are also important. Changes at larger spatial scales are more difficult to anticipate than those at local and regional scales. It is not too late for us individually and collectively to change our course to obtain a sustainable lifestyle. To adapt to the troubled waters and water-related resources, we need to make careful water management plans, secure additional water sources and water storage, conserve water and energy, improve water usage efficiency, improve energy sources, promote more renewable energy, and recycle materials to promote sustainable lifestyles. Severe competition and conflicts exist among various water users—agriculture, industries, and nations. To address these water resource conflicts, coordination and collaboration among water stakeholders will be needed.

REFERENCES

Alvarez, R. (2005). *Reducing the risk of high level radioactive wastes at Hanford.* hanfordchallenge .org/cmsAdmin/uploads/2005_Reducing_the_Risk_of_HLW_Full_Version.pdf.

Beasley, T. M. (1995). Gamma-ray spectroscopy, transuranic radionuclides, iodine-129, and technetium-99. In J. Morgan & L. Codispoti (Eds.), *Department of Defense Arctic Nuclear Waste Assessment Program: FY 1993–94.* Arlington, VA: Office of Naval Research, pp. 2–14.

Chernobyl Forum. (2005). *Chernobyl legacy: Health, environmental, and socio-economic impacts: and recommendations to the governments of Belarus, the Russian Federation and Ukraine.* Vienna, Austria: International Atomic Energy Agency.

Forman, S. L., Polyak, L., Smith, J., Ellis, K., Matishov, G., Bordikov, Y., & Ivanov, G. (1995). Radionuclides in the Barents and Kara sea bottom sediments: Distributions, sources and dispersal pathways. In J. Morgan & L. Codispoti (Eds.), *Department of Defense Arctic Nuclear Waste Assessment Program: FY 1993–94.* Arlington, VA: Office of Naval Research, pp. 67–73.

Gephart, R. E. (2003). *Hanford: A conversation about nuclear waste and cleanup.* Richland, WA: Pacific Northwest National Laboratory.

Hamlet, A. F., Mote, P. W., Clark, M. P., & Lettenmaier, D. P. (2005). Effects of temperature and precipitation variability on snow pack trends in the western United States. *Journal of Climate, 18,* 4545–4561.

Hanf, R. W., Morasch, L. F., Poston, T. M., & Diston, R. L. (2004). *Summary of the Hanford sites: Environmental report for calendar year 2003.* Report Number PNNL-14687-SUM, Richland, WA: Pacific Northwest National Laboratory.

Intergovernmental Panel on Climate Change (IPCC). 2007. Climate change 2007: Synthesis report: Summary for policymakers. In *Fourth Assessment Report of the Intergovernmental Panel on Climate Change.* New York: United Nations.

International Atomic Energy Agency (IAEA). (1991). The International Chernobyl Project: Technical report of the advisory committee. Vienna, Austria: Author.

Ishihara, T. (1993). Various problems of Russian radioactive waste. *Genshiryoku Kougyou, 39*(11), 71–78.

Lovelock, J. (1979). *Gaia: A new look at life on earth.* Oxford, UK: Oxford University Press.

Mayhew P. J., Jenkins, G. B., & Benton, T. G. 2007. Long-term association between global temperature and biodiversity, origination and extinction in the fossil record. *Proceedings of the Royal Society B,* pp. 1–7.

Micklin, P. P. (1988). Desiccation of the Aral Sea: A water management disaster in the Soviet Union. *Science, 241,* 1170–1176.

New Scientist. (1989). *Soviet cotton threatens a region's sea—and its children.* Retrieved January 27, 2010, from http://www.newscientist.com/article/mg12416910.800 -soviet-cotton-threatens-a-regions-sea—and-its-children.html.

New York International Bible Society. (1978). *NIV Pictorial Bible: New International Version.* Grand Rapids, MI: Zondervan Bible Publishers.

Onishi, Y., Kivva, S. L., Zheleznyak, M. J., & Voitsekhovich, O. V. (2007a). Aquatic assessment of the Chernobyl nuclear accident and its remediation. *Journal of Environmental Engineering, American Society of Civil Engineers, 133,* 1015–1023.

Onishi, Y., Voitsekhovich, O. V., & Zheleznyak, M. J. (2007b). *Chernobyl: What have we learned? The successes and failures to mitigate water contamination over 20 years.* Dorrdrecht, The Netherlands: Springer, pp. 9–47.

Polonsky, A. (2009). *Climate changes in the Black Sea region.* Proceedings of the U.S. National Academies and National Academy of Sciences of Ukraine Joint Workshop on Water Sector Adaptation for Climate Change. Washington, DC: National Academies.

ScienceDaily. (2010). *Hydrocarbons deep within earth: New computational study reveals how.* http://www.sciencedaily.com/releases/2011/04/110415104540.htm.

University of Idaho. (2005). *Changing climate, changing watersheds.* Watershed Management Council, University of Idaho.

University of Washington. (2004). *Overview of climate change impacts in the U.S. Pacific Northwest.* Seattle: Climate Change Group, University of Washington.

U.S. Geological Survey (USGS). (2009). *Science for the changing world.* Retrieved January 27, 2010, from http://ga.water.usgs.gov/edu/earthwherewater.html.

Washington State Office of Health. (2004). *Radionuclides on the Columbia River.* Olympia, WA: Environmental Health Programs, Hanford Health Information Network. www.doh.wa.gov/communityandEnvironment/Radiation/EnvironmentalSciences/ HanfordEnvironmentalRadiationOversightProgram.asf.

3

Our Atmosphere: Friend or Foe?

Robert A. Muller

Understanding our traumatized world today requires understanding our atmosphere. Fortunately, more people are becoming aware of a crucial aspect of our environment: climate change. They have heard the words but often do not have a broad picture and a deeper comprehension of the concept. This chapter explains this aspect of our traumatized world.

Our atmosphere is connected with just about everything that takes place on the surface of the earth: weather and climate, the oceans and ice caps, the biological realms including plants and animals, and all human activity. This chapter begins with a brief overview of radiant energy from the sun and its transformations for heating the surface and the atmosphere, with attention to the role of atmospheric carbon dioxide in the heat budget of the atmosphere as well as the controversial environmental and political issues associated with the greenhouse effect or global warming. Geological evidence, however, proves that over the last few million years, the earth and atmosphere have experienced extraordinary cyclical temperature swings that resulted in ice caps covering most of Canada, the northern United States, and northern Europe. These frigid times were separated by shorter periods when temperatures were about as warm as today. So much seawater was locked up in ice that sea levels were more than 400 feet lower than now, and during the warm "interglacials," so much ice melted that sea levels were about 200 feet higher than today, with Gulf of Mexico waters reaching close to Memphis.

In this chapter, we focus primarily on climatic change and variation in the scale of human lifetimes, over the last 150 years or so, essentially the history of rapid industrialization based on the burning of fossil fuels: coal, oil, and natural gas. We will also consider examples of shorter periods of 2 or 3 up to 30 years duration when regional climates, long-term averages of weather, became much wetter or drier, or colder or warmer than "normal," resulting in environmental and economic disasters as well as dislocation of human settlements. We will also examine extreme weather events, some of which occur with limited prediction or warning, producing widespread destruction and loss of life. Finally, we also consider how the fluid atmosphere acts like a sewer, disbursing concentrations of pollutants from densely populated industrial centers for hundreds of miles downwind, with consequences far beyond the initial sources of pollution.

THE CONNECTED ATMOSPHERE-EARTH SURFACE SYSTEM

Our atmosphere is a relatively thin envelope of air that allows for transmission of solar radiation to the earth's surface as the primary source of energy and heat for our earth as well as for the life-giving process of photosynthesis that is essential, directly or indirectly, for most living things. The atmosphere also acts somewhat like a translucent blanket that absorbs much of the "return" radiation from the earth's surface, preventing much of it from escaping to space and thereby maintaining near-surface air temperatures at levels compatible with the lives of people, plants, and animals. The atmosphere also shields people and animals at the surface from most of the dangerous ultraviolet solar radiation that is often associated with development of skin cancers, especially among sun lovers at the beaches, and even with farmers and ranchers who spend many of their years outdoors.

The lower "sphere" of the atmosphere is the zone of horizontal and vertical mixing, technically called the troposphere. In the tropics, the troposphere extends upward from the surface to more than 50,000 feet, but in subpolar latitudes, the troposphere is less than 30,000 feet thick. Temperature is normally warmest at the surface and decreases on average 3.6 degrees Fahrenheit per thousand feet through the troposphere. At times, especially near the surface and overnight, the temperature profile reverses, with lower temperatures just above the surface. These conditions are called inversions. When they occur, pollution generated at the surface is prevented from being dispersed aloft because colder air is denser and does not rise. This results in much higher pollutant concentrations that are often dangerous to the health of people, animals, and plants. Above the troposphere, where temperature normally does not decrease with increasing altitude, is the stratosphere, where there is mostly horizontal rather than vertical mixing of air.

Many people appreciate the cooler temperatures of uplands and nearby snow-capped mountains. In colonial times of the seventeenth and eighteenth centuries, Europeans established secondary colonial mountain capitals in the humid tropics, where the climate was considered to be more healthy. Except for astronauts and pilots of high-flying aircraft, we spend our entire lives in the troposphere.

The three primary gases of the troposphere—nitrogen, oxygen, and carbon dioxide—are well mixed vertically and geographically. On the other hand, water vapor, which is directly responsible for cloud development and precipitation, is most abundant near the surface, especially over the oceans. It varies greatly from high concentrations in the humid tropics to low values over deserts and cold polar regions. Carbon dioxide, water vapor, and especially clouds absorb outgoing radiation from the earth's surface and return much of the radiation back to the surface in what is commonly called the atmospheric greenhouse effect. This atmospheric absorption results in a much warmer surface and troposphere than there would be without an atmosphere. The concentration of these gases has not changed significantly over the last 2,000 years or more. The exception is carbon dioxide, with a well-documented steady increase associated with the beginning of the industrial revolution and the widespread burning of fossil fuels that began about 200 years ago. In the northern hemisphere, carbon dioxide has increased from 310 parts per million in 1955 when accurate sampling was begun near the summit of Mauna Loa in Hawaii to about 375 parts per million in 2010, an increase averaging about 1.2 parts per million per year, or about a 21 percent increase. There is widespread scientific agreement that atmospheric carbon dioxide is directly associated with absorption of thermal radiation from the earth's surface; thus, more carbon dioxide results in more warming in the troposphere and at the earth's surface. Because of increasing use of fossil fuels worldwide in the twenty-first century, carbon dioxide concentrations are predicted to rise dramatically, with probable greenhouse warming. Warming could also be influenced by other greenhouse gases, especially water vapor, that should also be increasing.

The relationship between the earth and sun through the annual cycle produces an unequal distribution of heating and cooling at the earth's surface, resulting in energy and heat gains in equatorial regions and net losses in polar regions. Nevertheless, these regions do not continue to become dramatically warmer or colder through time. The dynamic atmospheric circulation patterns, together with ocean circulations, transport and redistribute excess tropical heat to the higher latitudes and polar regions and colder polar air back to the middle latitudes. Storms play a significant role in this transport of warm tropical air pole-ward and cold polar air equator-ward.

REGIONAL CLIMATES OF THE EARTH AND CLIMATE CHANGE

If the surface of the rotating earth were all water, the resultant climates would feature a broad, warm and humid tropical zone astride the equator. Pole-ward in subtropical latitudes, there would be warm deserts with minimal vegetation cover. Still further pole-ward, in middle latitudes, would be humid regions with well-defined winter and summer seasons. There would be short and long runs of days and even weeks with back and forth outbreaks of colder polar air and warmer tropical air. Closer to the poles of both hemispheres would be belts with short, cool summers, with icecap climates centered at the poles.

The irregular patterns of continents and ocean basins, together with mountain chains and higher plateaus, result in the complex geographical climatic regions described in textbooks. The southern hemisphere is mostly oceans with a continent at the pole, so the climatic regions there more closely represent the idealized all-ocean belts described previously. The northern hemisphere, by contrast, is mostly land, including the massive Eurasian continent and North America, and a small Arctic Ocean at the pole. The resultant climates are not the idealized belts but instead are continental over the lands and maritime over and adjacent to the oceans.

After the middle of the nineteenth century, scientists recognized that climates over much of the earth have varied spectacularly in the recent past. Relic landforms associated with glaciers have been identified in regions without present-day glaciers, in Wisconsin and northern Germany, for example. Making use of an assemblage of dating methods in a textbook chapter, Aguado and Burt (2004) show that as recently as 12,000 years ago, an ice cap thousands of feet thick with a center near the Hudson Bay that extended southward to New York City and almost to St. Louis was still in place. About the same time, a similar ice cap with a center over Scandinavia reached the British Isles and almost to the Alps in central Europe. Furthermore, there have been at least five major individual surges of ice advance over the last 800,000 years. These were separated by shorter interglacial periods that were about as warm as today. These dramatic surges and retreats of ice are related to systematic regular variations in the orbit of our earth around the sun. These glacial and interglacial climatic changes were on geographic and temporal scales that enabled migrations of people, animals, and plants. Such migrations in today's densely populated world would be extremely difficult if not impossible, even if warning time was theoretically sufficient.

National networks of climatic stations where daily observations of maximum and minimum temperatures and precipitation are recorded were first organized in the late nineteenth century in the industrializing countries and some of their colonies. These climatic data allowed for the establishment of 20- or 30-year monthly temperature and precipitation "normals" for each station. The normals were merely averages, but much of the thinking at that time was that the normals were relatively stable with no long-term upward or downward trends, and that the ice ages were over. Of course, at each location in the middle and higher latitudes, there were runs of years that were warmer or colder, or wetter or drier, than normal, but the general professional and business understanding was that the climate was relatively stable and would always return again to the normals.

Beginning with the development of computers capable of processing massive climatic data sets in the middle of the twentieth century, climatic indexes of temperature and precipitation through time and their departures from the normals were developed for nations, hemispheres, and, indeed, for the entire earth; one single number, for example, representing the annual temperature of the entire surface of the earth. In the early 1970s, we learned that a distinct cooling trend had set in during the previous 20 or so years. Some climate scientists and science writers began to write about a "snow blitz" that within decades could result in expanding full-year snow cover with centers around the Hudson Bay and Scandinavia. This included areas with permanent settlements. Using a somewhat dramatic style, Nigel Calder ably presented these ideas in *The Weather Machine* (1974). This dramatic climatic change would, of course, have been catastrophic, especially for the inhabitants of most of North America and Europe. But there would have been some benefits to the economies of the nations of the subtropical and tropical realms, where temperature and rainfall averages would represent more favorable environments than what we have now.

Within a few years, however, the cooling subsided, and it was followed by a more or less global warming that persisted for about 20 years until the beginning of the twenty-first century. In the minds of many climatologists and environmentalists, this warming was mostly because of rising levels of carbon dioxide caused by industrialization, and drastic worldwide environmental and economic measures are needed to decrease the ever-rising carbon dioxide levels. During the most recent decade, however, the warming appears to have leveled off, and the winter of 2009 to 2010 was very cold with record-breaking snows across much of the eastern United States, Europe, and China. One of six great snowstorms ("nor'easters") with blizzard conditions along the east coast of the United States brought Washington, DC and the U.S. government to a halt for several days, and Washington, Baltimore, and Philadelphia broke their more than 100-year records for seasonal snowfall (LeComte, 2011).

The severity of the most recent winters in the densely populated regions of eastern North America and northern Europe has provoked questions about global warming and whether the warming is due to natural climatic variations or mostly due to human-induced increases of carbon dioxide. Nevertheless, there is little doubt that the earth is warmer today than in the mid-twentieth century, especially in northern polar regions. For example, in northern Alaska, summer and winter temperatures have increased much more than across middle and tropical latitudes, the extent and thickness of Arctic sea ice is decreasing, and there are warnings by some professionals that most of the Arctic Ocean could become ice free during the summer in 30 to 50 years. An open Arctic would accelerate temperature increases because snow and ice cover reflect most of the incoming solar radiation, but open water absorbs most of the solar beam. Many environmental and ecological impacts have been associated with warming as well. Some of the permafrost underlying most of the Arctic lands is melting, damaging the foundations of buildings, roads, and bridges, and at the same time, releasing vast amounts of methane, another greenhouse warming gas, into the atmosphere. Animals, fish, and plants from more southern areas have been moving in, disrupting local food chains and threatening the livelihoods of indigenous populations who depend on hunting and fishing for survival.

Disappearing alpine glaciers have been noted worldwide, in places as widely distant as Glacier National Park in Montana and Mount Kilimanjaro near the equator in eastern Africa. Because of melting ice from the continents and thermal expansion of the warming seas, sea levels have been creeping upward, threatening the survival of the low-lying Maldive Islands in the Indian Ocean, densely populated deltaic regions of the Mississippi and Ganges Rivers, and the infrastructure in many of the world's great commercial seaports (Aguado & Burt, 2004).

The most controversial issue, however, is whether the late twentieth century warming is solely or mostly a response to increasing carbon dioxide levels, or whether other geophysical interactions are the primary culprit. Some global warming enthusiasts have used the shape of a hockey stick politically to represent the shape of a graph of nearly steady global temperatures over the last 800 years followed by increasing temperatures beginning in the min-nineteenth century and rapidly increasing temperatures during the most recent decades. However, temperatures have cooled and warmed significantly over these last 800 years, and it is widely accepted that temperatures around the northern coasts of the Atlantic Ocean were considerably warmer 1,000 years ago than today, without the massive burning of fossil fuels (Aguado & Burt, 2004). This Medieval Warm Period allowed the Vikings to sail and colonize first Iceland, then Greenland, and finally to explore the maritime coasts of Canada and New England. In these same regions, however, climates returned to a much colder Little Ice Age from about 1200 to 1850, when the settlements in Greenland were abandoned. The uplands in the British Isles and Scandinavia lost most of their inhabitants because of summer-season failures of traditional crops, resulting in poverty, starvation, and out migration. With the return to warmer climates in recent decades, prosperity for a smaller population base in the highlands of Scotland, Ireland, and Scandinavia increased. Spectacular landscapes and tourism have replaced the widespread poverty of the nineteenth century.

The climatic naysayers, or contrarians, focus mostly on the historical evidence for natural variations of climate, the inaccuracies of the hockey stick representation of climate change, and the various adjustments to the raw data by climatologists developing global and regional data sets. They fear that the global plans of the environmentalists for scaling back carbon dioxide emissions are not only devastating for global economies but also ineffective relative to natural climatic variation. These scientific and political differences will not be resolved quickly or easily, as described by Mooney (2007). Hence, forever changing global climates need to be recognized and prepared for.

EXTREME WEATHER AND CLIMATE EVENTS

On a time scale of human lives, climates do vary significantly. The most obvious change is often the amount of precipitation. Runs of years with regional wetter or drier seasons or years are common, and the worst can severely impact human lives and the economy. In the middle latitudes, these runs of unusually persistent weather or climate are usually influenced by the location of jet streams that circle the northern hemisphere from west to east in the upper troposphere. The polar jet stream is a narrow ribbon of air racing around the northern hemisphere. It is positioned much farther south in winter, sometimes over the Gulf of Mexico, and much farther north in summer, usually over central Canada. Much of the time, these jets flow through great lobes, or waves, of air with higher atmospheric pressure ridges to the right of the flow and lower pressure troughs to the left. Normally, there are three or four waves around the northern hemisphere, with stormy and colder weather associated with the troughs, and fair and warmer weather with the ridges. The winter and spring storms follow the jet stream tracks, dragged along underneath the jet stream currents.

The ridges and troughs occur at usual, or normal, positions around the northern hemisphere, but they tend to drift from time to time. When they relocate for extended periods of weeks and even months, the weather and climate at the surface becomes unusual and occasionally extreme, with devastating environmental and economic consequences for some regions. During the first six months of 2011, the persistent unusual polar jet stream pattern brought heavy snows to the Pacific Northwest, flooding rains to the Missouri and upper Mississippi River basins, repeated outbreaks of violent weather and devastating tornadoes to Tuscaloosa, Alabama, and Joplin, Missouri, and widespread record droughts across the South from Arizona east to Florida. Atmospheric and oceanic scientists do not fully understand the causes for the dislocations of the ridges and troughs, but it is clear that warmer and cooler ocean temperatures are involved. One example is the recurring El Niño and La Niña events, that is, warmer or cooler than normal water across the tropical eastern Pacific. These events can persist for a year or more and are significantly correlated to weather and climate patterns across much of North America and the North Atlantic Ocean. The atmospheric and oceanic circulations are closely interrelated, and the patterns are interconnected around the globe.

The potential for disaster is especially great in subhumid climatic regions where rainfall is marginal for the maintenance of a natural vegetation cover of trees, and forests are replaced by natural grasslands. The Dust Bowl of the 1930s in the American Southwest is a lesson of environmental disasters and some ultimate recovery. On average, the Great Plains of Texas, New Mexico, Colorado, Oklahoma, and Kansas are classified as a transition from subhumid to semi-arid climatic types. They were covered with tall natural grasslands and were originally populated by vast herds of grazing buffalo. Through the latter half of the nineteenth century, buffalo were killed and replaced with beef cattle. However, during and after World War I, the demand for grains and a run of regional wetter than normal years encouraged the clearing of these natural grasslands for production of commercial grains. Initially, the profits were high, and farmers and those who provided supporting infrastructure prospered. In the early 1930s, however, the southern Great Plains turned extremely dry, with not enough moisture to sustain commercial crops. The natural grasslands had protected the soil from wind erosion, but the bare grain fields became open to relentless winds that whipped the soil up into one dust storm after another for about seven years. The progression of events is vividly told in *The Worst Hard Time* (Egan, 2006). The region and the environmental and economic devastation became known collectively as the Dust Bowl. The atmosphere carried dust all the way to Gulf and Atlantic coasts of the United States. The environmental degradation combined with the economic depression of the 1930s to force most of the farmers off their land, many of whom left for the West Coast nearly penniless, as was vividly described in the historical novel *Grapes of Wrath* (Steinbeck, 1939).

Rainfalls returned during the World War II years, and yields and profits were again high. Another run of dry years occurred in the mid-1950s, but this drought, sometimes called the Little Dust Bowl, was not as widespread or severe as that in the 1930s. Conservation and "dry-farming" practices, irrigation from the geographically extensive Ogallala aquifer, and some federal disaster support programs prevented another round of devastating economic failures. Nevertheless, there are continued fears that withdrawal of groundwater from the Ogallala aquifer far exceeds recharge from rainfall, and that in the long run, irrigation cannot be sustained at current rates of withdrawal (Egan, 2006). Climatic variation with clusters of wetter and drier years is to be expected on the Great Plains, but the lesson that, hopefully, has been learned is that land use and conservation practices are absolutely necessary for the maintenance of a stable agricultural economy, together with the use of external energy in the form of fossil fuels that support tilling, planting, irrigation, harvesting, and transportation to markets.

Extended runs of drought years are not limited to semi-arid climatic regions. Humid climatic regions, the northeastern United States for example, experience extended droughts from time to time that result in significant economic and environmental impacts. In the twentieth century, the first widespread severe drought in this region occurred during 1930 and 1931. For the next three decades, northeastern droughts were shorter and more localized, and in 1960 the New York metropolitan region had been so wet and groundwater levels so high that many basements on Long Island flooded; cynics joked about indoor swimming pools. The flooding rains suddenly shut off, however, and precipitation over the next five years was well below normal across a wide region that extended from West Virginia northeast into New England, with the most severe conditions about 1965 (Namias, 1966). For most of this region, this drought was the most severe of record, particularly because of its duration, with devastating environmental and economic impacts.

The metropolitan centers depend mostly on surface waters and reservoirs for public water supplies, and as the dry climatic pattern continued without abatement, reservoir storage became dangerously low. Water-use restrictions, such as banning car washing and lawn and garden watering became the rule rather than the exception. Property owners with green lawns were suspected of illegal use of scarce water and subject to fines when found guilty. Public and private water supply companies were forced to improvise emergency storage facilities, and in central New Jersey, two new reservoirs on tributaries of the Raritan River, Round Valley and Spruce Run, were constructed quickly to receive water diversions from the Delaware River, which was also very low (New Jersey Water Supply Authority, 2005). In fact, water flowing from the Delaware River into Delaware Bay was so low that brackish seawater, a little more dense than freshwater, spread upriver underneath the freshwater flow and threatened the water intakes for the city of Philadelphia. In northern New Jersey, usable storage in the reservoirs on the Pequannock and Wanaque Rivers that provided potable water for the city of Newark and surrounding suburbs was at one time down to less than a three-week reserve. The extended drought conditions also heavily impacted the ecological stability of undeveloped areas, especially upland forests. Stressed trees were lost, swamps and marshes dried out, and plants and animals died off. Expensive landscaping in suburban areas was also severely impacted.

In this humid climatic region, climatic variability continues to produce droughts with significant impacts to the region. Another serious but much shorter drought occurred in the Northeast a little more than 30 years, later during 1998 and 1999. Hence, we must recognize that climatic variability, even instability, is a characteristic of these humid climatic regions, and that plans and provisions for reoccurrences of these more extreme conditions need to be kept up to date.

In these same humid climatic regions, persistent atmospheric flow patterns can also generate excessively wet seasons that eventually result in massive river basin floods. Such was the case in the late summer, fall, winter, and spring of 1926 and 1927 in the Mississippi River Valley. Beginning in August 1926 and continuing off and on until late April 1927, extremely unusual repetitive flooding rains across most of the Mississippi drainage basin resulted in the most massive flooding on record along the Mississippi southward from Cairo, Illinois, to the Gulf in Louisiana. During the flood crest in April, it seemed like a repeat of the biblical flood of Noah, with the flood wave nearly 60 miles wide from Vicksburg, Mississippi, westward to Monroe, Louisiana. Day-by-day events are recounted in vivid detail in *Rising Tide* (Barry, 1997), with the U.S. Army Corps of Engineers focused finally on getting the floodwaters past New Orleans. The resultant loss of life, the sudden displacement of close to a million residents, and the enormous property losses initiated the development of a nationally organized lower Mississippi River flood control system by the U.S. Army Corps of Engineers that has proved to be successful during a succession of major floods in the deltaic region of Louisiana, especially in 1973, 1983, and 2011. The operation of the various diversion structures and floodways in 1973 is recounted based on interviews of scientists, engineers, and local residents and told in *The Control of Nature* (McPhee, 1989). Daily management of the diversions and floodways not only prevented the flooding of New Orleans but also the most likely sudden "natural" diversion of much of the flow of the Mississippi into the Atchafalaya River, a steeper and much shorter route to the Gulf. Had the diversion taken place, Morgan City near the mouth of the Atchafalaya would have been destroyed, and the present channel of the Mississippi from above Baton Rouge downstream past New Orleans to the Gulf would have become a brackish estuary of the Gulf, unable to provide for the freshwater water needs of the urban populations and the oil refineries and petrochemical complexes that line the river between Baton Rouge and New Orleans as well as serving as major ports as they do today.

During the spring of 2011, an unusually persistent jet stream pattern generated heavy rains and snows across the Midwest, resulting in another record-breaking flood along the Mississippi from St. Louis to Louisiana, with the floodways again opened to prevent massive flooding of New Orleans. The same storm systems produced record outbreaks of tornadoes across the Midwest and the South, including the deadly tornado events at Tuscaloosa, Alabama, and Joplin, Missouri. These together were the most costly seasonal tornado events in the United States in more than 60 years.

Similar climatic variability is also evident in the frequency of tropical storm and hurricane occurrences over the North Atlantic, including the Caribbean and the Gulf of Mexico. There have been extraordinary clusters of strikes along coastal regions, as detailed in *Hurricanes of the Gulf of Mexico* (Keim & Muller, 2009). The most shocking example is the high frequency of hurricane strikes along the east coast of Florida during the 1920s, 1930s, and 1940s. At Miami Beach, for example, there were 13 hurricane strikes between 1926 and 1950, essentially one every other year. But since 1950, there have been only seven strikes! Similar clusters of frequent strikes are on record for the Outer Banks of North Carolina during the 1940s, 1950s, and 1960s, and again since 1985. For the entire Atlantic Basin, the counts of tropical storms and hurricanes have been well above long-term averages since 1995, with 28 named storms in 2005, the most in recorded history, including four category five hurricanes. The clustering of major hurricane strikes during the 2004 and 2005 seasons along the central Gulf Coast, Ivan, Dennis, Katrina, and Rita, is remarkable and especially illustrative of shorter-term climatic variation.

The frequency and tracks of major hurricanes over the North Atlantic are affected by areas of warmer and cooler ocean water temperatures not only across the Atlantic but in the eastern tropical Pacific as well. Between 1945 and 1969, a period of 25 years, North Atlantic waters were warmer than usual, and 80 major hurricanes were identified over the Atlantic Basin. Between 1970 and 1994, in contrast, North Atlantic waters were cooler than normal, and only 37 major hurricanes were counted. In addition, El Niño and La Niña conditions over the tropical eastern Pacific affect the development and sustainability of major hurricanes over the Gulf and Caribbean; during El Niño seasons, stronger than normal upper troposphere winds from the southwest cut off and dislocate the tops of strong thunderstorm cells that are necessary for the maintenance and further development of hurricanes.

The shorter or longer intervals between hurricane strikes at beach resorts have encouraged residents to rebuild at places that are again vulnerable to future strikes. The federal flood insurance program has required much improved construction standards at sites prone to damaging storm winds and especially storm surges, but at the same time the program inadvertently has encouraged even more development through federal insurance subsidies to help cover much of the risk. Barrier islands along the Atlantic and Gulf coasts are now covered with wall-to-wall high-rise condominiums and hotels, where in earlier years mostly family camps were nestled among the dunes. Summer-season populations are so great now that more lives are at risk. Evacuation routes could be overwhelmed, and the potential property and infrastructure losses represent a burden that is shared by citizens far beyond the at-risk coastal areas. It is not clear how climate change affects the frequency and intensity of hurricanes, whether the next season will be more or less active than the long-term averages, or whether sections of the Atlantic and Gulf coasts will be more or less vulnerable.

ATMOSPHERIC POLLUTION AND ITS DISPERSION

Up to now, the focus has been on how the atmosphere, interacting with the oceans especially, affects climate change and variability in terms of temperature and precipitation for thousands or hundreds of years, decades, seasons, months, or even just a few extreme days.

We turn now to focus on the ability of the atmosphere to transport whatever is in it. The dynamic atmosphere serves to dilute and redistribute pollution concentrations and smog away from the source, whether the pollution source is entire metropolitan areas responsible for the pollutants in the first place, isolated industrial plants that produce pollutants, volcanic eruptions, or just dust being blown from arid fields. A classic example is smog from the Los Angeles basin that sweeps eastward from time to time across the deserts of Nevada, Utah, and Arizona, causing visibility at the Grand Canyon to be perceptively diminished, much to the disappointment of tourists. Consider another example: residents of the Great Plains assert that there is nothing but barbed wire between them and the North Pole and also the Gulf of Mexico. One winter day can have warm, humid weather from the Gulf with thunderstorms and the threat of tornadoes, and the next day may have icy gales and blizzard conditions with subzero temperatures from the Canadian Arctic. The atmosphere is extraordinarily interactive and mobile, with moving air at one place directly and indirectly connected to every other place.

Smelting operations of mineral ores in humid climatic regions can illustrate the dispersion properties of the lower atmosphere. Undisturbed natural environments in humid climatic regions are covered by forest vegetation, but vegetation around smelters without modern pollution controls has been killed by toxic sulfur-dioxide fumes, leaving the heavily impacted areas looking out of place as well as bizarre and barren without plants—very much like desert landscapes.

The Ducktown Desert in southeastern Tennessee provides a shocking example of the effects of smelting (EPA, 2005). The mining of high-sulfur-content copper ore was started in 1843, with ores placed on open smoldering wood fires for weeks to months, with plumes of acidic smoke drifting over adjacent areas. The location of the plume depended each day on wind direction and speed, and whether inversion conditions prevailed. By about 1900, all of the vegetation over an area of about 60 square miles had been destroyed, leaving a highly eroded naked red and orange landscape. Pollution controls and conservation practices were introduced in the 1930s, with reforestation plots initiated by the Civilian Conservation Corps (CCC) and the Tennessee Valley Authority (TVA). As part of a main route between Asheville, North Carolina and Chattanooga, Tennessee, U.S. Highway 64 crosses the basin, and in the 1960s, tourists were still shocked by the transition from lush forests to desert-like landscapes. By the turn of the twenty-first century, however, a young forest cover had become reestablished, and most tourists now would not be aware of the lengthy reclamation of the valley.

Much the same deforestation occurred around Sudbury, Ontario, which is located north of the Georgian Bay and about 200 miles north of Toronto in the northern boreal forest region of Canada (Smith, 1996). The nickel deposits there are considered to be the richest in the world, and mining and smelting that began there about 1880 has continued to the present time. Open-roast bedding smelting was banned in 1928 because of widespread forest damage within a radius of about 10 miles around the operations. A super stack 1,247 feet high was erected in 1972, allowing for some ecological recovery in the vicinity. But the emissions of pollutants higher in the atmosphere have resulted in more distant diminutions of air quality along with some negative impacts on the forests.

Concentrations of the iron and steel industries in the late nineteenth century at especially favorable locations with dense populations led to much larger domes of pollution over larger regions and affected residents' health and life spans. In the United States, the more than 100-mile industrial corridor from Pittsburgh, Pennsylvania, to Cleveland, Ohio, suffered from devastating bouts of pollution. At times, atmospheric temperature inversions prevented the normal dispersion of pollutants over larger areas. During an extreme case in October 1948, at Donora, an industrial suburb nestled in the deep and narrow valley of the Monongahela River, 24 miles south of Pittsburgh, 24 people died and more than one-third of the population became seriously ill during five days of a thick yellowish toxic smog trapped by an inversion. The deadly smog was believed to be associated with fluorine gas from a nearby zinc works; during the fifth day, the air was cleared by a rain event and lifting of the inversion. Until late in the twentieth century, less deadly smog events occurred from time to time in the English Midlands around Birmingham and Manchester; in the Ruhr Valley in western Germany, which is famous for the iron and steelworks of Krupp and Thyssen; and in Upper Silesia in southeastern pre–World War II Germany, now southwestern Poland.

During the later twentieth century, massive cleanups of the soot, smog, and general pollution produced spectacular results, with, for example, the cities of Pittsburgh and Essen, Germany, in the Ruhr serving as models for recovery from blighted and unhealthy environments. Our atmosphere is so effective in transporting pollution from industrial centers to much larger regions that before the cleanups had become effective, it was believed that the forests of Germany and eastern Europe, and even the southern Appalachians around Mt. Mitchell in North Carolina, would die out because of deadly acid rains. These recoveries are testimony to what can be accomplished by more effective pollution controls with joint public and private cooperation and dedication.

The atmosphere is even capable of intercontinental transport. Thin veils of dust lifted off the desert terrain of western Africa can be traced by satellites across the Atlantic Ocean, where these dust clouds can inhibit the development of tropical storms and hurricanes over the western Atlantic Ocean and Caribbean Sea. Similarly, atmospheric pollution originating in eastern Asia has also been seen crossing the Pacific Ocean for thousands of miles and reaching western North American coasts. And several times in recent years, ash from volcanic eruptions in Iceland forced cancellations of air traffic over northwestern Europe for safety considerations.

The atmosphere also supports the transport and migrations of insects and birds on favorable winds for surprisingly long distances, even over water where there are no opportunities for rest stops. History has documented plagues of locusts moving from place to place north and south of the Mediterranean Sea, even arriving on strong southerly winds in central Europe and the British Isles. Similarly, the seasonal migrations of Monarch butterflies and destructive corn earworm moths from Central America and Mexico with favorable wind currents all the way to the northern United States are well known. Much the same can be said about the seasonal migration of birds from tropical and subtropical environments in winter to summer locations thousands of miles to the north.

LOOKING FORWARD

In summary, the thermal and moisture properties of the troposphere, and especially the circulation patterns, are in a continuous state of variation and change from previous conditions. Further change must be expected and anticipated. For more than the most recent 150 years, temperature and rainfall data show significant natural variation and longer-term trends possibly associated with the well-documented steady and persistent increases of greenhouse gases. Regardless of the causes, the greatest global variations have taken place across the Arctic, where there is much environmental and ecological evidence of recent warming. But there is also evidence of worldwide warming that has the potential to impact environmental and socioeconomic infrastructures everywhere.

Much shorter-term extreme events such as tornadoes, hurricanes, flooding, and droughts are usually not predictable much in advance. Despite very costly storms, floods, and droughts, 2010 and 2011 were estimated on a global basis to have been just about the warmest and wettest for the data sets extending back into the mid-nineteenth century, resulting in increasing seawater temperatures and levels, less volume and extent of Arctic sea ice, and more rapid melting of the Greenland ice cap. During this same period, the earth has also been plagued by an unprecedented run of costly deadly events. In the United States, examples include more intense and frequent winter and spring storms associated with killer tornadoes, record rains and snows, and record flood levels across the Mississippi River Valley, and, at the same time, widespread droughts and fires occurred across the deep south, from New Mexico eastward to Florida. Extreme events from other continents are often in the news: the record-breaking droughts and heat in central Russia; the floods in Pakistan and in Queensland, Australia; and storms over northwestern Europe.

Public and private sector emergency responses for the shorter-term disasters are so much more doable than deciding on and implementing social and economic policies for mitigating some of the impacts of the predicted trends of temperature, precipitation, and sea-level rise that are associated with increasing levels of carbon dioxide due to our growing worldwide industrial societies of the last 150 years and into the future.

REFERENCES

Aguado, E., & Burt, J. E. (2004). *Understanding weather and climate* (3rd ed., Chapter 16). Upper Saddle River, NJ: Pearson Education.

Barry, J. (1997). *Rising tide: The great Mississippi flood of 1927 and how it changed America.* New York: Simon & Schuster.

Calder, N. (1974). *The weather machine.* New York: Viking Press.

Egan, T. (2006). *The worst hard time.* Boston: Houghton Mifflin.

Environmental Protection Agency (EPA). (2005). Copper Basin Mining district: Case study. Retrieved May 27, 2012, from www.epa.gov/aml/tech/copperbasin.pdf.

Keim, B., & Muller, R. (2009). *Hurricanes of the Gulf of Mexico*. Baton Rouge: Louisiana State University Press.

LeComte, D. (2011). U.S. weather highlights of 2010: A year of extremes. *Weatherwise*, May–June, pp. 13–20.

McPhee, J. (1989). *The control of nature*. New York: Farrar, Straus, & Giroux.

Mooney, C. (2007). *Storm world: Hurricanes, politics, and the battle over global warming*. Orlando, FL: Harcourt.

Namias, J. (1966). Nature and possible causes of the northeastern U.S. drought during 1962–65. *Monthly Weather Review, 94*(9), 543–554.

New Jersey Water Supply Authority. (2005). *Raritan Basin water supply system, safe yield evaluation, and operations model: 2005*. Retrieved May 22, 2012, from www.njwsa .org/Raritan_Basin_Riverware_Model.pdf.

Smith, M. (1996). The reclamation of Sudbury: The greening of a moonscape. *Restoration and Reclamation Review, Student Online Journal, 1*(4), 1–11.

Steinbeck, J. (1939). *The grapes of wrath*. New York: Viking Press.

4

Our Planet Earth: Understanding the Big Picture

Donald F. Nemeth

We usually personally understand what it takes to keep our homes in order, yet the earth is our global home. Do we understand what it takes to care for our earth home? Change on a global scale affects us both individually and collectively. This chapter offers an understanding of the earth, our home, how it changes, and what is necessary for its healing and rebuilding.

Planet earth nourishes us and sustains us. It is the only home we have. People who live close to the earth, people whose lives are dependent upon their immediate surroundings, are well dedicated to respecting and maintaining their environment. In western societies, the worth of a region is not judged by what it is; the worth of a region is determined by how much monetary return it can yield regardless of whether the end result is sustainable.

BACKGROUND

From the beginning, life forms have left their mark on the earth. Solid evidence of past forms of life is found abundantly preserved in the earth's rocks as fossils. Many plants and animal species left evidence of their presence in their paleoenvironment and changed the earth in some way, as have all creatures since then. Present day humans, however, are unique in the ways we can profoundly modify the earth. We can alter the course of a river, change the shape of a mountain, drain wetlands, build on active faults, and alter the composition of the atmosphere. Every change we impose has consequences, some good and some bad. To maintain our existence on this earth, it is imperative that we understand and respect it, and learn from the past. There are many natural phenomena over which we have little or no control, such as earthquakes, volcanic activity, and massive landslides. Geologic and recorded history holds the key to preserving the earth. Research into the geologic past yields information that helps us know what to expect in the future. A large body of scientific information is presently available that, via computer modeling, research, and a commitment to environmental preservation, gives us the ability to preserve the world (at least to some degree) as we know it today. Research leads to knowledge; knowledge leads to insight. We must be cognizant of the modifications we make to our environment and the outcome of our actions, positive or negative.

The concept of time can be easily conceptualized by the human mind in terms of hours, days, and years. When we enter the realm of thousands and billions of years, understanding becomes difficult. The average human life span in the United States is 78 years. This span of time is infinitesimally short compared to the earth's age of 4.54 billion years (USGS, 2007).

To understand the earth, we must look at it as a whole. On a recent trip to China, my Chinese guide relayed the story of how, as a school child, he first heard of America when his teacher told the class, "If you dig a hole in China all the way through the earth, you will come out in America." I remember my teachers in the United States telling me the same story in reverse. What is in the interior of the earth, and how does it affect what happens on and near the surface?

COMPOSITION

First we will delve into the structure of the earth, which can be conceptualized as a series of nested spheres having a common center (i.e., concentric); next the general nature of each spherical layer; and last the rock near the surface. It is within this last zone that the most dynamic forces shaping the earth's surface operate.

The internal structure of planet earth has been deduced partly from the composition of meteorites and how earthquake waves (i.e., seismic waves) travel through the earth. The innermost part of the earth, the inner core, which is also the heaviest part of the earth's interior, is believed to be predominantly iron and nickel. Surrounding the inner core is a liquid outer core, which, in turn, is encircled by a solid mantle. Above the mantle is the crust, which is composed of continental crust and oceanic crust. The continental crust, when compared to oceanic crust, is predominantly composed of minerals that are lighter in weight.

The uppermost solid rock below the earth's surface, the lithosphere, is made up of continental crust, oceanic crust, and the upper part of the mantle. The upper portion of the mantle, known as the asthenosphere, is a zone of solid rock that can flow plastically due to high temperature and pressure. This zone is analogous to modeling clay. It remains a solid, but it can still flow (i.e., plastic flow).

In the early twentieth century, Alfred Wegener, a German meteorologist, proposed that continents were moving. The theory, known as continental drift, was not widely accepted. After the 1950s, however, a large body of evidence was amassed and indicated that continents and the seafloor are on the move.

Oceanographers have been able to determine the age of the ocean basins' rocks. They have also studied the magnetic properties of the rocks. Geophysicists have determined the structural nature of continental boundaries and the seafloor. From this body of data came first the theory of seafloor spreading, followed later by the theory of plate tectonics.

Submerged and mostly out of sight below the surface of the Atlantic Ocean is one of the greatest physical features on the planet, the mid-Atlantic Ridge, which is a mountain range rising above the, seafloor. It extends from the Arctic to the Antarctic and its top surfaces above the Atlantic Ocean as Iceland, the Azores, and other locations. This mountain range's name does change with location, and it extends through all of the earth's oceans, from the Atlantic into the Pacific and Indian Oceans (Menard, 1965).

Below the oceanic ridges, within the earth's mantle the asthenosphere comes near to the seafloor. Heat convection within the asthenosphere brings molten rock (i.e., magma) near the surface and feeds volcanic activity. From oceanographic studies, we know that the seafloor increases in age away from the mid-ocean ridges. The seafloor is spreading. The seafloor is able to move because of plastic flow within the asthenosphere. The active forces generating volcanism tear the earth's surface apart along the axis of the ridges (i.e., a line running parallel to the trend of the ridge), forming rift valleys, linear depressions where the valley floor has dropped down relative to the surrounding mountains. Mid-ocean ridges are sites of active volcanism, rift valley formation, and earthquake activity.

An overall view of the earth's surface reveals prominent physiographic features such as mountain ranges (e.g., the Himalayas), ruptures in the earth known as faults (e.g., the San Andreas), mid-ocean ridges (e.g., the Mid-Atlantic), deep trenches along continental margins (e.g., off the coast of Chile), deep trenches and island arcs (e.g., Japan), to name a few. These features often, but not always, delineate the boundaries of tectonic plates that encompass the earth's entire surface. The plates are analogous to the segments making up the surface (i.e., shell) of a fractured egg. The eight largest of these plates in decreasing size are Pacific, North American, Eurasian, African, Antarctic, Australian, South American, and Nazca (Dinwiddie, Lamb, & Reynolds, 2011). The earth's surface is fractured into as many as 47 recognizable named plates (Dinwiddie et al., 2011) made up of the rocks of the lithosphere. In some instances, these plates are composed of almost entirely oceanic crust, while others are composed of oceanic and continental crust. At one time in the distant geologic past, all the continents of the earth were joined as one landmass. The present configuration of the continents is a direct result of the fracturing of the earth's surface, the addition and destruction of crustal rocks along plate boundaries, and the movement of tectonic plates. From globally positioning satellite data, it is even possible to determine the rate of plate movement (USGS, 1999).

When the edge of a plate is an oceanic ridge, the addition of new volcanic rock along the ridge causes the plate to expand. We know the earth's surface area is not increasing. Yet material is being added to the plates. So what is compensating for the increasing size of the plates? In some cases, it is as simple as the collision of the subcontinent of India with Asia and the formation of the Himalayas. A more common mechanism, however, is the formation of deep trenches along the margins of continents and/or island arcs. These trenches, known as subduction zones, are areas where the edges of plates are moving downward (i.e., subducting) into the mantle to be melted and recycled, leading to active volcanism and earthquake activity. In subduction zones, the earth's surface is being compressed, thereby accounting for the extension to the plate by the addition of new oceanic crust along oceanic ridges and the formation of rift valleys.

A map of the undersea oceanic ridges system shows that often oceanic ridges are offset, that is, they are broken into linear segments and are displaced along transform faults. A transform fault is a break in the earth surface along which horizontal movement has occurred.

A part of the oceanic ridge system in the Pacific Ocean is the East Pacific Rise that extends from the Antarctic through the Pacific Basin to the Gulf of California (located between the mainland of Mexico and Baja, California). In the Pacific, the East Pacific Rise is a spreading zone, From the Gulf of California northward into the Salton Trough, it is a rift valley, a characteristic of oceanic ridges. Northward, however, the ridge system is offset by a transform fault (i.e., the San Andreas) which runs two-thirds of the length of California, The fault then joins with the South Gorda oceanic ridge (USGS, 1999). The San Andreas fault, although it occurs on land, displaces laterally an oceanic ridge system. The horizontal movement occurring along the San Andreas fault and its effects can be comprehended by considering the geographic locations of Los Angeles and San Francisco in relation to the fault. The cities of Los Angeles and San Francisco are approximately 350 miles apart, Los Angeles is on the west block moving northward, and San Francisco is on the east block moving southwards, Over the last 10 million years the average rate of movement is 1.97 inches per year (USGS, 1999). If this rate of movement continues, in approximately 11 million years the site of Los Angeles will be adjacent to the site of San Francisco. It is not surprising that California is referred to as earthquake country.

The floor of the Salton Trough is more than 200 feet below present sea level. This valley, located partly in northern Mexico (Mexicali Valley) and partly in southern California (Imperial Valley and Coachella Valley), is an active seismic area. On April 4, 2010, an earthquake with a magnitude of 7.2 shook Mexicali and was felt as far as San Diego and Los Angeles (USGS, 2010). It is an area of frequent earthquakes and an area where heat is rising from within the earth to the surface. In the Mexican part of the trough is the inactive Cerro Prieto Volcano and the nearby Cerro Prieto geothermal field. This area of hot springs was first recognized by the early Spanish explorer Melchor Diaz in 1540 (Quijano-Leon & Gutierrez-Negrin, 2003). It was not until the 1960s that the Mexican government began to harness this geothermal energy. Today, the Cerro Prieto field ranks among the largest geothermal producer of electricity (Alles, 2007).

Another manifestation of active volcanism along an oceanic ridges occurred in April 2010 when eruptions in Iceland spewed volcanic ash into the atmosphere and disrupted air traffic across much of the northern Atlantic Ocean and Europe.

The land area encircling the Pacific Ocean, a region of active volcanism and earthquakes, is referred to as the Ring of Fire. Unlike the oceanic ridge system which is a zone of spreading the Ring of Fire is a zone of compression. On March 11, 2011, the sixth largest earthquake to ever be recorded, with a magnitude of 8.9, occurred off the coast of Japan. The quake resulted from movement within the subduction zone of the Japanese Trench. It generated a destructive tsunami. A tsunami is a wave that, at sea, can pass under a ship and hardly be detected but can reach destructive heights in a harbor or bay. The tsunami, in this case, was particularly destructive because deep embayments (i.e., indentation) along the coast amplified the height of the wave (USGS, 2011).

Living in active volcanic areas like the Ring of Fire presents many perils. Volcanoes in this region are especially known for their explosive activity and earthquakes. Mount St. Helens, the most destructive eruption of a volcano in the lower 48 states in recent time, occurred on May 18, 1980. Volcanic eruptions of stratovolcanoes (e.g., Mount St. Helens and Mount Fuji in Japan) present many dangers: earthquakes and lava flows; the ejection of debris, ash and gases into the atmosphere; and mudflows of volcanic materials. In 1883, the volcano Krakatoa in Indonesia exploded with a series of eruptions that sent volcanic ash an estimated 25 miles up into the atmosphere ("Krakatau," n.d.). The volcanic ash remained in the atmosphere for several years, blocking out the sun's rays and leading to cool summers and unusually cold winters in the northern hemisphere. It was not until five years later that the climate returned to its pre-eruption condition. In the immediate vicinity of the volcano, more than 36,000 people died from the eruption and ensuing tsunami (Gray et al., 1978).

A particularly destructive and dangerous phenomenon occurs when water, volcanic ash, volcanic debris, and gases mix and form a type of mudflow known as a lahar. Lahars can reach great size, as occurred in Colombia in 1985 when more than 23,000 people were killed (USGS, 2009). Strato volcanoes are not limited to the circum-Pacific. They also occur in the Mediterranean region (e.g., Mount Etna) and Africa (e.g., Mount Kilimanjaro, Tanzania) to name a few. The destruction of Herculaneum (a town near Pompeii) by Mount Vesuvius in the time of the Romans occurred due to lahars (Geography Site, 2006).

I remember, in the summer of 1963, arriving in the village of Heredia, Costa Rica, and smelling and feeling the volcanic ash falling from the eruption of Mount Irazu. A day or two later, I stood on the brink of the Irazu crater as it spewed ash and gases into the air. Like thousand of other tourists, I felt reasonably safe knowing the prevailing winds would blow the expelled materials away from me. A year or so later, I learned that all it took was a shift of the wind to expose the touring bystanders to the deadly asphyxiating gases. We learn to live with danger all around us. In some cases, we even find it exciting. Catastrophic events that occur with little warning however, are the ones to which we are most likely to succumb.

We live on a dynamic earth that rotates on its axis daily and revolves yearly around the sun. It is an earth with a fractured surface of moving continental and oceanic rock which is being torn apart by molten masses rising from the mantle. It is an earth that always has the potential for catastrophic events. Luckily, catastrophic change is not the norm. It is the exception.

A Changing Arctic

On a cold winter day in February 2011, I listened to a radio announcer report that one-third of the lower 48 states was in the grip of a major winter storm. I almost could not image that planet earth's climate was warming. Yet in the Arctic, a region far removed from most of our lives, average yearly temperatures are increasing faster than anywhere else on earth (Hassol & ACIA, 2004). On a global scale, the average surface temperatures for the years 2005 and 2006 were the warmest recorded since temperature recordkeeping began in 1880. The trend continues when 2011 tied with 2005 (Arctic Change Indicator, Global, n.d.).

Sea Ice

Sea ice blankets the surface of the Arctic Ocean. Most of this ice remains from year to year; however, in the summer, ice melts along the shore and retreats. It refreezes and advances to again form a completely ice-covered Arctic Ocean in the winter. Sea ice forms from the freezing of the surface waters of the ocean. It can vary in thickness from just a thin film to a maximum of 6.5 to 13 feet (Scott, 2009). Greater thicknesses are attained along pressure ridges where masses of floating ice have collided. Sea ice also forms at high latitudes outside of the Arctic Ocean and occurs in winter as far south as the Hudson Bay and James Bay, Canada.

The existence of sea ice in the Arctic has profound effects on the ecology, oceanic circulation, and climate. Sea ice, with its white surface, reradiates a significant part of the sun's energy back into space, keeping the Arctic cool. Sea ice also acts as a blanket to prevent the transfer of heat from the oceanic waters to the atmosphere (Arctic Change Indicator, Global, n.d.). When sea ice is not present, the water, with its darker surface, absorbs a large portion of the sun's energy, and the oceanic waters warm. Since 1979, satellite data have been collected on the time of formation and extent of sea ice. The University of Colorado's National Snow and Ice Data Center publishes a monthly online newsletter on the status of Arctic sea ice. Data presented in these reports indicate that, as of July 6, 2011, the extent of sea ice was the second lowest since records began in 1979 (National Snow and Ice Data Center, 2011). Fluctuations in the extent of sea ice do occur from winter to winter, as happened in the winter of 2011 to 2012 when sea ice extent was greater than the previous winter. However, the general downward trend in extent continues (National Snow and Ice Data Center, 2012). Sea ice formation has also been found to begin later in the year, with the approach of winter, and melt earlier in the season, with the approach of summer (Hassol & ACIA, 2004). Recently, there has been a net loss in the square miles of surface covered by sea ice and the length of time the sea ice remains. This general trend has persisted regardless of the severity of winters in North America and Europe. It has been estimated that by the end of the twenty-first century, the Arctic Ocean will be entirely free of ice during the warm portion of the year. The National Oceanic and Atmospheric Administration reports that new data analysis indicates the Arctic Ocean may be free of ice in 30 years (NOAA, 2009).

The length of time it takes to form sea ice and the length of time the ice remains also impact Arctic shorelines, especially their stability. The longer sea ice remains along a coast, the longer that coastline is protected from the direct impact of storm waves. Alaskan coastal erosion has increased in recent years, forcing some coastal communities to consider relocating to a more favorable site (Beck, 2005). As early as 1994, the community of Newtok, Alaska, began planning to relocate with construction at the new site to begin in 2011. As of December 2011, the Newtok Traditional Council announced the intent to solicit bids for infrastructure construction (Lincoln, 2012), and the villagers have approved the building of a new school at the relocation site (Alaska, 2012). It is reported that the per-household cost of relocation will be approximately $2 million (Feifel & Gregg, 2010). In addition to facing relocation, the indigenous peoples of the Arctic coast will also experience the consequences of ecological changes that threaten their traditional way of life.

Permafrost

The Arctic land area is underlain by frozen ground known as permafrost. Permafrost is ground and rock that is permanently frozen for two or more years. Defrosting solid rock that remains below freezing from year to year (although it is permafrost) does not have the same long-term impact on global climate as does defrosting permafrost soils. Permanently frozen soils are a gigantic storehouse of organic carbon. Approximately 61 percent of all organic carbon in North American soils occurs in permafrost (Tarnocai, Ping, & Kimble, 2007). Once it is no longer frozen, permafrost has the potential to contribute a significant amount of carbon dioxide and methane to the atmosphere.

The greatest expanse of permafrost is found in the northern hemisphere, where a staggering 24 percent of the land is underlain by permafrost (GRIP-Arendal, 2007). Permafrost occurs in a continuous band surrounding the Arctic Ocean and extends southward across Eurasia and North America, wherein it progresses into patchy zones of discontinuous occurrence. Arctic permafrost has been in place for hundreds of thousands of years (Alaska Public Lands Information, n.d.). In the Fairbanks, Alaska, area, it can extend from the surface down 150 to 500 feet. Further north, it is known to occur at depths greater than 2,000 feet (Arctic Change Indicator, *Permafrost*, n.d.). Though most extensive in the Arctic, permafrost is also found in rock and soils at high altitudes, such as in the Andes and on the Tibetan Plateau.

In the past, water tied up in the glaciers caused sea level to fall. It fell as much as 325 feet, exposing the continental shelf adjacent to the Arctic Basin (Alaska Public Lands Information, n.d.). Permafrost then formed. This permafrost that is now submerged due to the subsequent rise in sea level with the melting of the glaciers poses another danger from a warming Arctic Ocean. The warming of the Arctic Ocean will allow heat transfer to this zone of permafrost and subsequent melting.

If you have never been in an Arctic environment and have never experienced permafrost, it is hard to imagine. During the warm portion of the year, the sun melts the upper foot or so to form what is known as the active layer. This is a layer of muck, which refreezes with the approach of winter. In the high Arctic, near the Arctic Ocean, I was once involved with the excavation of a hole. An oil drum with its top removed was ultimately to be placed in the hole. To make the hole deep enough to accommodate the drum, an excavation had to begin several years prior to when it was needed. The excavation required exposing the upper portion of the permafrost, allowing it to melt, removing the loose material, and allowing the new surface to defrost. This process was repeated until we had the proper size hole. It was a long and tedious process. Ultimately, however, it would become the site of our new outhouse. Permafrost, even in a warming environment, will not disappear overnight. Permafrost that does melt, however, has the potential to significantly add greenhouse gases to the atmosphere. These gases will have an additive effect on the atmosphere, further increasing temperatures.

Other Arctic Problems

When Siberian Arctic lakes thaw, gas bubbles rise to the surface. The bubbles are composed of carbon dioxide and methane (Walter et al., 2008). Methane is 25 times more times powerful as a greenhouse gas than carbon dioxide. Methane, however, remains in the atmosphere for about 12 years, whereas carbon dioxide remains for hundreds of years (Moore, 2008).

Life in the Arctic presents unique challenges. Special engineering practices must be followed to construct buildings, roads, pipelines, and other structures. The builder must always be aware that heat transfer to the unfrozen ground can cause melting and uneven sinking of the structure into a sea of muck. Special precautions must be taken with pipelines that could rupture as permafrost melts. Travel over land in the summer months becomes a challenge when a myriad of lakes form across the tundra surface, usually with the proliferation of millions, possibly billions of mosquitoes. This terrain is almost totally impossible to traverse in summer. In winter, when the surface is frozen solid, however, it provides an excellent vehicular surface.

The discovery of hydrocarbons on the north slope of Alaska has led to extensive exploration, which calls for heavy equipment transport across the tundra, a treeless region underlain by permafrost. The frozen Arctic surface that provides a firm base for travel is defrosting sooner and remaining unfrozen longer in response to warming—a situation similar to the duration of sea ice. The opening of tundra roads in Alaska is now occurring two months later in the winter than previously (Arctic Change Indicator, *Roads*, n.d.).

Warming affects frozen soils most when they are exposed in deep cuts, whether natural or made by humans. Natural exposures, as in riverbanks, are particularly vulnerable. The cuts expose the frozen soils, including ice, to atmospheric heat and the sun's rays. Frozen water occurs most commonly in permafrost as fillings of voids between grains, as horizontal lenses of ice, and as vertical ice wedges. Melting poses problems for the environment. The quantity of water released is probably not as significant as the loss of stability of riverbanks and sea cliffs. Melting will profoundly alter the immediate surroundings and possibly alter the course of rivers, change drainage patterns, and change coastline configuration.

The Arctic, a unique frozen land, will not change overnight. Permafrost will not degrade in an instant. Probably no one can predict the rate of change. If global warming continues, what does appear to be a certainty is that the Arctic Ocean will be free of ice during the summer.

Another vast Arctic area of potential change is the ice sheet covering the island of Greenland. This sheet is massive, having an estimated volume of 683,751 cubic miles (Church et al., 2001), a mass so great that its weight depresses the earth's underlying crustal rocks. The Lamont-Doherty Earth Observatory has been monitoring the occurrence of earthquakes in Greenland. This is not a seismically active area; yet, since 2002, the number of local earthquakes has more than doubled, with most occurring in the summer months of July and August (Kostel & Bradt, 2006). This is the time most likely for glacial melt and the movement of large masses of glacial ice, exactly what we would expect with a warming climate. If the Greenland ice sheet were to melt entirely, global sea levels could rise by almost 24 feet (Church et al., 2001). An even larger quantity of water is locked up in the Antarctic ice sheet.

RISING SEAS

One of the greatest dangers from the addition of glacial melt water into the oceans of the world is sea-level rise. If global warming continues, sea levels will continue to rise. This rise will be further amplified by thermal expansion of the warmer oceanic water, making the problems even worst. Thieler and Hammar-Klose (1999) reported that, based on climatic modeling, the best estimate is a rise of 1.64 feet by the year 2100. The impact of an increase of this magnitude will further be amplified by the tidal range of a particular coastline and its vulnerability to storm action.

Because more than one-third of the world's population live within 62 miles of current sea level (Belt, 2011), a large portion of humanity will be impacted by rising seas. If you live in this zone, the most crucial factor will be elevation, that is, how high you are above sea level. Rising seas will cause increased coastal erosion. Coastlines will advance landward, placing areas that were once protected from wave and storm action at risk. Although rugged coastlines may provide the advantage of height, they too will recede with time. Recognizing the problems that are likely to occur with sea level rise, the U.S. Geological Survey (USGS) has classified U.S. coastal areas according to their vulnerability to change (Thieler, Williams, & Hammar-Klose, n.d.). Awareness of the consequential environmental changes is essential when determining where and when initial remedial steps must be taken to minimize both the social and monetary impact on humans. The classification is based on several factors: mean wave height, mean tidal range, coastal slope, whether a coastline is undergoing erosion or deposition, and relative sea level change. What is apparent from the USGS maps is that all U.S. coasts are vulnerable, but the most vulnerable are near sea level areas that are nearly flat and gently sloping.

One of the most economically important coastal features is the delta. Deltas—with their fertile soils, natural habitats for wildlife, and easy access to the sea, provided a hospitable environment for ancient humans. Ancient civilizations such as Mesopotamia flourished in the deltaic region of the Tigris and Euphrates Rivers of Asia Minor. The Egyptian civilization developed on the Nile delta. In fact, deltas are named for the shape of the Nile delta, which resembles the Greek letter delta.

The great rivers of the world (e.g., Mississippi, Rhine-Meuse, Yangtze) have built deltas where they enter the sea. Deltas have become major sites of agriculture, commerce, and manufacturing. Great modern cities have developed as ports (e.g., New Orleans; Rotterdam, the Netherlands; and Shanghai, China). All depend on marine commerce with sustainable port facilities. The Chinese government has poised Shanghai to become the number one financial center of Asia (Winston & Strawn, 2009). The Chinese government is committed to the importance of this deltaic region. Deltaic processes that maintain the Yangtze delta, as with all deltas, must be understood if the sites of cities such as New Orleans, Rotterdam, and Shanghai are to remain viable. All face the threat of sea level rise.

Deltas are gently-sloping features built near sea level by rivers where they flow into the ocean (deltas do also form in lakes and ponds). When a river enters the ocean and meets oceanic water, the rate of flow is slowed. The decrease in the velocity of the river water causes the particles being transported to drop. The largest, heaviest particles are dropped first. Then the lighter particles are carried out further into the body of water. As the particles are dropped, the particles that were deposited earlier are forced closer and closer together by the weight of the newly deposited overlying particles. This brings about a compaction of the sediment with the expulsion of water that once filled spaces between the grains. The compaction decreases the volume and results in subsidence. The surface decreases in elevation. If you were to take a slice through the earth below. In deltaic regions such as the Mississippi River delta, you would find that the underlying deposits consist of many deltaic lobes. A lobe would most likely consist of river channel deposits, natural levee deposits, freshwater swamp deposits, and marsh and shallow marine deposits. The lobe is a record of an episode of delta building by the river (U.S. Army Engineer, 1958). Through time, the river has built many lobes. In each case, the process is approximately the same. From the river mouth, a deltaic lobe is built further and further seaward until, probably when it floods, the river breaks through its channel, finds a shorter route to the sea, and builds a new lobe on the side of the former lobe. The former abandoned lobe is no longer nourished by the river, and it slowly subsides into the sea. Through time, the river builds lobes, with the lobes shifting back and forth along the coastline. Over thousands of years, thousands of feet of sediment accumulate. The weight of the sediment becomes so great that it depresses the earth's crust, bringing about regional subsidence, that is, subsidence of the entire coastal area. Along the Louisiana coast, geologists recognize a feature that they refer to as a hinge line. It is like a seesaw. North of the line (where Baton Rouge is located), the land is moving upward; south of the line (where New Orleans is located), the land is moving downward (Gagliano, 1999). Only through periodic flooding and the accompanying nourishment of the coastal area with sediment can the coast of Louisiana (i.e., the area on the downward-moving side of the hinge line) keep pace with the subsidence brought about by compaction and regional subsidence.

Human Alterations

New Orleans and the surrounding delta and coastal areas is a classic example of how humans have altered the environment to meet perceived needs without consideration of the long-term consequences. Today this coastal area is undergoing active submergence with substantial daily land loss. What is happening along the Louisiana coast may well provide the scenario of what to expect as global sea levels rise.

Land loss along the Louisiana coast can be attributed to several factors. One of the primary factors is the levees built to prevent Mississippi River flooding. An extensive system of levees lining channels is in place. The channels now act as conduits for the transport of sediment into the deep part of the Gulf of Mexico. The present delta of the Mississippi River at its furthest extremity is known as the Bird-foot delta. The Mississippi River has built this delta across the continental shelf almost to the continental slope. No longer is the sediment load of the river building up the deltaic area. It is now ending up in the depths of the Gulf of Mexico. This has led to sediment starvation for the coastal area, with the loss of cypress forests, marshes, and barrier islands, Subsidence is now outpacing delta building. Land loss has also been accelerated by the oil and gas industry. To explore, develop, and produce hydrocarbons from the marshes and offshore areas of Louisiana, petroleum companies dug extensive linear canals through the marshes. These canals provide an easy and quick means for the transport of supplies and personnel to the Gulf of Mexico. These channels, however, have an adverse effect on the marshes. As the wind blows across the canals, it generates waves that erode the channels, the channels increase in size, and they ultimately coalesce as an open body of water. These channels also impede the tidal flow that is so important in these marshes. At times of severe storms, such as hurricanes, the impact is severe. Salt water can now intrude into the coastal marsh and freshwater swamp. The freshwater swamp and cypress forest slowly die, and wetlands are then destroyed.

The wetlands surrounding the city of New Orleans have acted as a natural protection from the high winds and storm surge that accompany hurricanes. With the loss of marshes and cypress swamps surrounding the city, the coastline has been moving closer and closer to the city. In recent years, as evidenced by Hurricane Katrina, without this protective barrier, the effects of storms have been particularly severe.

An active and concentrated effort has been underway to restore and preserve the deltaic environment of south Louisiana. Several approaches are being undertaken. One is to dredge sediment out of river channels and then pipe the sediment into the wetlands and lakes to build new land (Addison, 2005). Another involves re-establishing the natural sedimentation regime by strategically positioned breaches in the levees, thereby facilitating flooding and deposition. This method can be used only in the remote, uninhabited regions of the delta. This approach has encountered a new obstacle. The Baton Rouge newspaper *The Advocate*, reported that two breaches have been closed. Shoaling had occurred in the adjoining main shipping channel. Monies budgeted for dredging a channel of the proper depth were about to run out (Wold, 2011). In the short term, the cost of maintaining the shipping channel won out over restoring the land area. The final fate of this portion of the delta may be complete land loss.

The Bird-foot delta of the Mississippi River is the furthest extremity of the delta into the Gulf of Mexico. One paved road, Louisiana Highway 23, gives access to this area. It traverses the last community on the delta, Venice, a marine and air support center for the offshore oil and gas industry. On a hot, humid, Louisiana summer day in 2010 after the BP oil spill, I drove through Venice, passed over the levee that was protecting the town from flooding and storm surge, and descended onto the unprotected delta surface. The road, which ran parallel to a canal, was bordered on the far side by a ridge of marsh grasses and a few living bald cypress trees interspersed with the remains of many dead bald cypress trees. These trees had been killed by subsidence, land loss, and the incursion of salt water from the open Gulf of Mexico. As I drove on, the road began to resemble a canal; small water puddles became larger, more numerous, and ultimately all joined completely, submerging the road. Only trucks could go beyond this point. I turned my car around, having never reached the end of the paved road. I had the feeling that if I continued, I would descend into the Gulf of Mexico. With rising seas, active compaction, and regional subsidence, this part of the delta will soon be lost to the sea.

As mentioned earlier in this chapter, the East Pacific Rise extends up the Gulf of California into the Salton Trough. Millions of years ago, the Colorado River began to build its delta across the Salton Trough. Through time, the delta formed a natural barrier separating the upper reaches of the oceanic Gulf of California from the present dry, below sea level Salton Trough. Today the trough is a rich, irrigated agricultural region existing in a desert climate. The irrigated fields of southern California's Imperial and Coachella Valleys as well as the irrigated fields of northern Mexico are possible only with the diversion of Colorado River water. To have a dependable water supply, it was necessary to build dams and create reservoirs. Dams (e.g., Hoover, Glen Canyon) were built to impound the river. Sediments carried by the river are now deposited behind these dams, and the river now flows almost clean when it enters the Gulf of California. Delta building has virtually ceased. With the filling of upstream reservoirs, water flow to the delta has substantially diminished. The lack of fresh water entering the Gulf of California has changed the salinity in the upper gulf water. It has also altered the circulation pattern and reduced the introduction of nutrients (Alles, 2007). This may have long-term adverse effects on the ecosystem. The thickness and aerial extent of the Colorado River delta is enormous. It is, however, no longer being built by the river and is now being eroded by wave and tidal action.

Dam construction on the Colorado River has had other unsuspected consequences. The formation of Lake Mead behind Hoover Dam placed a great load on the earth's crust. This load was so great that as the reservoir filled, adjustments in the rocks below the lake generated localized earthquakes in the Las Vegas area (Hiltzik, 2010). The earthquakes, though unexpected, could have been predicted.

Lake Mead, with its sapphire-color water, is a sharp contrast to the surrounding southern Nevada desert. The desert, a barren landscape of unsurpassed beauty, is often overlooked for the glitter of Las Vegas. Plush casinos graced with fountains, irrigated lush green landscaping, and irrigated golf courses are made possible with water from Lake Mead.

In late March 2011, I flew over Lake Mead in a helicopter and was shocked by how low the water was. The former height of the reservoir could be readily ascertained by the water-stained rocks that were now exposed like a bathtub ring around the lake. The reservoir has suffered from a regional drought that has lasted for more than 10 years. The lake was only half full, and the water level had fallen 100 feet below the high water mark (McKinnon, 2011). The spring snow melts in the Rocky Mountains, the source of Lake Mead's water, had not yet begun at the time of the fly over.

The winter of 2010 to 2011 had record snowfall levels. With the spring melt the reservoir rose 30 feet (Shine, 2011). The drought appeared to be over. However, this was not to be. The winter snowpack of 2011 to 2012, however, was below normal, and the lake level was expected to drop 13 feet (U.S. Department of Interior Bureau of Reclamation, 2012). To prepare for the future, the city of Las Vegas had begun considering a new water intakes, 200 feet lower than the lowest of two current intakes (Wallis, 2008), at a cost of over $800 million (Shine, 2012).

In a desert environment, even a reservoir will not guarantee an adequate water supply. With global warming, deserts are expanding. It is estimated that as many as a billion people may be threatened by desertification (U.N., 1997).

The Brahmaputra River is one the great untamed rivers of the world. At least, this was the case until November 2010. The Brahmaputra headwaters are in the Himalayas of Tibet. The river then flow across the Tibetan Plateau, through the Himalayas into India, and on to join with the Ganges River to form a common delta. This deltaic area comprises almost all of the territory of present-day Bangladesh, one of the most populous nations on the planet.

In November 2010, China dammed the Brahmaputra River for the first time. This was done to construct the first large hydroelectric plant in Tibet. According to the Chinese government, this facility will have little effect on downstream water flow (Raman, 2010). The facility will reportedly generate power by using the natural drop in elevation of the river to turn the turbines ("China Dams Brahmaputra," 2010). Water is essential for China's development. More than a quarter of China's land area is desert. Tibet has a vast supply of fresh water stored in Himalayan glaciers. This water could greatly alleviate China's water needs. One way to maintain a dependable water supply is to create a reservoir, a bank that stores water that can be drawn upon when needed for irrigation as well as domestic and industrial use. Another benefit is regulating stream flow, which prevents flooding.

In 2008, I traveled along the Yarlung Tsangbo River, the Tibetan name for the Brahmaputra, and learned from my Tibetan guide that most of the villages along the river are either relatively new or older communities expanded by an influx of people moving from the mountains, where life was becoming harder and harder. The villages along the river are connected by a well-maintained paved highway. They have electricity and other modern conveniences. The Chinese government is modernizing the region's infrastructure. Is this partly in anticipation of dam building and creation of reservoirs? If this is the case, what will be the effects downstream? What we have learned from the Colorado and Mississippi Rivers and their delta should give us some answers. One of the immediate effects will be a decrease in the amount of water and sediment carried downstream by the river. If in addition to China, India were to decide that it needed to manage the water resources of the Brahmaputra, the active building of the delta in Bangladesh would probably decrease. This would add to the woes of Bangladesh, a land of increasing population and decreasing area due to rising sea levels (Belt, 2011).

In low-lying regions of other parts of the world, similar circumstances are likely to occur. It is projected that by 2050, as many as 250 million people may be forced to relocate away from submerging coastal areas (Belt, 2011). Where will all these people go on a planet with shrinking habitable land?

Sustainability

The *National Geographic* magazine, an excellent source of information on our changing planet, reports that earth's population will soon reach 7 billion people. By 2045, the population is projected to reach 9 billion (Kunzig, 2011). Can our changing planet sustain this many people?

Planet earth does not have inexhaustible supplies of natural resources. Resources needed for our very survival surround us every day—the atmosphere, soil, and water. Soil, or dirt, is essential to our existence. Without soil, most of the plants we eat would not grow. Soil takes generations to form, yet we can scoop it up with a bulldozer in a matter of hours or days. We do not give much thought to destroying productive farmland to build shopping centers and subdivisions and abandon the inner cities. Is concrete really better for us than soil? The rich, productive soil of the Midwestern United States was scooped up by the continental glaciers of the ice ages. It came from Canada and was dropped in the United States. These glaciers left Canada with many bare rock surfaces, which are inadequate for food production. We must preserve our productive soil. There may not be another suitable place for migration. The lack of productive soil may catch up with us by the time the planet has 9 billion people. Water is also essential. Rights to water in rivers flowing through multiple nations often lead to disagreements and even conflicts, especially during times of scarcity. Last, our burning of fossil fuels has polluted the atmosphere and has threatened the planet as we know it today. Do we even begin to understand? What measures are we willing to take to correct our problems? How much are we willing to change to save our earth?

SUMMARY

The earth is over 4 billion years old. It is not static. It is always changing. Powerful and potentially destructive forces are continually active in the earth's mantle and crust, volcanism occurs and new seafloor is produced, continents and oceanic crust are moving, and crustal rocks are being sucked back into the earth, melted and recycled. Most of the time, these changes occur slowly, so slowly that they are almost imperceptible. These forces can be activated in an instant with catastrophic consequences. The composition of the atmosphere is changing, the planet is warming, Arctic frozen soils are defrosting, glaciers are melting, sea levels are rising. Rivers are being dammed and levees are being created. Deltas are being changed. Frequently, little thought is given to the long-term consequences of such actions. Humans' motives for altering the earth are frequently self-serving. Little emphasis is given to sustainability. Because we humans generally live for less than a hundred years, it is difficult for us to perceive the damage we are doing to our global home, the earth. For each of our shortsighted actions, we are damaging our planet exponentially, not additively. A cypress forest here, a marsh there; what difference does it make? Our planet can no longer save us from ourselves. It is our turn; we must now save our planet. Only then will the, Mother Earth, continue to sustain us.

REFERENCES

Addison, J. D. (Ed.). (2005). The nuts and bolts of pipes and pumps. *Water Marks: Louisiana Coastal Wetlands Planning, Protection and Restoration News, 29*(August), 5–7.

Alaska Public Lands Information. (n.d.). *Permafrost.* Retrieved July 28, 2011, from http://www.alaskacenters.gov/permafrost.cfm.

Alaska. (2012, January 4). *Alaska village votes yes on school relocation.* Retrieved June 6, 2012, from http://www.topix.com/city/newtok-ak.

Alles, D. L. (Ed.). (2007, August 6). *Geology of the Salton Trough.* Retrieved from http://fire.biol.wwu.edu/trent/alles/GeologySaltonTrough.pdf.

Arctic Change Indicator. (n.d.). *Global temperature trends: 2011 summation.* Retrieved February 4, 2011, from http://www.Arctic.noaa.gov/detect/global-temps.shtml.

Arctic Change Indicator. (n.d.). *Land: Permafrost.* Retrieved July 29, 2011, from http://www.Arctic.noaa.gov/detect/land-permafrost.shtml.

Arctic Change Indicator. (n.d.). *Land: Roads.* Retrieved February 20, 2011, from http://www.Arctic.noaa.gov/detect/land-road.shtml?page=land.

Beck, F. A. (2005). In C. Werner (Ed.), *What does climate change mean for the Arctic? How is Alaska being affected?* (Congressional Briefing Summary 2005). Retrieved May 22, 2012, from http://www.scscertified.com/lcs/docs/Arctic%20Climate%20Change%20%20ACIA%20Briefing%20Summary.pdf.

Belt, D. (2011, May). The coming storm. *National Geographic, 219*(5), 58–83.

China dams Brahmaputra River in Tibet. (2010). Retrieved July 22, 2011 from http://www.indianexpress.com/news/china-dams-brahmaputra-river-in-tibet/712121/.

Church, J. A., Gregory, J. M., Huybrechts, P., Kuhn, M., Lambeck, K., Nhuan, M. T., et al. (Eds.) (2001). *Climate change 2001: The scientific basis. Contribution of Working Group I to the Third Assessment Report of the Intergovernmental Panel on Climate Change.* Cambridge: Cambridge University Press.

Dinwiddie, R., Lamb, S., & Reynolds, R. (2011). *Violent earth.* New York: DK Publishing, pp. 26–27.

Feifel, K., & Gregg, R. M. (2010, July 3). *Relocating the village of Newtok, Alaska due to coastal erosion.* Retrieved July 28, 2011, from http://www.cakex.org/case-studies/1588.

Gagliano, S. M. (1999). Section 3: Faulting, subsidence and land loss in coastal Louisiana. Retrieved May 22, 2012, from http://www.coastalenv.com/final_faulting__subsidence_and_land_loss.pdf.

Geography Site. (2006). *Lahars and pyroclastic flows.* Retrieved August 5, 2011, from http://www.geography-site.co.uk/pages/physical/earth/volcanoes/pyroclastic%20flows.html.

Gray, W. R., Loftin, T., Melham, T., Ramsay, C. R., & Rinard, J. E. (1978). Powers of nature. *National Graphic.*, Special Publication, pp. 40–41.

GRIP-Arendal. (2007). *Permafrost extent in the northern hemisphere.* Retrieved July 15, 2011, from www.grida.no/graphicslib/detail//permafrost-extent-northern-hemisphere.

Hassol, S. J., & Arctic Climate Impact Assessment (ACIA). (2004). *Impacts of a warming Arctic: Arctic climate impact assessment (synthesis report).* Cambridge: Cambridge University Press.

Hiltzik, M. (2010). *Colossus: Hoover Dam and the making of the American century.* New York: Free Press.

Kostel, K., & Bradt, S. (2006, March 23). Glacial earthquakes point to rising temperatures in Greenland: Rise of seismic activity linked to the movement of glaciers may be response to a global warming. Retrieved July 17, 2011, from http://www.ldeo.columbia.edu/news-events/glacial-earthquakes-point-rising-temperatures-greenland.

Krakatau. (n.d.). Retrieved August 4, 2011, from http://www.photovolcanica.com/VolcanoInfo/Krakatau/Krakatau.html.

Kunzig, R. (2011). *National Geographic, 219*(1), 42–49, 60–63.

Lincoln, G. (Ed.). (January 18, 2012). For sale. *Delta Discovery, 14*(3). Retrieved from www.deltadiscovery.com/story/2012/01/18classifieds/for-sale/01182012195207236.html.

McKinnon, S. (2011, April 19). Lake Mead replenished by snow. *Arizona Republic.* Retrieved July 31, 2011 from http://www.azcentral.com/arizonarepublic/news/articles/2011/04/18/20110418lake-mead-replenished-by-snowfall.html.

Menard, H. W. (1965). The world-wide oceanic rise-ridge system. *Philosophical Transactions of the Royal Society of London: Series A: Mathematical and Physical Sciences, 258*(1088), 109–122.

Moore, L. (2008, February 26). *Greenhouse gases: How long will they last?* Retrieved May 22, 2012, from http://blogs.edf.org/climate411/2008/02/26/ghg_lifetimes/.

National Oceanic and Atmospheric Administration (NOAA). (2009). *Ice-free Arctic summers likely sooner than expected.* Retrieved July 25, 2011, from http://www .noaanews.noaa.gov/stories2009/20090402_seaice.html.

National Snow and Ice Data Center (2011). *Sea ice enters critical period of melt season.* Retrieved July 17, 2011, from http://nsidc.org/Arcticseaicenews/2011/070611.html.

National Snow and Ice Data Center. (2012). *Arctic sea ice news and analysis.* Retrieved June 10, 2012 from http://nsidc.org/arcticseaicenews/20/12/06/.

Quijano-Leon, J. L., & Gutierrez-Negrin, L. C. A. (2003, September/October). Mexican geothermal development: An unfinished journey. *GRC Bulletin*, pp. 198–203.

Raman, B. (2010). China defends decision to dam the Brahmaputra. Retrieved July 31, 2011, from http://www.southasiaanalysis.org/%5Cpapers42%5Cpaper4175.html.

Scott, M. (2009, April 20). *Sea ice.* Retrieved February 2, 2011, from http:// earthobservatory.nasa.gov/Features/SeaIce/.

Shine, C. (2011). Lake Mead's Water level rises 30 feet after wet winter. Retrieved July 19, 2012, from www.lasvegassun.com/news/2011/aug/17/lake-meads-water-level-rises/.

Shine, C. (2012). State Officials investigating cause of fatal tunnel breach. Retrieved July 19, 2012, from www.lasvegassun.com/news/2012/jun/12/state-officials-investigating-cause-fatal-tunnel-b/.

Tarnocai, C., Ping, C., & Kimble, J. (2007, November). Carbon cycles in the permafrost region of North America. In *The first state of carbon cycle report (SOCCR): The North American carbon budget and implications for the global carbon cycle.* (Synthesis and Assessment Product 2.2 Report by the U.S. Climate Change Science Program and the Subcommittee on Global Change Research). Retrieved May 22, 2012, from http://www.climatescience.gov/Library/sap/sap2-2/final-report/default.htm.

Thieler, E. R., & Hammar-Klose, E. S. (1999). Introduction. In *National assessment of coastal vulnerability to sea-level rise: Preliminary results for the U.S. Gulf of Mexico coast* (U.S. Geological Survey Open-File Report 00-179). Retrieved July 29, 2011, from http://pubs.usgs.gov/of/2000/of00-179/.

Thieler, E. R., Williams, J., & Hammar-Klose, E. S. (n.d.). *National assessment of coastal vulnerability to sea-level rise.* Retrieved July 28, 2011, from http://woodshole.er.usgs .gov/project-pages/cvi/.

UN launches decade-long efforts to tackle desertification. (2011). Retrieved August 1, 2011, from http://www.globaltimes.cn/www/english/sci-edu/world/2011-04/564417.html.

United Nations, Special Session of the General Assembly to Review and Appraise the Implementation of Agenda 21. (1997). The United Nations Convention to Combat Desertification: A New Response to an Age-Old Problem. Retrieved June 9, 2012 from www.un .org/ecosocdev/geninfo/sustdev/desert/htm.

U.S. Army Engineer Waterways Experiment Station Corps of Engineers. (1958, July). *Geology of the Mississippi River Deltaic Plain Southeastern Louisiana.* (Technical Report No. 3–483, Volume 1). Vicksburg, MS: U.S. Army Engineer Waterways Experiment Station Corps of Engineers.

U.S. Department of the Interior Bureau of Reclamation. (2012). *Water operations: Current status.* Retrieved June 7, 2012, from www.usbr.gov/uc/water/crsp/cs/gcd/html.

U.S. Geological Survey (USGS). (1999, May 5). *Understanding plate motions*. Retrieved August 3, 2011, from http://pubs.usgs.gov/gip/dynamic/understanding.html.

U.S. Geological Survey (USGS). (2007, July 9). *Age of the earth*. Retrieved August 1, 2011, from http://pubs.usgs.gov/gip/geotime/age.html.

U.S. Geological Survey (USGS). (2009, June 24). Description: Nevado del Ruiz eruption and lahar: 1985. Retrieved August 3, 2011 from http://vulcan.wr.usgs.gov/Volcanoes/Colombia/Ruiz/description_eruption_lahar_1985.html.

U.S. Geological Survey (USGS). (2010, April 4). *Magnitude 7.2: Baja California, Mexico*. Retrieved August 3, 2011, from http://earthquake.usgs.gov/earthquakes/recenteqsww/Quakes/ci14607652.php.

U.S. Geological Survey (USGS). (2011). *Magnitude 9.0: Near the east coast of Honshu, Japan*. Retrieved July 14, 2011, from http://earthquake.usgs.gov/earthquakes/eqinthenews/2011/usc0001xgp/.

Wallis, S. (Ed.) (2008). Lake Mead No 3 intake tunnel awarded. Retrieved July 19, 2012, from www.tunneltalk.com/Lake-Mead-No-3-intake-tunnel-awarded-php.

Walter, K. M., Chanton, P., Chapin III, F. S., Schuur, A. G., & Zimov, S. A. (2008). Methane production and bubble emissions from Arctic lakes: Isotopic implications for source pathways and ages. *Journal of Geophysical Research, 113*. doi:10.1029/2007JG000569.

Winston & Strawn. (2009, September). Shanghai as an international financial centre by 2020. *Greater China Law Update*. Retrieved from http://www.winston.com/siteFiles/Publications/China_Law_Update_Sept09.pdf.

Wold, A. (2011, June 6). Sediment discussed. *Advocate*, pp. 1A, 4A.

5

Our Providing Biosphere: Flora, Fauna, and More

Robert B. Hamilton

LOOKING BACK TO THE PAST TO UNDERSTAND CHANGE

About 4.5 billion years ago, the earth was formed through the coalescing of matter and its included energy. This mass of space debris eventually morphed into the world as we know it now, 4.5 billion years later (Dalrymple, 2001). As time passed, on this originally featureless planet, tremendous transformations occurred. Land, continents, and seas developed, as did an atmosphere and organic molecules. About 3 billion years ago, the chemical processes that had been occurring, along with other changes, proceeded far enough for living, cellular beings to develop (Brasier et al., 2006). Later living things continued to develop and diversify to occupy almost all conceivable areas that had a supply of requisite materials and a supply of energy. Species evolved and became extinct. Types and groups of living beings evolved and persisted for a period of time, then either became extinct or evolved to newer versions that continued to adapt to the changing environment, and to compete for resources and survival. This process led to the evolution of human-like beings appearing on the planet about 250,000 years ago. Modern humans have existed for only about 10,000 years.

When the human species appeared the earth's habitats were somewhat similar to those with which we now are familiar. While details are certainly different; many transformations occurred and accumulated over time, any habitats we know today existed long ago. Specifically, many plants and animals were at least superficially similar and ecosystems functioned similarly to the way they do now. In comparison, humans developed more than other species, becoming omnivorous and obtaining energy by eating both plant and animal material. In addition, humankind developed differently from other animal species by walking upright and having an opposable thumb and an enlarged brain.

Despite these differences, all organisms require energy and materials. Plants as well as animals require a source of energy (biomass) and oxygen. For example, plants require carbon dioxide, water, and sunlight in addition to nutrients that are usually available in the soil to generate their own biomass and oxygen through photosynthesis when the sun is shining. All organisms are also similar in that whether plant or animal, they change their environment in the process of acquiring the resources to sustain life by competing with others or consuming others fully or in part. In doing so, they change the environment in either small or larger ways. Certainly in combination, the changes become large. For example, a forest is formed as individual tree seeds develop in proximity to each other, and a beaver dam can cause the formation of a small pool or lake. These are examples of changes that living things make in the process of living and staying alive.

When human beings appeared in the environment, the initial changes they made were similar to those made by animals of similar size and diet. But soon, humans discovered ways to manipulate the environment that other species could not do. We harnessed the use of fire, developed tools, and became increasingly sophisticated with what we could produce. We domesticated animals and used them to do work and supply some of our needs. We eventually learned to make machines powered by internal combustion energies that use fossil fuels as an energy source to accomplish many tasks. We went from hunter-gathering to family farms to the giant industrial farms we have today. We discovered electricity and developed schemes to distribute it efficiently. We harnessed energy to do work and move materials throughout the world. Now, much of our food is not grown on our farms or in gardens near our homes; rather it comes from other states or other countries where it can be more efficiently produced. We transport seeds, herbicides, pesticides, and fertilizer as well as the machines necessary for own farming endeavors. When we harvest a crop, usually with machines, we ship it all over the world, often in refrigerated vehicles. Our effect on the environment that was originally local is now international.

As a consequence of all these processes, we have greatly affected our environment. We have harvested much of the primary forest in the world, which can mostly not be replaced, especially in the short term. Even in the long term, some species that were original inhabitants have become extinct. We have replaced natural habitats with human-made ones. Even much of the meat we eat is produced in situations more like factories than the natural habitats the animals originally occupied.

The Present State of Our Environment

As a result of these changes, much of the original habitat has been lost. Species are becoming extinct for various reasons, but primarily because of loss of their habitat. Where we live now bears only slight resemblance to the habitat of our forbearers. For example, parks now remind us of our origins, and we have had to pass conservation laws to protect endangered lands and species as well as to increase biological diversity. These steps have been necessary because we have lost our natural habitats and have had to re-create diversity that once was natural. Diversity is primarily related to environmental complexity and the size of natural habitats, both of which have been enormously reduced by modern agriculture and other human activities, even though the size of industrial farms is becoming larger. When farms were first established, the fields were relatively small, replacing natural habitat. These agricultural fields were not particularly good habitats, except for the species that occupied the edges between the fields and their surroundings, which also were eventually lost as fields enlarged. Other species were decimated by activities associated with these changes. For instance in the United States, the numbers of peregrine falcons, bald eagles, and brown pelicans were greatly reduced by reproductive problems caused by the use of chlorinated hydrocarbons like the insecticide dichlorodiphenyltrichloroethane (DDT). Many fish and other species were also negatively affected. As proof of the danger of pesticides, and the hope for the survival of living beings, many of these animals recovered after use of these pesticides was stopped.

As another example, breeding opportunities of cavity-nesting birds decreased when natural forests were converted to industrial forests, especially those that grow trees of the same age and harvest them together. Many natural cavities were lost when the native trees were harvested and replaced. The newly planted trees take years to develop suitable cavities. In addition, many species cannot construct their own cavities, causing them to become endangered: some native species that nest in cavities (or holes) were out-competed for the limited supply of cavities by the European Starling, an exotic bird species introduced to the United States by settlers from England. Even-aged forestry also resulted in all trees in an area being of the same age, thus resulting in the cavities being concentrated in stands, or groupings, of the same ages.

Thus, modern agriculture and forestry practices result in the elimination of natural habitat, replacing it with industrial agriculture and tree farms. Both greatly reduce habitat diversity, with the result that many of these places are not suitable for many wild species of plants and animals. An ever-growing human population causes creates additional demands for food and energy as well as needs for particular industrial commodities and cause conflicting decisions on the use of land.

In the case of land use, the result of changing events presents tremendous challenges for our future. At a time when there is increasing concern for biodiversity, we are encouraging energy alternatives like ethanol and biofuels that require large amounts of land. In some cases, these alternatives seem to be encouraged over drilling for fossil fuels that needs less land. Wind farms to produce energy also negatively affect habitat availability. Environmentally-conscious groups are simultaneously encouraging more habitat use for biodiversity and endangered species, and advocating setting aside land for the development of wind, solar farms, or alternative fuels. These energy-producing practices reduce the availability of land that can be used for increasing biodiversity. Both goals cannot be achieved simultaneously.

The environmental problems we face today are inter-woven like an interconnected web, difficult to untangle as each issue is enmeshed in another. We understand the importance of reducing use of fossil fuels to minimize adding carbon dioxide (CO_2) to the atmosphere, but ignore the consequences of developing alternatives. Demands for sources of energy are increasing to support an ever-growing human population and to make energy use more comparable between rich and poor nations. Water use is expanding, and its availability is becoming a major problem.

The combination of all these factors can lead to potential crises. These must be avoided. Making matters worse, some crises cannot be anticipated. What can be done? Because change is so ubiquitous and our environment is so complex, we must be flexible enough to respond appropriately to any challenge. We must be careful to ascertain the motives of those encouraging particular agendas, especially if those proponents will be enriched by the plans on a personal or organizational level, or if the plans are being sold through propaganda, demagoguery, and obvious marketing. All decisions should be thoughtful, based on accurate information, and devoid of emotional or manipulative appeals that seek to take advantage of the masses' vulnerability or lack of information about the relevant issues. All solutions need to be considered from a holistic point of view, taking into account the best interests of all living beings and all peoples.

Why Change Happens

So far, we have examined our physical environment and some of our uses and abuses of it. We now examine our biological environment and our history as a species. The fundamental question addressed in this book is: Will we be able to deal with the natural and inevitable changes that we cannot control as well as to manage our environment to minimize future damage from unexpected change and maximize our ability to adapt to an ever-changing world?

The first step toward being able to manage change in our environment is to understand the nature of such change. Change is based on energy and the availability of material resources. Our material resources are finite. For example, the earth only has so much oil. The other contribution to change is energy. Some unplanned changes occur because of energy stored in our planet that occasionally is released unexpectedly, as happens in the form of earthquakes and volcanic eruptions as well as energy produced when solar radiation interacts with our environment in ways that we cannot control, as happens in the case of hurricanes, other storms, floods, and occasional naturally caused fires.

Humans harvest stored energy in various ways and use it to accomplish specific goals. When energy is used, some of it is inevitably lost. Because our perceived energy needs are increasing, we need to continuously acquire energy and deal with the problems that occur with its acquisition and use.

Our condition as a species is constantly changing. Much of the change has been facilitated by our increasing ability to manage energy acquisition and use to accomplish our goals. Many of the changes we have overseen have greatly changed our environment and our relationship to it. Many of the changes we have fostered, deliberately or not, have also affected other species and our landscapes. Hopefully, the world that we are continuously changing by our efforts will be as suitable for us in the future as the world we have evolved in.

BIOLOGICAL BACKGROUND

All living things require materials and energy. Biology, in many ways, is the study of energy acquisition, production, and use in living systems. There are about 100 basic materials (elements) that are the building blocks of all matter. Except for radioactive elements, none of these can be naturally converted to others, and the total amount available of each is finite. This is why we can discuss global carbon, for example. Each element has its own distribution and may be common in some places, and rare or absent in others. Because life is almost everywhere, its main constituents—carbon, oxygen, hydrogen, and nitrogen—are also available almost everywhere. Life also requires energy. In nature, plants through photosynthesis convert carbon dioxide (CO_2) and water (H_2O) into energy-containing biomass by utilizing energy from sunlight. Animals cannot directly utilize energy from the sun to live. Many animals (herbivores and omnivores) consume all or part of the energy-containing compounds in plants. These animals, in turn, can be consumed by other animals (carnivores). Carnivores consume other carnivores. Respiration is the process of converting energy-containing biomass to the energy required by all living things for use in growth, metabolism, respiration, and so on. Energy flows from one organism to another. The biomass that is not soon utilized by plants and animals is eventually utilized and provides energy for decomposers that release nutrients back into the soil. In the distant past, when conditions were right, some biomass was not consumed or decomposed; instead it was buried, fossilized, and converted into energy-containing compounds like petroleum, coal, and natural gas. Thus plants, because of their ability to convert energy from sunlight to biomass, supply the basic energy needs for almost all plants and animals as well as for many aspects of our modern economy and existence.

The biosphere, which includes the earth, all of its constituents, including all living things, is a closed system. Little material enters or leaves it, but there is a constant input of energy from the sun and export of energy to the solar system.

This constant energy input supports life on our planet primarily through the production of energy-rich biomass through the process of photosynthesis. Much hydroelectric energy generated by dams is possible because of the evaporation of water caused by the sun and its deposition uphill through precipitation. Energy from wind is possible because of air movement caused by heating from the sun. Even tidal energy is possible because of the tidal influence of the sun and the moon.

Energy Flow in the Biosphere

Plants and animals have evolved and diversified. They now occupy our land, sea, and air as living constituents of our biosphere. Energy flows in all systems from the sun through plants to herbivores, omnivores, and carnivores. When energy is used, some of it is lost for further use at every step of the utilization, whether it be metabolism and growth of individuals or transfer to other organisms, through predation or parasitism. Energy flow from plants through herbivores to the largest carnivore is called a food chain. Energy is lost at all levels of the food chain because the energy in biomass is being used continuously to sustain life. At any level, the energy coming in is always less than the energy going out. Total energy available is much less (approximately 10 percent) at every level than the prior level. Thus, the most energy is available at the first level, plants, and the least at the last, top carnivore. That is why plant biomass is higher in all habitats than animal biomass, and why there are more herbivores (antelope, gazelles, zebras, and so forth) biomass on the African plains than carnivores (lions, hyenas, and so forth) (see *Why Big Fierce Animals Are Rare: An Ecologist's Perspective* [Colinvaux, 1978]). From our viewpoint, there are many implications. For example, if energy available to produce food becomes scarce, we can produce more food by harvesting and consuming the first level, plants (vegetables and fruits), nuts before the energy is lost as it passes down the food chain. Eating plants or their products rather than meat reduces energy loss in the system and allows more people to be fed. Doing this might become necessary if food or energy becomes scarce in the future.

The raw materials for the basic energy conversion equation of photosynthesis are carbon dioxide, and water. Other elements such as nitrogen, phosphorus, potassium, and others in small amounts (micronutrients) are constituents of the compounds that are necessary for plants and animals. For example, hemoglobin, an important component of vertebrate blood, contains iron. A shortage of red blood cells is often treated by taking iron. Goiter, a problem related to the thyroid gland, is usually caused by shortages of iodine, which is locally rare on our planet. The worldwide incidence of goiter was greatly reduced after iodine began to be routinely added to table salt. We can increase production of plants by fertilizing them, usually with nitrogen, potassium, phosphate, and some micronutrients that are locally rare. Applying fertilizer is a way to compensate for essential materials that are naturally in short supply and those that are removed when a crop is harvested.

Habitats

After life evolved from its precursors, its manifestations continuously increased as forms evolved and adapted to an ever-changing world. New species and groups evolved. Plants and animals evolved into a variety of forms that were suited to the environments they occupied as others became extinct. These forms occur together in familiar and predictable associations. Typical examples are pine forest, tropical rain forest, grassland, marsh, lake, desert, and tundra. These associations are not located randomly but occur at particular places with particular conditions. These conditions are affected by location and topographic features that affect climate, which is the main factor that determines the nature and location of these associations. Temperature and soil-water availability are the primary climate factors that affect plant distribution, but others such as soil type and seasonality are also important. Areas with similar climate have similar associations of flora and fauna, even on different continents or hemispheres. Specific types of plants and animals occur together in each separate association: plants and animals in deserts are similar to each other but different than those that occur in marshes and swamps. All forms in a habitat have specific adaptations for that habitat. Forms in deserts are adapted to low water availability; those in swamps and marshes are adapted to wetter conditions.

In many places, these original associations are no longer present but have been replaced by various alternatives that are managed by people for specific purposes. The original prairies have been replaced by grain-growing agriculture, which is similarly affected by climate. Grain fields do not differ much from the original prairies. Commercial forests are similar to the natural ones they replaced. Drier areas may also be used for commercial forestry or agriculture if sufficient irrigation water can be supplied. Wetter areas like swamps may be drained and also converted to agriculture or other uses.

Various factors can influence climate both locally and globally. If the climate changes, the locations of associated habitat adapted to these climatic conditions will move with its characteristic flora and fauna. Some climate changes could result in the loss of some associations because prerequisite conditions may no longer be present anywhere, but new habitats could also develop. Species occupying new habitat types may not be as characteristic as those in preexisting habitats because they may not have yet evolved or adapted. For agriculture or forestry, crops or varieties can be changed as the habitat changes. This is much easier now than in the past because of recent advances in genetic engineering.

Ice ages are examples of what has happened and could happen again during times of climate changes. Long-term heating and cooling resulted in ice-sheet formation and movement. Sheets of ice moved toward the equator but eventually retreated toward the poles. In the United States, during the last ice age, the ice sheets came almost as far south as the Gulf coast. Despite this, there was no large-scale extinction or permanent habitat loss. Habitats (controlled by climate) moved as the climate shifted. Plant and animal species survived by moving along with their habitats and the appropriate climate. The time scale of the climatic changes was long enough to allow movements of habitats and the accompanying flora and fauna. At the time of the ice ages, habitats were not fragmented by human activity, and movement was thus not inhibited. Other environmental changes have been more sudden and were accompanied by catastrophic changes of flora and fauna. The extinction of dinosaurs is thought by many to have occurred after a meteor impact affected their habitats.

If global warming or another ice age were to happen now, in theory habitats (either natural or made by humans) could move as the appropriate conditions moved. Recent human-induced habitat changes have fragmented habitats and made migration of habitats with the climate changes more difficult or impossible than they would have been with unfragmented ones. In addition, land ownership and local traditions would make the establishment of an appropriate route difficult if not impossible, but the long time frame available for people to accommodate would perhaps allow them to solve the route problem, and suitable corridors could be established. In addition, people could assist further by actively assisting the movement of plants and animals.

Succession

As we have seen, the types of animals at any one place with specific climate and conditions are known and predictable. When we discuss and name habitats, we often include the dominant plants and animals that usually occupy them and are characteristic. What we are thinking of is the last stage in a series of changes that begins when an area is colonized. The final stage is stable and will remain relatively the same until the area is again disturbed or the climatic conditions change. The final stage is called the climax. Because the climax is stable, individual plants and animals may die, but they will be replaced by similar ones, and the habitat thus stays the same. The sequence of changes that precede climax is somewhat predictable. In other words, there is a succession of different associations of plants and animals because the plants and animals affect their environment and each other in predictable ways. In time, colonizing species are replaced by other species. These species, in turn are replaced by others. Eventually, the climax is reached if there is no disturbance.

Changes That Occur during Succession

When a field is cleared in the southeastern United States, succession occurs from annual plants through biennial (every two years) and perennial (every year) plants, through a pine forest to a hardwood forest. The succession may take more than 100 years to complete. Often the pine are harvested, the debris burned, and the process repeated without climax ever being attained.

At any particular location, the stages that occur during succession follow a predictable pattern. The earliest stage consists of adaptable species with good dispersal abilities. Biomass is low, and life spans are short. Biomass production exceeds respiration, and biomass accumulates. This stage lasts only a year or two and is unstable, as are all other stages except climax. Visually it is a weedy field.

As succession proceeds, biomass and life spans increase. Species increasingly become better competitors. Productivity and respiration become more equal, and productivity still exceeds respiration. The rate of biomass accumulation declines.

At climax, productivity equals respiration, and there is no net change of biomass. The dominant vegetation is long-lived, and the environment is stable. In the southeastern United States, the dominant forms at most locations are hardwoods. The forest is often stratified (layers of vegetation at different heights), and species diversity, a measure of the variety of plants or animals, is high. Respiration equals productivity, and there is no net carbon accumulation. Species composition at climax can vary by site because of variation in slope, soil, and other conditions.

A popular way to reduce atmospheric carbon dioxide takes advantage of the changes that occur during succession by planting trees or other vegetation (McDermott, 2008). As the trees grow, the carbon in the biomass of these trees comes from the atmosphere and carbon is captured (sequestered) through photosynthesis. Individuals or organizations can buy carbon credits based on the amount of carbon dioxide that is tied up in the biomass of these trees. There are several problems, however. As carbon accumulates, more noxious greenhouse gases than carbon dioxide are released from the soil (van Groenigen, Osenberg, & Hungate, 2011). When climax is reached, net carbon sequestering stops because the sequestered carbon (productivity) is balanced by carbon use (respiration). To continue the benefit, the trees could be harvested and the process repeated, but what happens to the harvested trees? Carbon dioxide is produced if the trees are burned. The trees or the wood must be stored forever, or the benefit of growing them disappears. The sequestering process can be prolonged by burying the accumulated biomass (Zeng, 2008). In addition, biomass can be accumulated faster by growing faster-growing vegetation like algae, but if the biomass produced cannot be readily stored, it will be soon utilized and the benefit removed.

Climax in forested habitats is often completely harvested for use as wood. The harvested site is usually converted to other uses like agriculture or commercial forestry because it takes too long for succession to produce the next climax, and other uses produce shorter-term profit. If the vegetation is burned, carbon will be released. This is a serious problem now with tropical rain forests. In many other areas, the climax has already been harvested and the land is managed for crops, commercial forestry, or human habitation and infrastructure. The clearing of climax habitats has increased atmospheric carbon dioxide (Fearnside & Laurance, 2004) and decreased biodiversity.

People and the Environment

Early humans were hunters and gatherers. Wildlife were food, competitors, and even predators of humans. Survival of plants, animals, and humans depended on the condition of the environment, which includes plants and animals. People's influence over the environment was originally not much different than that of other animals, but we walked upright, had an opposable thumb, and possessed an enlarged brainthat facilitate our ability to control our environment.

Changing Relationships with Our Environment

Humans' connection to our original environment now is not as direct as it was in the past. Our distant ancestors obtained their energy as other animals in the environment did through hunting and gathering plant parts, such as fruits and nuts. Soon we learned to utilize non-consumed parts of plants and animals to provide shelter, clothing, and tools. As we made new discoveries, like how to use fire and make weapons and other tools, our influence over the environment increased. We began to control it more and more.

Eventually, we increased productivity with controlled burns to provide nutrients and remove unwanted vegetation. We cleared land and tilled it to grow our own food. We expanded from the efforts of individuals and families of nomadic people with primitive tools, to a more stationary existence in which we used oxen and other animals to pull plows and other devices to till the land that we controlled and used to provide a more predictable existence. We bartered with our neighbors and others to increase our use of more distant environments and provide a market for excesses of what we found or produced. Eventually we established family farms and were no longer predominately nomadic. The environment on these farms was very much in our control. It was not the wild lands of our ancestors.

When the United States was settled, it was still relatively unmodified compared to the conditions in Europe from whence the colonists came. Although the indigenous people had modified the land some for their own benefit, it was viewed by the settlers as a wilderness with bountiful resources. They came from lands that had been modified previously, supposedly for their benefit. The settlers arrived on the coasts and settled there. As they modified land by clearing and making family farms, available land became scarce locally. Many were lured by opportunities to be found in the unsettled land to the west. As American newspaper editor Horace Greely reportedly (Berger, 1968) said in a July 13, 1865, editorial, "Go West, young man, go West and grow up with the country." Our attitude was to take advantage of the bounty. We could always move to another unsettled place if needed. We originally viewed the wilderness as endless and took it for granted. We dominated it, but now it is mostly gone, and many of us miss what it was. It has mostly been replaced with agriculture and animal husbandry, especially in the more settled and moister East.

Modern Food Production

Food production can be increased by careful planting, tilling, and harvesting as well as by supplying pesticides, fungicides or herbicides to reduce competition, predation, and disease. All of these actions require raw materials as well as energy for production and, transportation. Thus, food production is increased by using energy extensively; there is an energy subsidy. This subsidy is more than it might seem when the energy used to make and use machines and the energy used to plant, fertilize, till and harvest, as well as the energy used to produce and manufacture fertilizer, fungicides, insecticides, and improved seed is considered. The use of genetically modified crops such as corn, soybeans, and sugar beets allows herbicides to be applied without harming the crop, which greatly increases yields. Research has helped us develop more productive crops and transfer genes to insert more desirable crop characteristics in them.

In modern times, the family farms of the settlers have, in many cases, been replaced by large corporate farms that supply most of our food. With the development of large machines, we are able to till enormous fields with our air-conditioned tractors. We developed mechanical planters and harvesters. We domesticated animals and tended and harvested them on large ranches, and fattened them in large food lots. Many of the foods we have today are produced on these large, corporate farms and ranches. We are no longer restricted to yard chickens; enormous poultry factory farms produce abundant eggs and meat in entirely unnatural and controversial conditions. In these large, commercial operations, relatively few people are required; the work is largely done by machines. We till, plant, grow, irrigate, fertilize, weed, and control pests to optimize production. We then harvest, prepare, and ship the food long distances to people who have mostly moved into large cities, perhaps in other countries or even other continents. Our environments are hardly recognizable; they are not the more or less undisturbed ones in which we originated.

Our Relationship Now with Nature

The majority of us now live in urban or suburban areas. In many of these areas, a few parks and green spaces, as well as the landscaping in our yards, are the only connections that we routinely share with our natural heritage; we are not as closely connected to wild habitats as we once were. Unaltered or slightly-altered habitats are not used to supply food as they once were. Many of our natural habitats have disappeared or almost so, but we still like to be close to nature.

As we move into cities and suburban areas, our connection with the environments in which our species evolved is getting more distant and tenuous. Many of us do not understand our natural heritage or even understand universal ecological principles. Many now actively oppose policies and practices that were accepted by our ancestors, who were closer to the land. The number of people eating a vegetarian diet is increasing due to nutritional and moral concerns, even though almost all natural food chains include carnivores. Our ancestors evolved as omnivores, and our teeth and digestive system have specializations for both meat and vegetable diets. There is opposition to use of leather and other animal products by many, even though they are natural, are used extensively by indigenous people, and are truly sustainable if harvest is controlled. That is not true of most, if not all, of the alternatives. Some people now even assert that animals have rights (Francione & Garner, 2010). The ways that natural systems function are being ignored. We are somehow now separate from nature. We still have needs. Natural systems function on the energy available to local systems and locally available resources. The energy and materials are limited in these systems and can support only a limited number of people on a sustained basis. There is no major energy subsidy. Now we import material from afar, employ huge energy subsidies, and change our relationship to the environment to support an ever-growing population with increased and increasing energy demands.

Close relationships with plants and animals are still maintained by some: hunters, fishers, bird watchers, nature photographers, and picnickers. In 2006, 87.5 million Americans over the age of 15 fished, hunted, photographed, fed, and closely observed wildlife and spent approximately $57.4 billion for trips to observe them (U.S. Fish and Wildlife Service, 2006). This was about 36.5 percent of our population (U.S. Census Bureau, 2006). Many enjoy a close relationship with our historic and biological environment. In addition, some recent researchers have found that time spent in natural habitats seems to benefit human health (Phillips, 2011).

This interest in nature is understandable—we evolved in natural systems, but many of us are no longer close to them, like those people who live in large urban areas where nature can be observed well only in parks or zoos. The occasional animals we observe often seem lost or are pests. Still, thousands of people log on to sites to observe hawks nesting on ledges of buildings or similar examples of nature. On the other hand, many pigeon fanciers seek to eliminate the occasional peregrine falcon that harvests them in some metropolitan areas. The importance we place on pets and gardening as well as encouraging birds and butterflies to live in our yards are indications of our heritage and our relationships with nature, as are our reactions to pests and occasional interactions with dangerous animals like bears, tigers, snakes, or crocodiles.

Humans still depend on plants and animals. We have changed incrementally from rather benign hunting and gathering that had minimal impact on environments to corporate farming and massive ranching operations that drastically alter the environment and operate on a larger scale than many natural systems.

In addition to hunting and fishing for sustenance or pleasure. We enjoy animals and plants in many other ways. We garden to produce food and beauty, and pay to visit commercial gardens. We keep animals for pets and use them to assist us in many ways. Ecotourism is a major business, and we construct and visit zoos. We travel to view nature at parks and preserves of many kinds. We whale-watch; we swim with dolphins. Our cities have green spaces and parks; we feed the pigeons in parks or other birds and butterflies in our yards. Wildlife and green space is an important part of our lives.

In addition, animal and plant products have important uses other than providing food. Clothing and pharmaceuticals are prime examples. Both plant and animal fiber are used in clothing. Many plant products are now used extensively as natural supplements and/or alternatives to traditional medicine. Many of the modern medicines developed, researched, and marketed by large pharmaceutical companies were first discovered in plants. That is one reason so many people are concerned by the loss of biodiversity and the resulting loss of potential chemicals that could benefit us. Plants and animals have always been essential components in our environment and are essential to our well-being. Even fossilized remnants of plants and animals are important as raw materials in the manufacturing of plastics, cosmetics, and other materials (Clifford, 2011).

Even now, when change has resulted in new ways to provide our food and other needs, plants and animals are an important part of our physical and psychological well-being. During Hurricane Katrina, 44 percent of people who decided not to evacuate did so because they could not take their animals with them. Both federal and state law now requires provisions to be made for pets at times of crisis (McCulley, 2007).

Many veterinarians perform the same services for animals that physicians do for people. Medicines and procedures are now available for treatment of many animal diseases and conditions. Some of these are very expensive.

Because the basic energy supply for natural systems comes directly from the sun through photosynthesis, we often do not require additional sources of energy, but we can increase production greatly with energy subsidies of various kinds. The quantity of sunlight available depends on the area of the earth's surface and solar output. The total surface of the earth is about 198 million square miles. Ultimately, energy striking the surface is a limiting factor. Because the energy striking the surface varies by season and position on the globe, the energy available varies by time and location. Much of the sunlight hits the ocean and is the prime source of energy for oceanic life.

Climax habitats have been selectively cleared and are now rare. Because they are the last stage of succession, it will take many years to reinstate them, if we were to do so; but we usually do not. The standing crop of biomass at climax was large; and that is why climax habitats were initially harvested. On the other hand, there is no net productivity, and a climax forest cannot really support many of us.

Habitat Change

People use habitats and alter them to accomplish specific goals. The short-term result of these changes is often considered positive by the people making the changes if the original goal is accomplished; However, habitats have many functions and characteristics, and changing one affects others. The stratification of forest habitats, the distance from the edge, the block size, the species composition of the vegetation, and other details are all characteristics that have been shown to affect species composition of specific habitat components such as birds. A small change in space or time may have a minimal effect, but an accumulation of small changes eventually results in drastic changes in the habitats related to both space and time. Incremental changes that we continually make are accumulating and we are decreasing biodiversity as some species are becoming rare or extinct.

Changes in habitats can cause changes that lead to other changes in time and/or space. For example, after a stream is channelized (i.e., modified to remove high water quickly and stop flooding of neighboring land), the excess water goes downstream faster than in the past; this water may in turn cause flooding down stream that did not occur there previously. Channelization occurs again to reduce the new flooding and the process repeats itself over and over. What was originally a meandering stream with occasional over-bank flooding now is a straighter, less diverse channel with rushing water at times of high rain fall. The accompanying plants and animals change. One habitat becomes another. Short-term effects for humans usually seemed positive because flooding was reduced locally, but when a stream becomes channelized, in the long-term, there are many changes that are not considered positive by many.

When an area is originally colonized by people, the habitat is likely to have been climax unless it has been recently disturbed by natural causes such as wind or fire. Disturbance can change the habitat to an earlier stage of succession. The area affected is the area that was colonized. Often the changes are not at the edge of a large patch of habitat but scattered throughout, and the habitat becomes fragmented (large block gets broken up into smaller blocks). This creates patches of earlier stage habitat within blocks of older habitat. The animals and plants in the disturbed areas are often different species than those of the climax and are less specialized with good dispersal abilities. There are some species that are specialized for these small gaps that are naturally caused by tree falls and occasional storms. The disturbed habitat will undergo succession until it becomes climax again or it is again disturbed. Many habitats are deliberately disturbed or harvested before climax is reached. Habitat edges are often particularly diverse because they contain species of the patches on both sides of the edges as well as some species that are adapted to edges.

Migration causes special problems related to the difficulty of finding suitable areas for breeding areas, winter areas, and migration stopover places.

Because of habitat loss, reserves have been established to accomplish many goals: to protect critical habitats of threatened and endangered species; to set aside areas for national parks, national forests, and wilderness protection; to establish wildlife refuges and preserves; to provide for large preserves to protect important habitats and still allow some human usage (biosphere reserves); and so on. Coordination among sponsors has often been minimal, and political and refuge boundaries often cause problems.

Endangered Species

Humans harvest, modify, and destroy habitats. As our numbers increase, the quantity of land and associated habitats affected by us increases and the undisturbed habitat decreases. Land quantity is finite, and availability can be limited. Many natural habitats are becoming extinct or increasingly rare. That is devastating to the flora and fauna of these habitats. Consequently, many species have become extinct or are endangered or threatened. Pollution and overharvest have also contributed to extinction. That is especially true for commercial fisheries.

Because climax habitats are stable, they often are occupied by threatened or endangered species that are not flexible in their requirements. The species are endangered because their habitats are becoming rare and because they often are not flexible enough to live in other habitats, especially unstable subclimax habitats. When habitats become extremely scarce, the species that occupy them also become scarce. Species need a certain number of individuals to have a reasonable chance of survival. Because climax habitats are now scarce and habitat fragments have gotten small and distant from each other, the numbers present in any fragment can get too low to ensure species survival. When the numbers get low, sometimes individuals are trapped and placed in zoos or other sanctuaries until their numbers have increased and they can be reintroduced into the wild, if suitable habitat becomes available. Whooping cranes (Erickson & Derrickson, 1981) and California condors (Snyder & Snyder, 2000) are well-known examples. Recently all California condors were trapped and bred in zoos before a successful reintroduction program re-established them in the wild.

Habitat occurs in blocks that are separated from other blocks by dissimilar habitats. Larger blocks hold more species than smaller blocks. Habitats that are structurally complex usually have more diversity than simpler ones (Wiens, 1992; MacArthur & MacArthur, 1961).

Many people are concerned about loss of plants and animals, and we are trying to protect them. In the United States, we have an Endangered Species Act and various lists of threatened species. We are trying to protect as many species as possible (i.e., preserve biodiversity). The reason many species are endangered is habitat loss, and the key to recovery is habitat recovery. There are other causes in our ever-changing world. Extensive DDT and related chemicals reduced numbers of many predatory birds at the top of the food chain and pelicans by thinning of their eggshells. Many like bald eagles, and peregrine falcons recovered after DDT usage was stopped.

Individual animals and small groups of animals can be protected in zoos and private refuges. Some like the California condor and whooping cranes (Erickson & Derrickson, 1981) have been bred in captivity and released into the wild. Individual nests and habitat can be protected (e.g., bald eagles, peregrine falcons, red-cockaded woodpeckers). Artificial nests can be used by species that have lost nesting habitat (e.g., bluebirds, ospreys, red-cockaded woodpeckers, wood ducks).

Threatened and endangered species can be protected in refuges established for them in critical habitats. These refuges must be large enough to ensure random events do not decimate numbers.

Refuges such as national parks, national forests, wilderness areas, state management areas, biosphere reserves, and privately managed the ones can protect plant and animal species, communities of plants and animals, and specific habitats. Many are now managed to protect biodiversity.

Long-Term Planning for Wildlife Reserves

Placement of refuges has been a matter of convenience, and habitat available for acquisition is often not optimal.

Succession and other factors may complicate management, but with careful planning, refuges can contain all succession stages. Climax may be rare, but can develop on refuges.

Climatic and/or other changes may cause habitat changes in refuges so that they can no longer accomplish the original objectives.

In the long term, conditions will change, but we may not anticipate the timing, direction, or intensity of the changes.

Because of concerns about climate change and global warming, many models predict future climate and habitats at particular refuges or protected areas. In almost all cases, the original goals of the refuge will be compromised with these changes. Other ecological processes can be affected by climatic shifts. Timing of breeding and food-supply availability are examples. These possible changes would be gradual and there should be time for habitats to change along with the climate and other conditions. Changes in surrounding areas could be more sudden and difficult to adjust for. That is a major reason for reserves to be very large so changes in the surroundings have a minimal effect.

Ideal Future Refuge Criteria

Ideally, future refuges should have the following characteristics.

Large Size

To provide for diversity, refuges should be as large as possible. The number of species a block of habitat can hold is a function of area. Large refuges can hold many successional stages and unique habitats, and there is room for large block sizes. They may contain critical habitats for endangered species and suitable habitats for target species such as waterfowl and upland game like quail and grouse.

Location

Refuges must have suitable climatic and other conditions and be near other available habitat so that interacting systems can be developed. Associated flora and fauna may need to move from refuge to refuge, so appropriate corridors are needed. Proper advance planning can help ensure opportunities to provide new habitat for future refuges or corridors is available in the neighborhood. For example, the location of planting for carbon sequestering or acquiring land for wetland acquisition can be used to fill habitat gaps or provide habitat corridors. Disturbance should be minimal or controllable at all refuges.

Landscape Ecology

With habitat loss, isolation, and fragmentation, it is imperative that refugees be at optimum locations and organized to maximize their usefulness. The principles of landscape ecology (which emphasizes location and interaction of habitats) can be applied throughout an area to optimize location, habitat, block sizes, and connectivity. These are frequently difficult to optimally accomplish because of (1) lack of required habitat types, (2) past patterns of land use,

(3) ownership differences, and (4) political boundaries. Coordination is required to establish landscape networks for perpetual and sustainable management.

Proper Habitats

We are required to provide critical habitats for endangered species and other rare and threatened species. We need suitable habitats for target species: waterfowl, upland game, need breeding, wintering, and stopover areas for residents and migrants, and so on.

Careful planning now will allow us to improve our refuge systems in the future. We should have suitable areas available for use when climate or other conditions change. Habitats and associated flora and fauna may need to move from refuge to refuge, so appropriate corridors are needed.

Landscapes Important in Planning

We have gone from areas with large blocks of similar habitat to scattered, fragmented patches of habitats that are mostly unconnected. Ideally, refuges should use landscape principles. Refuges should be aggregated into, landscape networks where refuges and other lands are spatially related to accomplish landscape goals. Good landscape planning requires coordination among various private and public entities. The United Nations and nongovernmental organizations (NGOs) are especially important in facilitating planning across national borders.

Biosphere Reserves

Biosphere reserves are in many ways ideal and are designed to protect our biodiversity while still allowing use in controlled ways. The main characteristic of biosphere reserves is large size that contains both protected and managed areas. They are supposed to be significant examples of important areas in the biosphere. They often contain critical habitats.

There are few biosphere reserves because of conflicting land use and unavailability of suitable areas. Changing climates, changing habitats, and so on may make these refuges unsuitable for their original species and objectives, but their large size gives some room for habitats to move.

It is desirable to have a global plan for a system of reserves throughout the biosphere. Habitats should be available so that flora and fauna can move when conditions change. Connecting reserves with appropriate corridors could increase their effectiveness for wildlife and humans. Biosphere reserves are in many ways ideal and are designed to protect our biodiversity while still allowing use in controlled ways.

Chapter 6 covers many aspects of the organization and management of the largest biosphere reserve.

Aquatic Habitats

In many aquatic environments, photosynthesis occurs primarily in small plants called phytoplankton that exist near the surface of the water where light intensity is highest. Phytoplankton are the basis of most aquatic food chains. They are consumed by small animals, zooplankton; these in turn are usually consumed by larger animals such as fish that may be consumed by even larger ones or schools of smaller fish like piranha. Sometimes large forms eat much smaller forms. This is true of the largest animal, the blue whale, which can be almost 100 feet long and consumes small aquatic animals called krill. Phytoplankton are the primary photosynthesizers in water. Submergent, floating, or emergent plants and algae can exist in shallow water and are also photosynthesizers.

Like terrestrial habitats, aquatic habitats vary and are influenced by temperature and salinity. Depth of water is also important. On land, the sun does not penetrate the surface and the productivity is primarily above ground. On the other hand, water cannot support emergent vegetation, so there is little above-water productivity except in shallow areas. Sunlight can penetrate water. The depth of penetration depends on the clarity of the water, which is affected by non-transparent inclusions in the water.

Most aquatic animals are surrounded by water instead of air and have different mechanisms for obtaining oxygen because most comes dissolved in the water. Aquatic forms need oxygen for respiration, like landforms. On the other hand, there is no water shortage, in water, but different mechanisms are used to obtain it in fresh-water and saltwater forms.

Marshes and estuaries are some of the most productive areas of our planet. Sunlight and nutrients are abundant, and availability is increased by an energy supplement provided by the tides and wind. It is these marshes that are valuable nursery grounds for shrimp and crabs as well as many saltwater fish such as speckled trout, redfish, spot, and croaker. They along with abundant offshore fish are harvested commercially and are an important food supply for our hungry world. In many cases, fishery managers believe fish are being overharvested, and the take is limited. In some cases, there is competition between commercial and recreational users over the amount each group can harvest. Many species of commercial fish are no longer profitable to harvest because of previous overharvest, and it will take aggressive management to provide fish supplies in the future. People have learned to grow and harvest many species in artificial ponds and cages. This is an important source now and may be the source of most edible fish in the future.

In contrast to land, most of the surface of the ocean is unowned (no one owns the resources there and the bounty is harvested in common). This leads to overharvest (Hardin, 1968) because anyone overharvesting benefits from the overharvest and when the resource is depleted, the loss is shared by all. There is no motivation to limit harvest by individual users of the commons. If the resource were owned, overharvest by the owner would also lead to depletion, but the owner would be harmed and the harm could be prevented by responsible harvest, and so it is in the owner's interest to harvest responsibly. In this way the commons lead to over harvest and ruin. The same logic applies to all commons; the original concept applied to open range for sheep. All oceanic species are subject to overharvesting because of the "Tragedy of the Commons" and many commercial species can no longer be harvested: whales (Encyclopedia Britannica, 2011), turtles, swordfish, salmon, tuna, speckled trout, redfish, red snapper, lobster, and so on. Seafood harvest is an important source of food for many of us, especially those living on islands such as Japan, so we must find ways to harvest responsibly.

SUMMARY

Our earth has been an extremely providing place. Our biosphere has nurtured us, providing energy and food needs for us and all living things. It, for the most part, has been welcoming. As humans have increased in numbers and expanded their horizons, their impact on the earth has increased and will undoubtedly continue to do so unless we decide to live more in harmony with our historical environments. As our numbers increase, our energy needs increase, and various materials essential to our well-being will become scarcer. Simultaneously, the world is becoming increasingly different than the welcoming one we evolved in.

We now try to manage our world and the use of our resources. As we manage the world to meet our needs, we must anticipate our future needs and the various problems that will inevitably occur as our environments change. We must keep our options open so that we and the earth's co-inhabitants will have the most reasonable chance to survive in whatever situation we find ourselves. Unintended consequences abound, often because planners do not consider the ramifications of their plans holistically enough, and they do not include in their plans a way to return to previously known hospitable conditions if their plans go awry.

Demands for energy and materials for our ever-growing population have resulted in fragmented landscapes that increasingly differ from the ones we evolved in. Areas available for present and future expansion are limited because the size of the earth does not change. When we expand our use by creating wind-farms or solar-panel farms or clear wild land for ethanol and bio-fuel production our ability to provide for biodiversity, wilderness and parks is reduced. We need to minimize conversion of land dedicated to conservation of biodiversity to other uses like energy production. The land is a limited resource just like energy and the materials we use to support growth of our population and standard of living. Harvesting subterranean resources does have the advantage of minimizing surface disturbance. Many "green" groups seem to not consider that. They should broaden their focus to minimize detrimental changes to our surface environment.

Because the path we are following is so dangerous to us and all life, we must all contemplate the future and the way to ensure our species' long-term survival in a world that depends on the interdependence of all life and resources. We all should participate in that discussion.

REFERENCES

Berger, Evans. (1968). *Dictionary of quotations*. New York: Delacorte Press, p. 745:2.

Brasier, M., McLoughlin, N., Green, O., & Wacey, D. (June 2006). A fresh look at the fossil evidence for early Archaean cellular life. *Philosophical Transactions of the Royal Society: Biology, 361*(1470), 887–902. doi:10.1098/rstb.2006.1835. PMC 1578727. PMID 16754605.

Clifford, S. (2011, June 26). New analysis: Oil oozes through your life. *New York Times*, Special Report, pp. 6–7.

Clover, C. (2011). *End of the line: How overfishing is changing the world and what we eat.* London: Ebury Press.

Colinvaux, P. A. (1978). *Why big fierce animals are rare: An ecologist's perspective.* Princeton, NJ: Princeton University Press.

Dalrymple, G. B. (2001). The age of the earth in the twentieth century: A problem (mostly) solved. *Special Publications, Geological Society of London, 190*(1), 205–221. doi:10.1144/GSL.SP.2001.190.01.14.

Encyclopædia Britannica. (2011). *Overharvesting.* Retrieved from http://www.britannica .com/EBchecked/topic/1377241/overharvesting.

Erickson, R. C., & Derrickson, S. R. (1981). Whooping crane (*Grusamericana*). In J. C. Lewis & H. Masatomi (Eds.), *Crane research around the world* (pp. 104–118). Baraboo, WI: International Crane Foundation.

Fearnside, P. M., & Laurance, W. F. (2004). Tropical deforestation and greenhouse-gas emissions. *Ecological Applications, 14*(4), 982–986.

Francione, G. L., & Garner, R. (2010). *The animal rights debate: Abolition or regulation?* New York: Columbia University Press.

Hardin, G. (1968). The tragedy of the commons. *Science, 162*(3859), 1243–1248.

MacArthur, R. H., & MacArthur, J. W. (1961). On bird species diversity. *Ecology, 42*, 594–598.

McCulley, R. (2007, June 6). Saving pets from another Katrina. *Time.* Retrieved from http://www.time.com/time/nation/article/0,8599,1629962,00.html.

McDermott, M. (2008). Can aerial reforestation help show climate change? Discovery project Earth examines re-engineering the planet's possibilities. Retrieved May 9, 2010, from http://www.treehugger.com/files/2008/08/aerial-reforestation-explored-in -discovery-project-earth-premiere.php.

Phillips, A. L. (2011). A walk in the woods: Evidence builds that time spent in the natural world benefits human health. *American Scientist, 99*(4), 301–302.

Snyder, N. F. R., & Snyder, H. (2000). *The California condor: A saga of natural history and conservation.* Princeton, NJ: Princeton University Press.

U.S. Census Bureau. (2006). *United States: Population and housing narrative pro-file*. Retrieved May 15, 2010, from http://factfinder.census.gov/servlet/NPTable?
_bm=y&-geo_id=01000US&-qr_name=ACS_2006_EST_G00_NP01&-ds_name
=&-redoLog=false

U.S. Fish and Wildlife Services. (2006). Net economic values of wildlife-related re-creation in 2006. In *Addendum to the 2006 National Survey of Fishing, Hunting, and Wildlife Associated Recreation* (Report 2006–5).

van Groenigen, K. J., Osenberg, C. W., & Hungate, B. A. (2011). Increased soil emissions of potent greenhouse gases under increased atmospheric CO_2. *Nature, 475*, 214–216. doi:10.1038/nature10176.

Wiens, J. A. (1992). *The ecology of bird communities: Volume 1: Foundations and patterns*. Cambridge Studies in Ecology. Cambridge: Cambridge University Press. (Original work published 1989.)

Zeng, N. (2008). Carbon sequestration via wood burial. *Carbon Balance and Management, 3*(1). doi:10.1186/1750-0680-3-1.

6

Our Biosphere Reserves: Conservation, Sustainable Development, and Preparation for Future Changes—Emphasizing the Mata Atlântica Biosphere Reserve in Brazil

João Lucilio Ruegger de Albuquerque

The purpose of this chapter is to describe the ecosystems that we live in, and how climate change in particular is affecting these ecosystems. This requires an understanding of some crucial issues in our environment today, including that of biodiversity and biospheres. One of the best natural laboratories in which to understand the impact of environmental changes is the Brazilian rainforest, one of the most threatened forests on the planet. My team is conducting work in this famous forest to preserve and conserve the environment. The Brazilian Atlantic Rain Forest, or Mata Atlântica (in Portuguese), as it is known internationally, stretches along Brazil's Atlantic coast, from the northern state of Rio Grande do Norte south to Rio Grande do Sul. This forest is famous not only to scientists but to the public, who flock to it to experience its majesty. The impact of dangerous environmental changes in this region is dramatic and traumatic, and therefore exceptionally important to understand and to forestall.

Our work in the Brazilian rainforest is presented here as a way to elucidate clearly for readers the global concepts of environmental change. In the Atlantic Rain Forest Biosphere Reserve, we are focusing on preserving the environment, promoting sustainable development, and improving quality of life in Brazil as well as on the planet. It is the biggest Biosphere Reserve of the MAB (Man and Biosphere) a Program of UNESCO (UN Economic, Scientific, and Cultural Organization) concerning biosphere reserve certification. Today there are about 590 biosphere reserves. The Mata Atlântica Biosphere Reserve is considered one of the most important biosphere reserves of the World Network of Biosphere Reserves.

To solve environmental impacts and the social and political problems generated by climate change and other environmental changes in Brazil, we must reinvent nature, society, and the city planning processes because cities need raw material and power. They are a magnet to inhabitants and consumers, who consume resources, generate waste, and cause other environmental problems. Overcoming those challenges is the main goal of the Atlantic Rain Forest Biosphere Reserve.

THE BIOSPHERE: THE NATURE OF GAIA, OUR PLANET

Many scientists and other people agree that climate change and global warming are currently one of the biggest threats to life as we know it on our planet. The world as we know it began from natural "magic" that appeared on earth about 4 billion years ago, probably in the ocean, in the form of bacteria from nucleic acid capsules (RNA and DNA) plus proteins, carbohydrates, and water.

We terrestrials—human beings—are approximately 600 million years old. We have been *Homo sapiens* for only 4 million years, and in this period, we have jumped by means of "intelligence" from a stage where we deemed ourselves to be part of nature to another where we deemed ourselves to be lords of nature. At that moment, the great degradation of our planet began.

Life on earth adapted and diversified to accommodate environmental differences and huge natural impacts, until we reached the condition today: 1.5 million currently known species, of which perhaps only 10 percent are described.

This is our Gaia, a biotic planet.

A unique and basic function of humanity, unlike other species, is the search for happiness. For this, we have invented economics, ethics, politics, culture, religion, and sexual desire. We have now become a society of consumption, where happiness is about gaining more and more material things.

To accomplish our goals, humans are the most successful invading species among all others when it comes to adapting to and manipulating the environment.

Biodiversity

Biodiversity is a term that describes the variety of life on earth. It refers to the wide variety of ecosystems and living organisms—animals, plants, their habitats and their genes—that are the foundation of life on earth. Biodiversity is crucial for the functioning of ecosystems that provide humans with products and services without which we could not live. Oxygen, food, fresh water, fertile soil, medicines, shelter, protection from storms and floods, stable climate, and recreation—all have their source in nature and healthy ecosystems. As such, we depend on biodiversity for our security and health, and it strongly affects our social relations and gives us freedom and choice.

Impacts

As humans, we occupy all continents and most ecosystems of the planet. We really believe "thou shall grow and multiply," and currently there are over 6 billion of us. We have 54 percent of earth's surface "domesticated" with agriculture, cattle raising, industry, and urbanization.

Now, for the first time in our history, we may be on the brink of a huge environmental impact created almost exclusively by ourselves. The impact will occur in the biosphere, the approximately 30-kilometer-long space surrounding the planet where life takes place in its land, water, and atmosphere ecosystems. *Economic and Political Agenda 21*, the document drafted at RIO-92—the UN Conference on Environment and Development, held in Rio de Janeiro in 1992, also known as Earth Summit—fails to mention that fact because it naively declared that by the twenty-first century we would have solved issues related to the aggression against biodiversity.

The International Panel of Climatic Changes (IPCC), which is a scientific foundation focused on biodiversity and also carbon negotiations, failed to consider global warming in its first report. It also failed to consider the Arctic's de-icing. Only afterward did the world's scientific community change its thinking regarding the climate changes. The report affirms that there is a 90 percent probability that human beings are responsible for global warming. Of the 360 environmental disasters known in 2005—which is 20 percent above the numbers in 2004—250 are believed to be connected to global warming. In 2011, this number grew larger.

Challenges

The great challenge, therefore, is that we must seek out and implement new strategies to reduce or eliminate the impacts of global warming and other environmental changes. This will be possible only with the integration of other sectors with conservation interests, even if such interests are not ideological but simply economic, to generate new conservation models to prevent global warming and other environmental changes or to reduce undesirable impacts if they occur.

We know that technological solutions, in addition to having questionable efficiency, often have a high cost that only a few countries can afford. We therefore have to seek realistic political and global solutions to this immense challenge.

Many of our problems are caused by the large number of people occupying urban areas. The world's urban population, which in 1950 was approximately 732 million, is now approximately 3.5 billion, of whom over a billion live in slums.

Predictions about Climate Changes in Brazil until the End of the Twenty-First Century

Brazil, which is a huge country with the highest biodiversity on the planet, has great agricultural potential but major social and economic problems. Eighty percent of the population lives in urban areas. This contributes to a drinkable water crisis, destruction of endangered biomes, and climate changes in general.

With a population of approximately 200 million, Brazil is the sixteenth highest issuer of carbon dioxide (CO_2) on the planet, if we take into account only chemicals, and the fourth highest issuer of forest burning. It is estimated that 75 percent of the origin of climate change in Brazil is due to misuse of forest reserves.

According to studies prepared by the Brazilian Ministry of Environment, the main predictions for the future of Brazil are terrifying. If climate change continues at the current rate. It is estimated that:

- Twenty percent of the Brazilian population (approximately 42 million people) will be affected by sea level increases, which will probably reach 0.50 meters (19.7 inches).
- The semi-arid region of the Brazilian northeast will become a desert, a process that is occurring now.
- In the southern and southeastern regions, there will be violent storms and coastal erosion, which already are occurring.
- "Savannazation" (the process of becoming like a desert) of the Amazon forest will occur due to temperature increases of up to 8°C (46.4°F) and vegetation removal (which is also currently occurring).
- The rates of tropical diseases—such as dengue, yellow fever, encephalitis, and skin cancer—will increase.

The anticipated changes described previously raise dramatic questions. What is going to happen to species that are confined to colder regions? Will we be able to define today where to create protected areas managed by government and migratory corridors to ensure that within 100 years areas occupied by the remnants of the Mata Atlântica are protected and connected?

In spite of the increasing number of researchers and projects every year, much information is still missing regarding the Mata Atlântica. This prevents us from improving tools that are required to precisely predict the consequences of deforestation and climate change, as well as to determine how biodiversity of ecosystems will be structured in the future.

CHALLENGES TO COUNTERACT CLIMATE CHANGES IN BRAZIL AND THE WHOLE PLANET

The grave challenges related to combating environmental destruction of our planet, highlighted by the issues in the Brazilian rainforest, are to:

- Stop quick degradation of our forests
- Increase awareness and environmental education, not only for the general population but also for those holding power
- Stop biodiversity loss, which is accelerating
- Control the appearance of emerging ecosystems
- Control unbridled urbanization

- Control the food supply
- Monitor long droughts and desertification
- Restructure our energy matrix, which may include but should not be limited to fire-wood and charcoal, oil, hydroelectricity, nuclear power, biofuel, solar and wind power (which is not used much), and also ideal energy and hydrogen fuel cells (which are primarily used on an on an experimental basis)
- Decrease social and political conflicts, which are huge in Brazil

From 1979, when the first International Conference on Climate was held, researchers have noted that the earth is undergoing a warming process. Monitoring by the IPCC highlights that changes are occurring faster than before. The average temperature on earth has already increased at least 0.5°C (33°F) in the last century. Several scenarios suggested that it will increase over 2 to 3°C (35 to 37°F) by late in the twenty-first century.

Along with temperature increase, there is a significant decrease in rain indexes in the region occupied by the Mata Atlântica is forecasted. Professor Carlos Alfredo Joly of the University of São Paulo reports that within 100 years, the Mata Atlântica will be warmer and drier. Questions remain:

Will there be time for redistribution of Mata Atlântica species?
Will we be able to predict this redistribution today?

An overriding challenge is that we must manage to find and implement new strategies to avoid environmental trauma, including global warming and/or climate change. Climate changes and/or global warming are currently major threats to life as we know it. New strategies will be possible only with the combined efforts of all stakeholders, whether their concerns are conservatory, economic, political, or ideological. Due to the monumental task at hand, including costs that are involved, solutions must be sought at all levels—from governments and civil society—to address this immense challenge.

We must reinvent our approach to this important challenge. This requires that we restructure our understanding of nature, society, and urbanization. With regard to the latter, although cities occupy only 4 percent of the earth's surface, they are the major producers of climate problems.

BIOSPHERE RESERVES

Biosphere reserves were created by UNESCO, in 1971 to promote knowledge, practice, and human values and to better understand the relationship between human populations and environments on earth. There are currently over 500 reserves that together form a worldwide network to carry out corporate research, preserve cultural and natural heritage, and promote sustainable development.

The Zoning of Biosphere Reserves

Reserves have a system consisting of three zones:

- Core zone: Formed by areas protected by law and defined as maximum protection areas, for example, federal, state, and local parks
- Buffer zone: Includes the core zone, with activities compatible with the conservation function of the core zone
- Transition zone: Surrounds the buffer zone; it is where activities should be implemented to promote sustainable development

The Brazilian Biosphere Reserves

Biomes are defined as the world's major communities, classified according to the predominant vegetation and characterized by adaptations of organisms to that particular environment. Six major biomes are freshwater, marine, desert, forest, grassland, and tundra. Biomes have changed and moved many times during the history of life on earth. More recently, human activities have drastically altered these communities. Thus, conservation and preservation of biomes should be a major concern to all.

In Brazil, there are seven big biosphere reserves, one for each of the country's major biomes. Biosphere reserves occupy 15 percent of the Brazilian territory. The seven reserves are:

- Biosphere Reserve of the Mata Atlântica, which was created in six steps from 1991 to 2009
- Biosphere Reserve of the Green Belt of the City of Sao Paulo, which was created in 1992 and which is an integral part of the Biosphere Reserve of the Mata Atlântica
- Biosphere Reserve of the Cerrado (Brazilian savanna), which was created in two steps from 1993 to 2000 and which has 73,389 acres
- Biosphere Reserve of the Pantanal (the biggest flood plain in the planet), which was created in 2000 and which has 63,505 acres
- Biosphere Reserve of the Caatinga (Brazilian semi-arid territory), which was created in 2001 and which has 49,420 acres
- Biosphere Reserve of the Central Amazon, which was created in 2001 and which has 49,420 acres
- Biosphere Reserve of Serra do Espinhaço (Highland Fields), which was created in 2005

The Mata Atlântica Biosphere Reserve

Biosphere reserves are dynamic (subject to constant change), therefore, reviewing them is always necessary. In the case of the Mata Atlântica Biosphere Reserve, such reviews were performed in six phases from 1992 to 2008. In 1992 (phase 1), its surface was about 6,177,609 acres with 882,162 acres of marine area, and in 2008 (phase 6), its surface was estimated to be about 153,995,442 acres with 39,907,355 acres of marine area.

Located in Brazil's most urbanized and industrialized region, including Brazil's two largest cities of Sao Paulo and Rio de Janeiro, this reserve requires institutional, territorial, and ecosystemic coordination on a uniquely large scale.

The Mata Atlântica is closely connected to the history of Brazil. Its very name originated from the endemic tree species named Pau brasil (*Cesalpinea echinata Lam-Leguminosae/Cesalpinoideae*).

Due to its great size, and the significant climate variation existing from the northeastern region to the southern region of Brazil, especially in regard to temperature and precipitation, the Mata Atlântica is directly impacted by the climate characteristics of each region. The climate on earth has varied significantly over the past 65 million years; however, the pattern of fluctuations has drastically changed since the industrial revolution in the mid-nineteenth century, and these fluctuations have significantly increased from the mid-twentieth century.

Therefore, due to its continental dimensions, strategic location, decentralized and effectively participatory management system, and a set of extremely broad-based, dynamic programs and projects, the Mata Atlântica Biosphere Reserve (RBMA) completely fulfills the three basic functions required by UNESCO biosphere reserves. Some of these contributions are summarized in the following sections.

Conservation

The biosphere reserve currently covers areas in 16 of the 17 states where the Mata Atlântica is found. There are 153,992,287 acres in land and 39,899,332 acres in marine areas, involving a great diversity of ecosystems. There are dense rain forests; ombrophylous (always green, without leaf falling) mixed forests, also known as araucaria forests; ombrophylous open forests; semideciduous seasonal forests; and deciduous seasonal forests.

A series of ecosystems associated with the Mata Atlântica is protected in the RBMA, such as mangroves, high altitude fields, rupestrine vegetation (rock outcrop), dunes, sand banks, caves, cave ecosystems, and many others located on ocean islands. The inclusion of all of these ecosystems in the RBMA demonstrates the country's commitment before the international community to comply with these duties. For this reason, the simple fact of an area being included in the RBMA and recognized by the MAB/UNESCO strengthens efforts put toward its conservation and encourages actions by the environmental movement (governmental and nongovernmental) in its defense.

The RBMA houses the most important remains of the Mata Atlântica, habitat of endemic species in danger of extinction, priority areas for the creation of protected areas, forest recovery areas, and forest mosaics and greenbelts. Two hundred seventy-six of 472 species of flora and 380 of 627 species of Brazilian fauna considered in danger of extinction are found in the Mata Atlântica. Out of these, 85 percent are protected in full protection conservation units of the Mata Atlântica, which compose the core zones of the RBMA. There are more than 700 conservation units, of which 246 are ruled by government (6,350,000 acres) and 466 are private reserves (255,500 acres). Added to other preservation areas defined by law (mangroves, riparian forests, and other sorts of vegetation) the core zones of the RBMA covers 18,000,000 acres.

In the buffer zones and in the transition zones, which together add to almost 178,000,000 acres, endangered species as well as land, coastal, and marine ecosystems are protected.

The administration of the conservation initiatives in the biosphere reserve is implement by means of the public policies and technical and scientific programs. It is as important as its inclusion in the RBMA and the creation of protected areas. Among these programs, those that deserve to be highlighted are related to research and conservation, waters and forests, mosaic and greenbelts, and restoration of the Mata Atlântica, all with various projects in the various regions of the reserve.

Sustainable Development

Natural resources of the Mata Atlântica have always served as raw material to be used by its inhabitants. Since the colonizers discovered Brazil, exploited resources have diminished at increasing rates. After exploitation started, devastation of the forests began. Today, 500 years of continued use and conversion of the forest into agriculture, animal husbandry, mining, infrastructure development, and urbanization has left only 7 percent of the original vegetation that covered the original Mata Atlântica Biome remaining well preserved.

Designating these areas as the Mata Atlântica Biosphere Reserve enlarges the sustainable use of the forest. The very concept of biosphere reserve implies the implementation of zoning and sustainable use of natural resources in its buffering and transition areas. To the extent that the promotion of ecotourism in protected areas and surroundings is encouraged, sustainable development is also promoted in the core zones of the RBMA. The biosphere reserve of the Mata Atlântica is recognized for its projects to provide ecotourism guide training and certification to hotels and inns in various regions. Projects that focus on youth, traditional communities, and small local businesspeople have been especially successful in some areas.

There are over 70 different indigenous groups in the Mata Atlântica, dozens of *Quilombos* (black slave–descendant communities), *caiçaras* (traditional fishing communities), and other groups of traditional fishermen, in addition to millions of small rural producers and extractive communities. This is the main audience for the RBMA's engagement. In this sense, the National Council of the Biosphere Reserve of the Mata Atlântica has 17 state committees (each State included in the Reserve has one RMBA committee) have been engaged in the formulation of public policies and fair market practices that promote the improvement of the quality of life of their traditional populations. For this, the RBMA has supported the creation of sustainable development reserves, extractive reserves and other protected areas that compose its buffer zones. An enormous effort has been made to provide government funds and programs to support community initiatives in agroforestry, organic agriculture, sustainable handling of native species, and sustainable agriculture. It has also been engaged in the formulation of policies for payments for environmental services (carbon, water, and biodiversity) in the Mata Atlântica.

Also focused on the local communities that inhabit its territory, the RBMA has an important program focused on the production and fair trade of products of the Mata Atlântica. The Mata Atlântica Market Program (check its Web site at the biosphere reserve's Web portal, www.rbma.org.br/mercadomataatlantica) registers, certifies with a specific seal, and supports the production and sale of handicraft, food products, and other items.

Although it prefers to focus on local communities, the RBMA also maintains projects and partnerships with business sectors to integrate quality economy into productive chains and the principles of sustainability. Examples include the reserve's partnerships with northeastern sugar and alcohol sectors and with various companies of other sectors that maintain advanced sites of the RBMA in conservation areas.

Knowledge and Management

Over a decade ago, the national council of the RBMA defined in its action plan that the formerly named logistics function prescribed by the MaB program for the biosphere reserves should be translated into three lines of action: (1) developing traditional and scientific knowledge, (2) promoting the community and environmental education, and (3) implementing a decentralized and participative management system.

The Mata Atlântica cooperates with the majority of the universities and research centers and researchers in Brazil. Therefore, the RBMA focuses its efforts on the systematization and dissemination of scientific information that contributes to the conservation and sustainable use of the forest. Likewise, it promotes the utilization of knowledge about the people of the forest and the managed species that are a fundamental part of our culture and the sustainable development of the biome. To this end, the RBMA has already promoted 12 national and international seminars, it maintains a Web portal, and produces vast environmental communication and education material (posters, folders, videos, etc.) as well as technical and scientific publications. The RBMA books series contains 40 volumes (dating back to 1993) published about the Mata Atlântica for the general public.

The RBMA's management system, with a national council, 16 state committees, 5 subcommittees, 3 regional committees, and 24 advanced sites in various states is currently the most comprehensive biome defense network of the Americas. There are over 300 government (federal government, states and cities) and civilian institutions (nongovernmental organizations [NGOs], local communities, businesspeople, and scientists) permanently engaged in an integrated manner.

This management system, which received UNESCO–Brazil's commemorative Environmental Award for 60 years of UNESCO and 30 years of the MAB Program, is certainly the RBMA's biggest achievement. It is what enables the management of a reserve with such enormous dimensions and provides a great capacity for political mobilization and articulation of conservation goals for the forest. This is also the network that ensures logistic, material, and human support for conservation and sustainable development in the RBMA's area.

The review and expansion of the biosphere reserve during phase VI is a direct result of this vast network that made the reserve what it is today, not only a priority conservation area, but also one of the most important institutions making a socioenvironmental impact in Brazil. Phase VI advances the Mata Atlântica biosphere reserve's goal of being an important instrument before the ministry of the environment for the implementation of public policies in the Mata Atlântica.

The rich participation process adopted when preparing for phase VI contributed to consolidating and strengthening the RBMA partnership network and its management system, as well as promoting and implementing the purposes of the MAB program. The RBMA has been a pioneer in the successful experimentation and enrichment of the new directives as defined in Madrid during the Biosphere Reserves Network Meeting in February 2008.

This complex of formations comprised by a set of ecosystems highly changed by human action results in a landscape mosaic with a variety of vegetal fragments of different sizes, forms, ecologic conditions, and conservation and pressure levels.

Among such natural mosaic areas, it is possible to highlight regions currently known as ecological corridors and mosaics of protected areas. These include the Jacupiranga Mosaic and the Serra do Mar and Mantiqueira Mosaics, within the limits of which almost all ecosystems contained in the Mata Atlântica are represented. Related ecosystems, such as insular and high altitude fields, are also included. All these corridors and the mosaics of protected areas are now a part of the Mata Atlântica Biosphere Reserve.

Currently there are over 500 reserves, which jointly comprise a world network that has as its purpose to promote knowledge, practice, and human values in order to establish relationships among populations and the environment on earth. Corporate research, conservation of cultural and natural assets, and the promotion of sustainable development are highlighted in these projects.

Areas of Concentration

The biosphere reserve of the Mata Atlântica contributes to the conservation, preservation, and sustainable development of the Mata Atlântica by means of its programs and projects. These are developed with governmental and nongovernmental funds for the purpose of cultural and ecological sustainable conservation of biodiversity and other forest heritage, including landscape and water resources, valorization of social diversity and cultural and ethnic heritage, and promotion of economic development so that it can be culturally and ecologically sustainable.

Support for demonstrative projects, production and disclosure of knowledge, environmental education and qualification, scientific research and monitoring, and, in particular, public policies have an important role in the organization of the biosphere reserve.

Contribution

We are involved in collaborating to inform and make populations aware of the mobilization and participation to disclose the meaning of citizenship and solidarity, which must be further developed in Brazil. The individual as consumer, professional, and citizen, and the collective work of NGOs, companies, and governments must be encouraged. Our projects contribute to public policies by creating discussions related to sustainability, regulation, planning, and channels for market inclusion and insertion by payment of environmental services, certification, and social responsibility. Finally, the search for sustainability is not only an action in favor of our planet, but also one for our own good. This must be the ultimate goal.

SUMMARY

I believe that the work we have been doing in Brazil contributes to diminishing the problems that beset our planet, which is the theme of this book: change. The Mata Atlântica biosphere reserve provides for the interaction of the Mata Atlântica biome with society and also encourages active participation among those involved.

What we have been searching for in our programs of the Mata Atlântica biosphere reserve is to recover the instinct of survival that has been obfuscated by the actions of our culture, our ambition, and our arrogance. We must use our collective skills to repair such past mistakes. Our mission in the Mata Atlântica biosphere reserve is to contribute to establishing a harmonious relationship between society and the environment, given the principle that humans are nature and nature is humans. This work constitutes a pact for the conservation of biodiversity, the promotion of sustainable development, and the mobilization of public policies that preserve the precious rainforest and our environment in general.

Part II

Our Human Resources: Coping with Environmental Changes

Humankind is currently suffering from an onslaught of environmental events leading to tragic aftermaths, including loss of lives and livelihoods. Some such tragedies are out of people's control, like earthquakes, floods, fires, tsunamis, and tornadoes. Other disasters occur as a result of a mixture of these uncontrollable events of nature exacerbated by people's actions, as in the case of faulty construction of water levees or nuclear power plants. Further compounding the disaster is a community's lack of resources or preparedness to respond to the danger. In spite of these conditions, people have been able to survive such tragedies. The chapters in this part of the book show us how individuals and communities cope with such drastic environmental disasters. Models for survival that are presented include building on individual resilience, strengthening community support, and following traditions of indigenous peoples who have long lived with respect for, and in harmony with, nature. In addition, a newly evolving perspective about survival from environmental tragedies takes into account a spiritual view of ecology and the world in which we live.

7

Our Robust People: Resilience in the Face of Environmental Trauma

Darlyne G. Nemeth and L. Taighlor Whittington[*]

Whether devastated by hurricanes, earthquakes, wars, or other natural or human-induced disasters, people inevitably find a way to regroup and to rise to the challenge. Their robustness, strength, and ability to endure great tragedy and survive great hardships are amazing examples of psychological resilience.

According to Cameron (2000), in the final analysis, one of the greatest impacts of environmental trauma is psychological (as cited in Nemeth et al., 2000). This concept is echoed by Onishi, Voitsekhovich, and Zheleznyak (2007) in their book reflecting on the twentieth anniversary of the Chernobyl nuclear disaster.

After the basic safety needs of food and shelter have been restored, people must begin anew both physically and emotionally. This requires a psychological process called coping, which is the ability to contend with and overcome difficult circumstances quickly. It is the essence of psychological resilience.

In this chapter, we address the importance of coping, resilience, perspective, and hope. We also discuss common behavioral maladaptations to trauma and change, derived and refined from our factor analytic studies over the past 10 years. We then hypothesize a six-stage recovery process, which we believe to be universal.

COPING

There are several steps in coping with environmental trauma. The first coping step requires people to identify, label, and share their feelings. Talking about their concerns and traumas in a safe place is an important part of this process. If people avoid this step, they remain in denial, which Campbell (1981) defines

[*]The authors wish to thank Amber Gremillion, Ashton Smith, and Chelsie Songy for their assistance in research and format preparation.

as the "refusal to admit the reality of, disavowal of the truth, or refusal to acknowledge the presence or existence of something" (p. 163). Remaining in a state of denial is one of the biggest impediments to coping. When people refuse to admit that something will occur, is occurring, or has occurred, they cannot move forward. For example, although many New Orleanians knew Hurricane Katrina was coming their way, they assumed that they could "ride it out" (Bergal et al., 2007; Horne, 2006). Many even planned hurricane parties (Brinkley, 2006). Because they were in denial, when Katrina and her aftermath hit, they were unable to move forward. They had not planned to evacuate. Many people and animals were simply washed away (Bergal et al., 2007; Brinkley, 2006). Bar-Levav (1988) titled his book, which addresses this process of not facing tragedy, *Thinking in the Shadow of Feelings*. This is an ineffective process. According to Bar-Levav, "rather than reflecting current reality, feelings express our expectations based on what we already know from before" (p. 116). He noted that feelings are "totally unreliable as a guide to actions in the present. . . . Normally we respond emotionally with little consideration of the real circumstances that confront us" (p. 116). This is not coping. Bar-Levav further states that "Remnants of feelings that have been denied and suppressed accumulate within us, since they find no legitimate outlet, and their pressure increases with time" (p. 116).

First Coping Step: Facing Feelings and Sharing Experiences

This first coping step should not be an in-depth process. Rather, Garrido (2007) points out that the purpose of this sharing experience is to assist people in calming down and in learning that they are not alone. It also allows others to bear witness to their tragedies.

Second Coping Step: Acknowledgment and Affirmation

Acknowledgment is taking notice of or recognizing something or someone as genuine or valid, and affirmation is confirming or validating something or someone. To acknowledge the reality of people's experiences is freeing. It helps to melt away denial. Having others acknowledge and understand our pain or loss allows us to admit what we have experienced. "Understanding cannot alter physiologic processes, but it can lessen that small portion of our anxiety that results from not knowing what plagues us" (Bar-Levav, 1988, p. 130). We can then move out of denial and experience the support of others, for "the more complete the denial the greater the danger" (Bar-Levav, 1988, p. 136). When unburdened by the support of others, people can make the decision to move forward. Without the support of others, people lose hope; yet hope is essential for rebuilding. Without hope, people become victims. Tragedy itself does not victimize people; rather, falling into a state of hopelessness, despair, and/or depression victimizes people. Depression is not inevitable. Although many people fall into a state of depression after environmental trauma, depression can be dissipated by affirmation. When we acknowledge how people are feeling and affirm, or give legitimacy, to what they are feeling, people have permission (yours and theirs) to move forward.

Third Coping Step: Solving Problems

Once people have been able to face their tragic losses and pain, and acknowledge their survivor's guilt, they are more emotionally available to think, to solve problems, and to create a plan for moving forward. Restoration of the environment that was once known and cherished may not be ideal. It may not even be appropriate or feasible. Frequently, people want to rebuild exactly what was lost. But rebuilding in the same physical environment is not always a resilient decision. For example, in the United Kingdom, long-range environmental destruction decisions have been made regarding which historic properties will be maintained and restored and which properties will be let go (Chang, 2006). These decisions were made with several considerations, including environmental issues, available financial resources, and the cultural importance of the structure. In the aftermath of Hurricane Katrina, many continue to wrestle with similar issues. Rethinking priorities and restructuring needs often serve people better than merely rebuilding what was.

Fourth Coping Step: Reassessing and Reprioritizing Needs

Learning from experiences, rather than merely repeating them, is a crucial coping strategy. We must remember the difference between doing what is wanted versus doing what is needed. This requires benefiting from history and being willing to change. Often, emotional attachments to the past prevent logical planning for the future. Restoration problem solving, which involves focusing on restoring/rebuilding what was regardless of present and future needs, is not good enough. It is not merely a matter of rebuilding a physical or cultural environment. Rather, it is a matter of carefully analyzing the situation, accepting what needs to be done, and reshaping the cultural environment so that people can flourish.

Resistance to this process is a major impediment to change. According to Billow (2010), resistance typically accompanies change and must be addressed to move forward: resistance "cannot be cured, overcome, or resolved . . . " for truth is infinite and continuity does exist as we attempt to "make, unmake, and remake our experiences meaningful" (p. 342). Specifically, Billow outlines five assertions about resistance: (1) Resistance regulates the development, expression, and usefulness of emotional truth. It keeps truth from becoming overwhelming. (2) Resistance is motivated by basic conflict between thinking and not thinking.

It is experienced through bodily arousal. Resistance is "motivated to reveal and to conceal, to develop and limit meaning" (p. 325). (3) Resistance involves the interplay between truth and falsity. It can facilitate building constructive relationships: "It is expectable in human relations that truth–seeking and falsification occur in chorus, in different degrees of awareness, and with conflicting intrapsychic and intrapersonal purpose" (p. 332). (4) Resistance, which is a social phenomenon, is intersubjective, involving multiple levels of interplay. Specifically, it involves "interactive mental relationships, intrapsychic, interpersonal and immediate, and also historic, cultural, and political" levels (p. 333). (5) Resistance is intersubjective, involving multiple levels of mental interplay. In the final analysis, however, the goal must be to work toward truth rather than to work through resistance.

Fifth Coping Step: Implementation

This step involves doing what is needed even though it may not be what is wanted. It is about working toward truth. For example, some Alaskan Eskimo villages are relocating out of necessity (i.e., truth). This is being done because of climate change, not because of the villagers' desire to relocate (Reiss, 2010). Louisiana's coastal dwellers have experienced similar phenomena (Davis, 2010). People must work together in a prosocial manner to achieve their goals. Individual efforts must lead to collective efforts.

In summary, successful coping begins with facing one's feelings and experiences, and moving out of denial. This is facilitated by the acknowledgment and affirmation of others. With affirmation, depression can be dissipated and people can begin solving problems. When creative thinking and planning begin, people must focus on their present and future needs. Often, this process is thwarted when people focus on the past and resist change. Last, doing what is needed at both an individual level and a community level is always a challenge. To achieve closure, special interests must be put aside, and a sense of the common good must prevail. Regardless of the specific intentions of the few, people's resilience is, in the final analysis, determined by the collective wisdom of the many.

RESILIENCE

Resilience is "the positive capacity of people to withstand stressors and to cope with trauma" (Walker & Heffner, 2010, para. 1). The ability to be focused on today, to learn from yesterday, and to imagine oneself in tomorrow is the hallmark of a resilient person. Adaptability. Flexibility. These qualities are inherently imbedded in resilient people.

Not all people are resilient. Those with little hope, those with little joy, those with little charity. They live only for today; they bemoan the past; and they see nothing but despair ahead. These are the people who usually do not survive trauma. If by chance they do survive physically, they usually do not survive emotionally. These are the people who passively exist and merely endure what is to come.

But passive endurance is not enough. It may allow physical survival. But it does not allow emotional growth. Growth requires mastery, and mastery is the hallmark of resiliency. But mastery is not over others, rather it is over ourselves. Even under the most traumatic circumstances, we have a choice to remain the master of ourselves or to succumb to the will of others. Again, this is a choice. Mastery over ourselves requires remaining in control of our feelings, our thoughts, and our actions. Regardless of the circumstances, we must never give up mastery. We must never lose hope. We must always stay future-oriented. To endure the present, we must see ourselves in the future. Tomorrow. Next week. Next month. Next year. When we can see ourselves there, we can plan to get there. Endurance with a plan is not passive. It involves the active process of thinking, dreaming, and hoping for a better tomorrow; for when hope is lost, the future is lost.

There are countless examples throughout history of people who have lost hope and vanished versus people who have maintained their belief in a better tomorrow and have flourished. People flourish by embracing change, accepting its inevitability, planning for it, and welcoming it. Just when things are calm and stable, chaos, whether human-induced or nature-induced, is likely to emerge (Gleick, 1987). Resiliency, determination, and cultural heritage, however, are the constants that ensure survival (Davis, 2010).

People who lack resiliency accept complacency. They expect that things will stay the same. When change occurs, people respond with rigidity and are easily broken. Broken people cannot cope. They cannot adapt. They cannot envision a different tomorrow. They are likely to succumb to depression, anxiety, and/or substance abuse (Bourque et al., 2006; Sattler et al., 2002).

GAINING PERSPECTIVE

Although respect for the past is useful, it must not prevent us from moving into the future. Active endurance of the present provides us with the creative thoughts we need for building a better tomorrow. Passive endurance depresses and fatigues, whereas active endurance invigorates and energizes. Staying in the present, while planning for tomorrow, allows people to manage their anxieties. The present is appropriately fleeting and ever so quickly becomes the past. It is just a moment in time, for "even very strong emotional reactions normally pass quickly if they do not connect with stored remnants of suppressed feelings from the past" (Bar-Levav, 1988, p. 135).

People who are mired in the past and who cannot see themselves in the future vanish. Perspective, however, must be gained from the past in order for one to embrace the future. Gaining perspective is an important process.

But how is this done?

After change has occurred, whether through chaos caused by a hurricane or a quiet evolution due to global warming or climate change, people must be willing to deal with their feelings. "The act of consciously inhibiting an impulse, affect, or idea, as in the deliberate attempt to forget something and think no more about it," (Campbell, 1981, pp. 611–612) or suppression of one's past feelings and traumas interferes with movement. People who remain "stuck" in the past are immobilized—they are unable to think about, plan for, and/or embrace the future.

People understand the power of hurricanes, the power of tsunamis, the power of brutality; yet people do not fully comprehend the cleansing power of feelings. On an individual basis, as well as on a collective level, this process of understanding our feelings must occur. As stated previously, Bar-Levav (1988) calls thinking in the shadow of feelings an ineffective process; yet this is a defense that many traumatized people use to cope. Why do so many shy away from experiencing this very cleansing emotional process? Gaining perspective requires it, yet people and institutions are usually afraid of it. Denial and suppression typically prevail. Frequently, spin, a process of repackaging information for special interest needs, enhances these defenses. But anything as powerful as feelings must be heard.

ROBUST VS. PSYCHOID LEADERS

Leaders play an important role in the creative process of coping. When people are unwilling to hear their own feelings, they may abdicate mastery and prefer to listen to the voices of others. At times of trauma or transition, individuals may rise to leadership roles by distorting the truth and saying whatever it takes to gain power. According to Bar-Levav (1988), "Irrationality is fast becoming an increasingly effective tool" (p. 120). Adolf Hitler and Saddam Hussein who are examples of psychoid leaders, ruled by fear and intimidation.

On the other hand, Winston Churchill and Franklin Delano Roosevelt, are examples of robust people who were capable of igniting the hope that individuals possessed. Robust leaders build upon their own and others' personal strengths and resources. They find a way to actively endure and to deal with the changes that must be made (Lopez et al., 2009). Robust people are strong, powerful, vigorous, and healthy individuals who find a way to survive, adapt, and change in order to meet the challenges that lie ahead. They have perspective. They honor the past, realistically address the present, and develop pathways to the future.

But sometimes, robust people are thwarted by leaders who wish to preserve the past, such as Osama bin Laden, or those who fear the future, such as

Moammar Kadafi. These individuals were also psychoid leaders. They are character-disordered individuals who desired power and control at the expense of others. They rise to positions of power by offering simple solutions to complex problems during difficult times. Vulnerable individuals who are unwilling to hear, let alone listen to, their own voices, fear the future. These dependent followers, who typically engage in group think, are susceptible to psychoid leadership.

This is another time in history wherein psychoid leadership is prevalent. In the last century, Adolf Hitler emerged to lead an economically devastated Germany. He did so with fear tactics and aggression. In this century, Osama bin Laden did the same thing. Hitler pitted Christians against Jews. Bin Laden pitted Muslims against Christians. They used half-truths and selected religious ideas to offer simple solutions to complex problems. The problems of today, however, are quite complex and the solutions are hardly simple.

Psychoid leaders prey upon the most vulnerable in society. Via spin, they can easily convince dependent followers of even the most illogical of ideas (Nemeth, 2005). Rather than uniting communities, further separations are fostered. At times of environmental trauma, this divisive process can present yet another barrier to recovery. Psychoid leaders can inflame pre-existing prejudices and invite extreme responses. Other disordered characters, such as militants, paranoids, religious fundamentalists, and corporate sociopaths, tend to emerge as well (Lamar et al., 2008). For example, Militants are prepared for every possible outcome. They stockpile food and weapons. They build bomb shelters and teach one another the latest war techniques.

Paranoid individuals usually withdraw from their families and communities. They perceive the world as a dangerous place and tend to allow little outside influence. As they drift into psychosis, however, they take action against the outside world. Ted Kaczynski, the Unabomber, is one such individual (*Ted Kaczynski*, 2011).

Religious fundamentalists fortify themselves in compounds and prepare for the end of the world as they know it. They are often led by psychoid leaders who desire power and control at all cost. Examples of this are the members of the Branch Davidian Compound in Waco, Texas, led by David Koresh (*David Koresh*, 2011).

But corporate sociopaths are perhaps the most dangerous of all. These corporate executives are willing to lie, cheat, deceive, and distort reality in order to line their own pockets. For example, the recent banking crisis was brought about by such individuals. The U.S. government, under the direction of President George W. Bush's treasury secretary, Henry Paulson, brokered a deal with top U.S. bank executives, with the understanding that their banks would use the bailout money to take the pressure off of their home mortgage holders (Sorkin, 2009). Did they? No. They kept the money, restructured their banks, and gave their executives big bonuses. Did any of them go to jail? No. Corporate sociopaths manage to avoid both responsibility and accountability. Oil company executives are now doing the same thing in the aftermath of the BP oil spill (Chediak, 2010). These character-disordered individuals seem to rise to leadership positions during times of crisis. Due to their lack of prosocial empathy, these individuals manage to either block or undermine meaningful recovery.

THE RECOVERY PROCESS

There appears to be a universal six-stage process that follows environmental trauma. These six stages are: shock, survival mode, basic needs, awareness of loss, susceptibility to spin and fraud, and resolution.

1. Shock

Hurricane Katrina. The Japanese earthquake, tsunami, and Fukushima nuclear disaster. The BP Gulf oil spill. The Tuscaloosa, Alabama, and Joplin, Missouri, tornadoes. These environmental traumas were immediately followed by the first psychological response: shock. Shock is a reaction to "a sudden physical or mental disturbance" (Campbell, 1981, p. 583). This is a natural response to disruption—no matter how simple or horrific the disruption is.

We tend to view our lives as predictable, stable, and secure. We expect the sun to come up each day, to go about our daily routines, to watch the sun set, to go to bed each night, and to begin the process all over again the next day. We expect to go to our workplace and for our lives to continue "as is." But these are merely false beliefs that we carry with us. Nothing is guaranteed—except for change. We are vulnerable in so many ways. For example, if we live near water, if we build in earthquake-prone areas, if we work in unstable drilling conditions, we are not safe from environmental trauma. Yet we expect the advantages to outweigh the risks. We are especially unprepared for change when it is more traumatic or intense than we had anticipated.

Again, New Orleanians knew that Hurricane Katrina was coming, but residents were not prepared for the human-induced problems that brought about the mass flooding and chaos after Katrina had passed. For example, one well-known French Quarter artist, Harold "Napoleon" King, was riding his bicycle to dialysis treatment when he found himself up to his neck in water. He was eventually rescued by a Coast Guard truck and taken to the Superdome. He was then bussed throughout the state to three different medical facilities. He eventually died while being transferred from the Leesville Rehabilitation Hospital, in Leesville, Louisiana, to a facility in Gretna, Louisiana (Wallie, 2005).

The Japanese did not expect a tsunami to extensively damage a nuclear power plant (Tabuchi & Wald, 2011). In Chernobyl, in spite of their proximity to the nuclear power plant, people had no warning at all of the disaster to come. Liakhovich (2006) stated, "There was absolutely no warning of the imminent danger.

Millions of people in Kiev, and throughout Ukraine and Belarus continued with their daily lives without the slightest notion of spreading radiation" (para. 5).

Recent tornadoes in Alabama, Georgia, Mississippi, and Missouri did not allow residents enough time to prepare. Some found safety in walk-in refrigerators, basements, and bathrooms (*Survivor stories*, 2011). Others, who did not have safe houses, found no safety at all. Specifically, the Jasper County, Missouri, emergency management director, Keith Stammers, reported that residents were given about 20 minutes' notice when 25 warning sirens sounded (Murphy, 2011). Missouri Governor Jay Nixon added, "The bottom line was the storm was so loud you probably couldn't hear the sirens going off" (Murphy, 2011, para. 14), so they were ineffective.

All of these people lived in danger zones, yet they expected that nothing would happen. They lived under the illusion of safety (Davis, 2010).

In all of these situations, people, property, and entire communities vanished in minutes. For those who survived, there was shock. Bar-Levav (1988) pointed out that "The sudden eruptions and storms of powerful emotions still cause us to lose our bearings" (p. 129). For example, in the aftermath of the terrorist attacks of the human-induced September 11, 2011, disaster, many people walked around the streets in a zombie-like state—dazed, disoriented, disheveled, and distraught. For those who watched from afar, via television or the Internet, there was disbelief. People were stunned. How could this happen?

When people are in shock, they act without thinking. Frequently they perform heroic feats at their own peril. These heroic actions, however, may have unintended consequences such as posttraumatic stress disorder and/or long-term health ailments that may include cancer, stroke, asthma, sleep apnea, neurological problems, cognitive difficulty, and respiratory disease (Prynn, 2010). In the rush to locate loved ones and to help others, many expose themselves to life-threatening air, contaminated water, radiation, and rubble. Often, the effects of this exposure do not show up for years. And when people get sick, it is not uncommon for authority figures to deny and/or disavow their illnesses. For example, after Hurricane Katrina, evacuees were placed in Federal Emergency Management Agency (FEMA) trailers. These trailers underwent air quality testing by the Occupational Safety and Health Administration (OSHA) and were found to contain elevated levels of the gas formaldehyde. Despite these findings, FEMA officials claimed that the trailers were safe and that there was no need to conduct air quality testing (Brunker, 2006).

In the 2011 U.S. Department of Health and Human Services (DHHS) twelfth Report on Carcinogens (RoC), prepared by the National Toxicology Program, formaldehyde's status was changed from "reasonably anticipated to be a human carcinogen" to "known to be a human carcinogen" (p. 195). The report went on to state that "studies have demonstrated a causal relationship between exposure to formaldehyde and cancer in humans" (p. 195).

2. Survival Mode

In a state of panic, most people do whatever it takes to survive. Walking miles without shoes, as so many did after Hurricane Katrina, is just one example. Many came for medical care with little skin left on the bottoms of their feet (Anonymous, personal communication, 2006). Yet, they were alive. They had an opportunity to plan for tomorrow.

For those who died in the April 20, 2010, BP oil explosion in the Gulf Coast waters, there was no warning, no opportunity to recover. This human-induced environmental trauma not only took the lives of 11 brave men, but it took the livelihoods of thousands of families dependent on the Gulf Coast of the United States for their income. It also severely impacted—and in some instances destroyed—the normal functioning of ecosystems in some very fragile areas (Davis, 2010). This trauma was totally preventable. As discussed earlier, corporate sociopathy, a business philosophy that values financial gain over all other considerations, was the culprit. Will these executives, who bypassed safety regulations, ever be held accountable? Even now, many Gulf Coast residents are still in survival mode. Why is it up to the victims to prove their losses? For those who died in the explosion, their families do not even have bodies to bury. What of their losses! Closure is a basic need for all survivors of trauma. Otherwise, either directly or indirectly, survivors tend to become victims.

In survivor mode, Garrido (2007) identified five types of victims: (1) those who are overwhelmed and in shock due to the emotional impact of the trauma; (2) those who tell their horrifying story while displaying no emotion; (3) those who feel guilty for having survived while others died or were injured; (4) those who believe that they (a) made the disaster worse somehow, (b) could have done something to help, (c) could have prevented it from happening, or (d) could have saved someone; and (5) those who have been victims of group violence.

According to Garrido (2007), to address the plight of survivors, it is necessary to understand which of the aforementioned emotional characteristics they display. By understanding how survivors are coping, responders can better know how to assist them. Effective intervention can preclude victimization and/or depression. Ineffective intervention, as was the case following Hurricane Katrina (Bergal et al., 2007), can increase physical and emotional pain and forestall recovery. Frequently, simply allowing victims to talk about their story or addressing their survivor's guilt can empower them to become active survivors, rather than passive endurers, of their experiences. In any case, the chaos that breeds victimization must be ameliorated as quickly as possible. When basic needs are re-established, victimization can be greatly reduced via this process, and people can begin to find a way to cope.

3. Assessment of Basic Needs

Typically, first or second responders assess basic needs. Initially, these needs include food, clean water, shelter, and safety. In the aftermath of Hurricane Katrina, the local chapter of the Salvation Army was effective and found ways to help (Bergal et al., 2007).

Local people do this best. They understand the culture of the people and they know how to assess their basic needs. Yet local people are often trumped by outside organizations that have little understanding of the culture. In the aftermath of Hurricane Katrina, local faith-based groups were effective. In contrast, the Red Cross was not (Bergal et al., 2007). A New Orleans coffee shop owner, Bob Patience, declared that "The Red Cross came too late, stayed too late, and were ineffective when they were here" (as cited in Bergal et al., 2007, p. 69). Furthermore, Red Cross volunteers set up a field hospital in Mumford Stadium at Southern University in Baton Rouge, yet they did not separate out those individuals who needed a diabetic diet or specialized medical care from others. A local physician took this responsibility upon herself. She rallied the Baton Rouge medical community to assist with food and supplies, for example, honey buns were replaced with more nutritious bananas (Anonymous, personal communication, 2006). Louisiana's high rate of diabetes was a well-known medical fact that should have been included in the Red Cross disaster response plan.

Safety is one of the most difficult conditions to re-establish. People all too quickly learned what it was like to be without real money. One year after Hurricane Katrina, during an Anniversary Wellness Workshop held in Baton Rouge, one man spoke of what it was like to be without cash money (Nemeth et al., 2012). Checks were useless. So were credit cards. Another man swore that, in the future, he would always carry enough cash for food and lodging. He estimated this amount to be at least $300. (A more in-depth description of the Hurricane Anniversary Wellness Workshops will be presented later in this chapter.)

As espoused by Karen Horney, a twentieth-century psychoanalytic theorist, the safety motive is a measure by which individuals attempt, either directly or indirectly, "to protect themselves from the hostility in their environment, and more broadly, to protect themselves from any kind of threat" (Wolman, 1989, p. 299). Lawlessness prevailed in the aftermath of Hurricane Katrina. Brinkley (2006) described the looting in New Orleans as "a once-in-a-lifetime 'shopping' opportunity. A couple of thousand people were wandering around, like sinister Santa Clauses, with bags of stolen merchandise over their shoulders" (p. 361). Many people were harmed, and violent crimes were committed. For example, Charmaine Neville was raped on a rooftop at knifepoint (Brinkley, 2006). She was one of many women to have suffered such indignities. No meaningful plans to address victims' basic needs had been put in place. Since they were forced out of their homes by the raging waters, many people were huddled into the

Superdome for shelter. Others were left on bridges with no place to go. The initial response to this regional nightmare eventually turned into a national disgrace (National Medical Association, 2005).

Postdisaster problems, however, exist worldwide. For example, the Fukushima incident has turned into a disgrace for Technical Porcelain and Chinaware Company TEPCO, the nuclear power plant operator (Wallace, 2011). It is clear that environmental trauma can be compounded by humans' poorly thought-out initiatives and inept responses. For example, the tsunami and hurricane in Japan were unpreventable, but the conditions of the Fukushima Daiichi Nuclear Power Plant, similar to those inadequate conditions of the canals and levees in New Orleans, Louisiana, were another matter—they were preventable. Coping becomes more difficult when natural trauma is compounded by humans' short-sighted actions. Verchick (2010) noted that Louisiana is losing about 6,600 acres of coastal wetlands each year due to shortsighted, human-made interventions, such as levees, navigational channels, and oil and gas infrastructure. Specifically, Verchick points out that Louisiana is losing a football field's worth of land, which is vital to protection against bad storms, every half hour. By not protecting the natural infrastructure, which shelters people throughout the world, the aftermath of hurricanes, earthquakes, tsunamis, and other natural disasters becomes even more traumatic.

Guillermo Garrido, MD, a Venezuelan psychiatrist, participated in a symposium at the 2007 UN Department of Public Information Non-Governmental Organizations' (UN/DPI/NGO) Fall Meeting in New York City. His address was titled "Trauma Resolution and Life Style Change." Dr. Garrido pointed out that "the severity of a great natural disaster lies in its collective tragedy." He noted that it is society's responsibility to create order; reduce chaos; identify, select, and organize available resources; and manage such a crisis. Dr. Garrido recommended that people's physical needs must be addressed first. These include: identify medical problems, provide needed medications, regulate the person's sleep cycle, and provide food that is consistent with the person's medical status (e.g., diabetics require special diets and, possibly, dialysis).

To ameliorate the immediate impact of trauma, Dr. Garrido recommends that the following interventions be implemented as quickly as possible: calm people down, soothe their fears, let them talk, keep them safe, and provide food and shelter. The realistic limitations and availabilities of services in crisis situations must also be discussed. Dr. Garrido cautions that crisis managers must not promise what cannot be delivered.

4. Awareness of Loss

After passing through the shock of a situation, finding a way to survive, and re-establishing their basic needs, people must become aware of their losses. This phase involves surveying the damage. This typically begins when people endeavor to find their loved ones, to locate their property, and to gain perspective. Then, when a major authority figure comes to acknowledge their pain by his or her presence, people can begin to settle down. For example, when President Obama comes to console the victims of a flood or a hurricane or a tornado in the United States (*Obama Pays Visit*, 2011), or when Emperor Akihito of Japan comes to address the prefecture of Fukushima and neighboring areas, people feel reassured (JiJi Press, 2011). This settling experience allows people to face their personal losses, including the loss of people, property, community, and even perhaps culture.

Becoming aware of the potential loss of culture is frightening. Why is it that many New Orleanians are trying so desperately to rebuild the Lower Ninth-Ward, which was devastated by flooding in the aftermath of Hurricane Katrina? Many outsiders would argue that this low-lying area should never have been built on to begin with; therefore, why rebuild it? But, it is not just about a geographic location or the loss of property; it is about the loss of an entire culture. Culture provides stability. It symbolizes the past, anchors us to the present, and helps us to prepare for the future. It is the legacy upon which our hopes and dreams are founded. We can survive the loss of loved ones, for we know how to grieve. We can survive the loss of property, for we know how to rebuild. But we cannot emotionally survive the loss of our culture. History is replete with examples of people being transplanted out of their culture; for example, the Cherokee Indians forced to march to Oklahoma on the Trail of Tears (*Trail of Tears*, 2010). (Please refer to Chapter 10 for further examples.) People who are forcibly displaced usually do not fare well. Often, they perish. People need roots; they need their culture; they need their foundation for living.

5. Susceptibility to Spin and Fraud

Just when people need to rebuild, to repackage themselves, and to reshape their lives and their culture, spin and fraud come knocking on the door. Whether it is government or industry trying to gloss over the truth, or "entrepreneurs" trying to take advantage of people's vulnerabilities, or insurance companies attempting to settle claims too quickly or deny them altogether, there are usually perpetrators of spin and fraud on the heels of an environmental disaster.

For example, in New Orleans, "contractors" were there to rebuild during the day and to steal during the night. Contaminated Chinese drywall was used during the day (Nolan, 2011), and copper wiring was stolen at night (McCarthy, 2010). People were being traumatized over and over again. Mold and mildew were making residents sick, while the chemicals used to get rid of that mold and mildew were often toxic (Fuller, 2007). Many who were housed in FEMA trailers were unknowingly being poisoned by formaldehyde (Brunker, 2006). Clearly no-win situations abounded.

It appears that some lessons, however, were learned from Hurricane Katrina. FEMA's responses to the tornadoes in Alabama and Missouri were less inept (Associated Press, 2011). Even the Red Cross, which underwent a dramatic restructuring post-Katrina, has been more a part of the recovery efforts and less a part of the recovery problems in these tornado stricken areas. But perpetrators of spin and fraud are ever-present post-disaster, and they greatly impede the recovery process for society's most vulnerable individuals.

Who is most vulnerable to such spin and fraud? According to Bourque and colleagues (2006) and Tang (2007), the most vulnerable are those who have been in the closest proximity to the disaster and who, therefore, have had the greatest exposure. They typically have a low socioeconomic status and poor coping skills. They may have had a previous history of mental illness and a poor social-support system. They may have experienced loss of family members or pets in the disaster. They may have had to relocate. They may have found themselves linguistically (e.g., now interacting with people who speak a different language) or socially isolated. The most vulnerable individuals have the greatest difficulty achieving resolution.

6. Resolution

Resolution can take a long time—from many months to many years. The beginning of the resolution phase is typically marked by an anniversary reaction. Borstein and Clayton (1972) define an anniversary reaction as something that occurs on or around the date of a past traumatic event and that involves reactions to an emotionally charged episode that holds tremendous significance for an individual or group. When the initial event is experienced as traumatic, individuals may then tend to become sensitized to re-experience those symptoms under reminiscent circumstances.

Anniversary symptoms typically include constant worry, irritability, tension, headaches, restlessness, sleep disturbance, sadness, and fatigue (Nemeth et al., 2011). According to Maccoll and colleagues (1999), intrusive memories, emotional numbness, and behavioral reactivity may also accompany reminders of the event.

ANNIVERSARY WORKSHOPS

After Hurricane Katrina, Nemeth and colleagues conducted anniversary wellness reaction workshops. These workshops were designed to help survivors cope with their unresolved emotional pain and to promote emotional healing. Because recovery is not a linear process, many attendees were still moving in and out of the first five stages of recovery. Rather, it is an emotional process whereby a person typically moves three steps forward and then two steps back. At anniversary times, however, a person often regresses to Stage one and has to begin the entire process of emotional recovery all over again. Anniversary reactions are powerful emotional experiences from which no one who has experienced trauma is exempt.

They may gather in families or in places of worship for support. Perhaps the only cue is the date of the disaster. For example, September 11 is a date that many in the United States will remember for the Twin Towers terrorist attack. August 29 is a date that many New Orleanians will remember for Hurricane Katrina. April 20 is a date that most Gulf Coast residents will remember for the BP oil rig explosion. March 11 is the date that most Japanese will remember for the earthquake, tsunami, and Fukushima disaster. Dates are powerful cues. People may believe that they are past the trauma and that they are moving on. Then, the first anniversary of the trauma occurs, and pent-up feelings surge to the surface. These survivors then realize that they were not in a completed state of psychological recovery. Rather, they were merely in the process of dealing with their recovery as best as they could.

In the anniversary wellness workshops, people were able to let down their guard and deal with their feelings (Nemeth et al., 2012). As Bar-Levav (1988) pointed out, true resolution is not possible without addressing one's feelings. Usually, people go through the first five stages without fully identifying their feelings. They just try to "get through it." But there comes a point where the philosophy of "buck up and deal with it" totally breaks down—a point that typically occurs on or around the anniversary date of the trauma. Usually, the strongest reaction occurs at the time of the first anniversary. Feelings and symptoms such as panic, grief, and conflict typically emerge (Nemeth et al., 2011). But if things remain unresolved—for example, if there is no physical body to mourn when a person is missing, as happened in the April 20 BP Gulf oil explosion, or if there is no opportunity to return home, as happened in the August 29 Hurricane Katrina aftermath—then no resolution can occur. Building a memorial at the site of the September 11 Twin Towers terrorist attack, for example, allows people to grieve and to gain perspective. It allows resolution.

But most victims of environmental trauma are not so fortunate. They are the poor, the disenfranchised, and the most vulnerable among us. These are the people for whom the anniversary wellness workshops were designed. They are for the "forgotten people," the socially disadvantaged and the politically disconnected. The majority of the participants who attended these workshops were still living in formaldehyde trailers. They were becoming sick, both emotionally and physically. They had been herded into small, camp-like fenced areas with guards. They were not accustomed to this lifestyle. For example, most New Orleanians relied on public transportation, but Baton Rouge (where the workshops took place and to where people were relocated from nearby New Orleans), like Los Angeles, is a commuter city where people use cars to get from here to there. Yet, few displaced New Orleanians had cars. Many did not even know how to drive.

Participants came to the workshops for the promise of a day out and a nice lunch. But to their surprise, they received much more. They received an opportunity to be heard, an opportunity that had been denied them for the past year. During this postdisaster year, many continued to be in crisis and did not have services available. Typically, no one cared about how they were feeling or what they wanted or needed. Any services that were provided were more on a "take it or leave it" basis. For example, in Gulfport, the "Mississippi cottages" for evacuees were deemed "too nice" for evacuees and were therefore found objectionable by many (Eaton, 2008). With the influx of homeless evacuees from New Orleans, Baton Rouge's population doubled after Hurricane Katrina (Haygood, 2006). Many Baton Rougeans did not like the changes in their city. They did not like accommodating the "Katrina people." They were distressed about traffic congestion, increased crime, and more people competing for jobs and services (Haygood, 2006). Sympathy toward the suffering quickly turned to scorn. Unfortunately, long-term charity (i.e., a year or more) did not sit well with Baton Rouge residents (Blass, 2007). Statements were echoed like "those people" or "why don't they get off their butts and get a job?" In traffic, locals made statements about the newcomers like, "They must be from New Orleans." Caring turned into aggravation. Many Baton Rougeans simply wanted the Katrina people to go away.

But the faith-based organizations stood their ground and continued to help even when helping became unpopular (Chideya, 2005). Help was also forthcoming from the mental health and medical communities, which continued to provide family services through programs such as InCourage long after the national Red Cross had departed (InCourage, 2011). Many of the local faith-based communities funded the anniversary wellness workshops. So on a wing and a prayer, the anniversary wellness workshops commenced (Kimbrell, 2006; Kern, 2006). Participant evaluations of the impact of the workshops revealed that the workshops ended on an impressive note. Both qualitatively and quantitatively, far more than expected was achieved.

Quantitative Findings

To see if participants had a reduction in anxiety, the State-Trait Anxiety Inventory (STAI) (Spielberger, 1983) was administered to 16 participants before and after the fourth anniversary wellness workshop. The STAI consists of two 20-item scales that measure anxiety in a specific situation (state anxiety) and in general (trait anxiety). State and trait anxiety scores were analyzed using appropriate statistical measures. A significant reduction of 6.4 points in state anxiety from pre- to post-workshop assessments [$F(1, 15) = 15.59$, $p < .001$]

occurred. A reduction of 3.4 points in trait anxiety from pre- to post-workshop assessments, however, was not significant [F(1, 15) = 2.30, p = .150]. These results support the hypothesis that the wellness workshop interventions reduced anniversary reaction trauma-related state anxiety (Nemeth, 2012).

Qualitative Findings

Participants identified, labeled, and shared feelings. They began to form communities and empower themselves. They were heard. Anxieties were greatly reduced, and resolution began. In just a seven-hour workshop—essentially one day—the world changed for these participants. They emerged from a fog of confusion and doubt. They voiced their feelings, and they began to plan. Reactivity gave way to empowerment, and communities were reborn. The veil of darkness was lifted and people, once again, saw the sunlight (Nemeth et al., 2012). This process was demonstrated in the many group drawings that came to symbolize the past, present, and hoped-for future.

A tripartite group process was used. It consisted of the following: (1) Psychoeducational material was presented in a group-as-a-whole format at the beginning and end of each workshop. In this format, participants were able to say hello and goodbye to one another and to the experience. (2) Small group structured exercises. (3) A fish bowl group format summarized the small group experiences.

Participants were able to deal with their unresolved emotional traumas. All sessions were free. Attendance was voluntary (Nemeth et al., 2011).

Seven exercises followed an experiential demonstration of balance being disrupted by chaos. These exercises, which are available from the primary author via email (dgnemeth@gmail.com), were as follows: (1) My Good, Bad, and Ugly Hurricane Feelings; (2) A RILEE Relaxation Exercise; (3) Saying Goodbye to Say Hello; (4) How I Feel; (5) My Hurricane Feelings Banner; (6) Our Banners; and (7) Group Banners. Groups drew banners that came to symbolize hope and resilience. Several of these drawings have now become a part of the Hurricane Katrina Collection of the Louisiana State Archives at the Cabildo Museum in New Orleans (Nemeth et al., 2011).

THE SIX-STAGE ENVIRONMENTAL RECOVERY PROCESS

Table 7.1 compares two hurricanes, two earthquakes, two nuclear disasters, and two oil spills. The six-stage recovery process is outlined for each: Hurricane Katrina, Hurricane Gustav, Haitian earthquake, Chilean earthquake, Chernobyl nuclear disaster, Fukushima nuclear disaster, Exxon Valdez oil spill, and BP Gulf oil spill.

Table 7.1
Estimated Onset Dates (EDOs) for the Six Stages of the Environmental Trauma Recovery Process

	A Hurricane Katrina B*	B Hurricane Gustav N*	C Haiti Earthquake N*	D Chile Earthquake N*	E Chernobyl Nuclear H*	F Fukushima Nuclear B*	G Exxon Valdez Oil Spill H*	H Gulf Coast Oil Spill H*
Stage 1: Shock	EDO: 8/29/2005	EDO: 9/1/2008	EDO: 1/12/2010	EDO: 2/27/2010	EDO: 4/26/1986	EDO: 3/11/2011	EDO: 3/23/1989	EDO: 4/20/2010
Stage 2: Survival Mode	8/30/2005	8/31/2008	1/13/2010	2/28/2010	4/28/1986– 6/30/1986	3/11/2011	3/24/1989	4/20/2010 4/21/2010
Stage 3: Basic Needs (Food, Shelter, and Safety)	8/31/2005	9/3/2008	1/13/2010	2/28/2010 & 3/1/2010	4/27/1986	3/12/2011	3/27/1989	4/20/2010 4/21/2010
Stage 4: Awareness of Loss	8/31/2005	9/3/2008 9/5/2008	1/14/2010 2/12/2010	2/27/2010 3/6/2010	4/26/1988	3/16/2011 4/03/2011	3/24/1989	4/23/2010 4/29/2010

Table 7.1 (Continued)

	A Hurricane Katrina B*	B Hurricane Gustav N*	C Haiti Earthquake N*	D Chile Earthquake N*	E Chernobyl Nuclear H*	F Fukushima Nuclear B*	G Exxon Valdez Oil Spill H*	H Gulf Coast Oil Spill H*
Stage 5: Susceptibility to Spin and Fraud	9/7/2005	9/2/2008	3/09/2010	3/3/2010	1986–1988	3/15/2011	1989–2008	10/29/2010
Stage 6: Resolution	8/29/2006	9/1/2009	1/12/2011	2/27/2011	4/26/1987	TBD	1990	TBD

*N = Nature-Induced Environmental Trauma *H= Human-Induced Environmental Trauma *B = Both **EDO = Estimated Date of Onset TBD = To Be Determined

Sources: A2 – (Indepth: Hurricane, 2005), A3 – (Ertelt, 2005) and (Indepth: Hurricane, 2005), A4 – (Indepth: Hurricane, 2005), A5 – (Ross, 2005), A6 – (Kimbrell, 2006), B2 – (Evacuation of, 2005), B3 – (Structural damage, 2005) and (Lowry, 2005), B4 – (Anderson, 2008), B5 – (University of Alabama, 2008), B6 – (Williams, 2009), C2 – (Romero, 2010), C3 – (Romero, 2010) and (Getting aid, 2010), C4 – (Haiti "will not die," 2010) and (Alpert & Robinson, 2010), C5 – (Strickler, 2010), C6 – (Haitians remember, 2011), D2 – (Chilean quake, 2010), D3 – (Kofman, Patria, & Blackburn, 2010) and (Thousands still, 2010), D4 – (More than, 2010) and (Thompson, 2010), D5 – (Hough, 2010), D6 – (Shoicket, 2011) and (Chile marks, 2011), E2 – (Marples, 1993), E3 – (The evacuations, n.d.,) E4 – (Chernobyl blast, 2008), E5 – (European Liaison Group, 1986), E6 – (USSR & Chernobyl, 1987), F2 – (As it happened, March 11, 2011) and (As it happened, March 13, 2011), F3 – (As it happened, March 13, 2011) and (Japan quake, 2011), F4 – (Japan nuclear, 2011) and (Johnson, 2011) and (A message from, 2011), F5 – (British Red Cross, 2011), G2 – (Appendix A, 1989), G3 – (Simon & Martin, 2010), G4 – (Appendix A, 1989), G5 – (Chang, 2010), G6 – (NOAA Office of Response, 2008), H2 – (National Commission, 2011) and (Vargas, 2010), H3 – (National Commission, 2011), H4 – (Goddard, Reid, & Pope, 2010) and (Coast Guard suspends, 2010), H5 – (Leinwant, 2010), H6 – (Jaffe & Parkinson, 2011)

131

Stage 1: Across all eight examples cited in Table 7.1, shock begins on the date of the disaster.

Stage 2: If there is forewarning, survival mode may begin shortly before the date of the disaster. For example, before Hurricane Gustav hit Louisiana, survivors from Hurricane Katrina went into survival mode by evacuating early (Evacuation of New Orleans, 2008). Another example of people entering survival mode can be found in the evacuation and rescue efforts of the crew members from the burning rig the night of the BP oil rig explosion (Deepwater, 2011).

Stage 3: When help arrives, the basic needs of food, shelter, and safety are re-established. For instance, in Chile after the devastating earthquake, the need for food and essential supplies was so great that Chile's president, Michelle Bachelet, ordered supermarkets to give away basic supplies to victims ("Thousands Still Without," 2010). In Chernobyl, the relocation of residents appeared to be the main intervention to re-establish safety.

Stage 4: Typically, however, the awareness of loss hits when an important official, by his or her behavior, recognizes the problem. In many cases, this occurs at the time of an official site visit, for example, when the president of Chile visited small towns, consoling residents devastated by the earthquake (Thompson, 2010). Awareness of loss is not just about acknowledging the loss of loved ones and material possessions, however. The first minimal contact of oil with the shoreline after the *Exxon Valdez* oil spill could also be considered an awareness of loss. In the case of Chernobyl, the suicide of Legasov on April 26, 1988, who worked on the liquidation of consequences of the Chernobyl accident, appeared to mark the end of denial.

Stage 5: Misleading information, lack of truth, and, at times, exaggeration of successes or failures greatly compounds people's susceptibility to spin and fraud. After Hurricane Katrina, fake websites made to look like Red Cross websites popped up on the Internet asking for donations (Ross, 2005). With the Chernobyl disaster, authorities downplayed the danger of radiation contamination. In fact, in the Vercherniy Kiev newspaper, the initial news report on the Chernobyl accident consisted of only a few lines in the weather section (Liakhovich, 2006).

Stage 6: In most cases, resolution typically begins on the first anniversary of the environmental trauma.

In regard to the two hurricanes, considerable progress in response systems (i.e., preparedness) was made between 2005 and 2008, allowing for a swifter recovery from Gustav. As there was little human-induced involvement in Gustav, the loss of life was minimal (Nemeth, 2008). In regard to the two earthquakes, more effective building codes in Chile greatly reduced the loss of life; whereas building codes in Haiti added to people's misery. Also, recovery efforts to re-establish basic needs occurred more swiftly in Chile. In both Hurricane Gustav and the Chilean earthquake, swift recovery responses made the difference. Both nuclear catastrophes were unexpected. Early intervention after the earthquake and tsunami in Fukushima has, to date, been instrumental in minimizing and ameliorating the damage. (Please refer to Chapter 2 for further details.) Interventions following the Gulf Coast oil spill, however, have been proceeding slowly while BP executive Tony Hayward got his life back (Somaiya, 2010). Yet even more than two years following this trauma, the Gulf Coast and its residents were still struggling. Many did not get their life back and resolution was yet to begin.

THE POWER OF HOPE

As mentioned earlier, one of the most important feelings involved in recovery is hope. According to Snyder (1989, 1994, 2000) and Snyder and colleagues (1991), hope fuels our pursuit of the good life (as cited in Lopez et al., 2009). Snyder and colleagues "characterize hope as a human strength manifested in capacities to (a) clearly conceptualize goals, (b) develop the specific strategies to reach those goals, and (c) initiate and sustain the motivation for using those strategies" (p. 37). Maintaining feelings of high hope allows individuals to see alternatives and solve problems. On the other hand, dissolving into hopelessness can lead individuals to get stuck in the present, to focus on the obstacles, and to eventually succumb to depression and anxiety. Instead, when individuals can see opportunities, they can set goals that allow experiencing, creating, getting, doing, and/or becoming (Lopez et al., 2009).

Hope does not rely on intelligence, but rather on a sense of internal and social competence (Barnum et al., 1998 as cited in Lopez et al., 2009). It is the decision to believe in oneself (Lopez et al., 2009). According to this view, hope is related to perceived competence and adaptive coping strategies. Feelings of hope, however, can be sabotaged by trauma and/or violence. Hinton-Nelson, Roberts, and Snyder (1996) conclude that children who have witnessed violence have lower levels of hope than children who have not witnessed violence (as cited in Lopez et al., 2009). Because of having experienced environmental trauma, these children, as well as many adults, have less resilience and are often unable to engage in hopeful thinking. Lopez and colleagues state that "when hopeful thinking is stymied, interpersonal struggles may result" (p. 42).

Researchers such as Collins and Bill (1997), Snyder (1994), Snyder and Feldman (2000), noted that "ruminations block adaptive goal-related thinking and cause increased frustration and aggression against others" (as cited in Lopez et al., 2009, p. 42). In New Orleans following Katrina, according to Osofsky, Osofsky, and Harris (2007), some children used magical thinking to cope. Over 30 percent of the children in their study developed symptoms of depression, loneliness, sadness, and anger, and about half of the children met the criteria for needing mental health services. Osofsky and colleagues (2007) concluded that a clear natural disaster plan for children and their families must be developed.

THE POWER OF PEOPLE

Thus, in the aftermath of environmental trauma, when hope is lost, chaos abounds. People become disoriented, displaced, discouraged, and distraught. Due to the lack of safety and of sanitary physical conditions, illness often results. Although mental illness is usually not caused by environmental trauma, a sense of hopelessness can greatly exacerbate any pre-existing mental health conditions (Nemeth et al., 2011).

At times of environmental trauma, however, many individuals can cope well. They are "high hope individuals" (Lopez et al. 2009, p. 38). High hope individuals are excellent leaders. They can not only see the future, but more important, they can flexibly develop plans to get from here to there. They have a sense of emotional, psychological, and social well-being. They possess qualities of mastery, authority, and purpose. They know how to successfully relate to and work with others. They are integrated, coherent, and actualized. They know how to accept others and con-tribute to the common good. They know how to move forward. They are strong and they remain so even during tumultuous times. For they are the robust people.

REFERENCES

A message from His Majesty the Emperor. (2011, March 16). Retrieved June 22, 2011, from http://www.kunaicho.go.jp/e-okotoba/01/address/okotoba-h23e.html.

Acknowledge. (2011). In Merriam-Webster Online. Retrieved July 12, 2011, from http://www.merriam-webster.com.

Affirm. (2011). In Merriam-Webster Online. Retrieved July 12, 2011, from http://www.merriam-webster.com.

Alpert, L. I., & Robinson, E. (2010, January 14). Haiti quake death toll could hit 500,000. New York Post. Retrieved July 14, 2011, from http://www.nypost.com.

Anderson, E. (2008, September 5). Death toll from Gustav grows to 23 with three deaths in St. Charles. Times-Picayune. Retrieved July 15, 2011, from NOLA.com Web site: http://www.nola.com/t-p/.

As it happened: Japan earthquake on Friday. (2011, March 11). Retrieved June 16, 2011, from http://news.bbc.co.uk/2/hi/asia-pacific/9422862.stm.

As it happened: Japan earthquake on Saturday. (2011, March 13). Retrieved June 16, 2011, from http://news.bbc.co.uk/2/hi/asia-pacific/9423417.stm.

Associated Press. (2011, May 3). FEMA seeking to redeem agency reputation with quick response to tornado outbreak. Retrieved July 13, 2011, from http://www.wkyt.com/home/headlines/FEMA_seeking_to_redeem_agency_reputation_with_quick _response_to_tornado_outbreak_121161699.html.

Bar-Levav, R. (1988). Thinking in the shadow of feelings: A new understanding of the hidden forces that shape individuals and societies. New York: Simon & Schuster.

Bass, E. (2007, February 22). Post-Katrina Baton Rouge struggles with its identity. Retrieved July 14, 2011, from http://www.usatoday.com/news/nation/2007-02-21-baton-rouge -cover_x.htm.

Bergal, J., Hiles, S., Koughan, F., McQuaid, J., Morris, J., Reckdahl, K., & Wilkie, C. (2007). City adrift: New Orleans before and after Katrina. Baton Rouge: Louisiana State University Press.

Billow, R. M. (July 2010). On resistance. International Journal of Group Psychotherapy, 60(3), 313–346.

Borstein, P. E., & Clayton, P. (2006). The anniversary reaction. *Diseases of the Nervous System, 33*, 470–472.

Bourque, L. B., Siegel, J. M., Kano, M., & Wood, M. M. (2006). Weathering the storm: The impact of hurricanes on physical and mental health. *Annals of the American Academy, 604*(1), 129–151.

Brinkley, D. (2006). *The great deluge: Hurricane Katrina, New Orleans, and the Mississippi Gulf Coast.* New York: William Morrow/HarperCollins.

British Red Cross condemns fraudulent Japan Appeal emails. (2011, March 15). Retrieved July 8, 2011, from http://www.redcross.org.uk.

Brunker, M. (2006, July 25). *Are FEMA trailers 'toxic tin cans'?* Retrieved July 12, 2011 from http://www.msnbc.msn.com/id/14011193/ns/us_newskatrina_the_long_road _back/t/are-fema-trailers-toxic-tin-cans/.

Campbell, R. J. (1981). *Psychiatric dictionary* (5th ed.). New York: Oxford University Press.

Chang, C. (2010, June 27). Alaska's present, after 1989 Exxon Valdez oil spill, might be Gulf Coast's future. *Times-Picayune.* Retrieved July 26, 2011, from http://www.nola .com/t-p/.

Chang, S. A. (2006, September/October). *Continental shift: Storms, floods, and rising tides threaten many historic structures in the United Kingdom. So why is Britain's National Trust so willing to let those buildings go?* Retrieved June 5, 2012 from http://www .preservationnation.org/magazine/2006/september-october/continental-shift.html.

Chediak, M. (2010, August 5). *BP may seek to avoid responsibility, Transocean says.* K. Jordan & C. Siler (Eds.), Retrieved June 5, 2012, from http://www.bloomberg.com/ news/2010-08-05/bp-may-seek-to-avoid-full-responsibility-over-rig-blast-transocean -says.html.

Chernobyl blast: Valery Legasov's battle. (2008, April 28). Retrieved July 22, 2011, from Chernobylee Web site: http://www.chernobylee.com/blog/2008/04/chernobyl-blast -valery-legasov.php.

Chideya, F. (2005, September 8). *Baton Rouge church helps Katrina victims.* Retrieved July 16, 2011, from http://www.npr.org/templates/story/story.php?storyId=4837194.

Chilean quake toll jumps to 708. (2010, February 28). Retrieved July 15, 2011, from http:// news.bbc.co.uk/2/hi/americas/8542122.stm.

Chile marks earthquake anniversary amid disputes. (2011, February 27). Retrieved July 15, 2011, from http://www.bbc.co.uk/news/world-latin-america-12592991.

Coast Guard suspends search for 11 missing oil rig workers. (2010, April 23). Retrieved June 16, 2011, from http://www.nola.com.

David Koresh. (2011). Retrieved July 13, 2011, from http://www.biography.com.

Davis, D. (2010). *Washed away? The invisible peoples of Louisiana's wetlands.* Lafayette: University of Louisiana at Lafayette Press.

Department of Health and Human Services National Toxicology Program. (2011). *Report on carcinogens* (12th ed. p. 195). Retrieved July 13, 2011, from http://ntp.niehs.nih .gov/index.cfm?objectid=03C9AF75-E1BF-FF40-DBA9EC0928DF8B15.

Eaton, L. (2008, April 13). Agency is under pressure to develop disaster housing. *New York Times.* Retrieved July 16, 2011, from http://www.nytimes.com.

Ertelt, S. (2005, August 31). *Planned Parenthood "helps" Hurricane Katrina victims with free morning after pills.* Retrieved July 14, 2011, from http://www.lifenews.com/2005/08/31/ nat-1578/?pr=1.

European Liaison Group. (1986). *The Chornobyl nuclear disaster.* Retrieved July 26, 2011, from http://www.infoukes.com/history/chornobyl/elg/.

Evacuation of New Orleans ordered for Sunday. (2005, August 31). Retrieved July 15, 2011, from http://www.msnbc.msn.com/id/26425142/ns/weather/t/evacuation-new-orleans -ordered-sunday/.

Fuller, R. (2011). *After the flood: How to remove black mold from water damage.* Retrieved July 16, 2011, from http://ezinearticles.com/?After-The-Flood:-How-To-Remove -Black-Mold-From-Water-Damage&id=456723.

Garrido, G. (2007, September). *Trauma resolution and lifestyle change.* Paper presented at the 60th Annual United Nations DPI/NGO Conference Midday Workshops, New York.

Getting aid to Haiti earthquake victims. (2010, January 20). Retrieved July 14, 2011, from http://news.bbc.co.uk/2/hi/americas/8468484.stm.

Gleick, J. (1987). *Chaos: Making a new science.* New York: Penguin Group.

Goddard, J., Reid, T., & Pope, F. (2010, April 30). *Gulf of Mexico oil spill reaches Louisiana.* Retrieved June 16, 2011, from http://www.timesonline.co.uk/tol/news/environment/ article7112465.ece.

Haiti "will not die": President Rene Preval insists. (2010, February 12). Retrieved July 14, 2011, from http://news.bbc.co.uk/2/hi/8511997.stm.

Haitians remember their earthquake dead a year on. (2011, January 12). Retrieved July 15, 2011, from http://www.bbc.co.uk/news/world-latin-america-12171707.

Haygood, W. (2006, August 25). After Katrina, Baton Rouge weathers a storm of its own. *Washington Post.* Retrieved July 13, 2011, from http://www.washingtonpost.com/ wp-dyn/content/article/2006/08/24/AR2006082401918.html.

Horne, J. (2006). *Breach of faith: Hurricane Katrina and the near death of a great American city.* New York: Random House.

Hough, A. (2010, March 3). *Chile earthquake: President Michelle Bachelet "failed to grasp scale of devastation."* Retrieved July 15, 2011, from http://www.telegraph.co.uk.

Indepth: Hurricane Katrina timeline. (2005, September 4). Retrieved July 14, 2011, from http://www.cbc.ca/news/background/katrina/katrina_timeline.html.

InCourage. (2011). Retrieved July 16, 2011, from http://www.fsgbr.org/programs/ incourage?

Jaffe, M., & Parkinson, J. R. (2011, April 20). *BP Gulf oil spill 1-year anniversary; Congress yet to pass any major laws on oil and gas drilling.* Retrieved July 15, 2011, from http:// abcnews.go.com/Politics/bp-gulf-oil-spill-year-anniversary-congressional-inaction/ story?id=13419389.

Japan nuclear plant owner confirms first deaths as workers fail to contain leak. (2011, April 3). Retrieved June 22, 2011, from http://www.foxnews.com/world/2011/04/02/japan -nuclear-plant-owner-confirms-deaths-facility-workers-fail-contain/.

Japan quake: Sendai residents queue for food and fuel. (2011, March 13). Retrieved June 17, 2011, from http://www.bbc.co.uk/news/uk-12725480.

Jiji Press. (2011, May 12). *Japanese emperor visits Fukushima.* Retrieved July 13, 2011, from http://www.nzherald.co.nz/world/news/article.cfm?c_id=2&objectid=10725125.

Johnson, C. (2011, March 16). Emperor comforts Japan in 1st TV talk. *Washington Times.* Retrieved June 22, 2011, from http://www.washingtontimes.com/news/2011/mar/16/ emperor-comforts-japan-in-1st-tv-talk/.

Kern, E. (2006, July 16). Mental-health storm approaches. *Advocate,* p. 6A.

Kimbrell, S. (2006, July 16). Storm survivors try to let go. *Advocate*, pp. 1–2B.

Kofman, J., Patria, M., & Blackburn, B. (2010, March 1). *Chile's president orders grocery stores to give food away after devastating quake.* Retrieved July 15, 2011, from http:// abcnews.go.com/WN/International/chile-earthquake-looting-rescues/story?id =9977178.

Lamar, C., Nemeth, D. G., Gilliland, V., Whittington, L. T., & Reeder, K. P. (2008, October). *Climate change questionnaire.* Paper presented at The 5th World Congress for Psychotherapy, Beijing, China.

Leinwant, D. (2010, October 29). First fraud case emerges from BP oil spill. *USA Today.* Retrieved July 15, 2011, from http://www.usatoday.com/news/nation/2010-10-29 -spillfraud29_ST_N.htm.

Liakhovich, O. (2006). *After the blaze: Chernobyl 20 years on.* Retrieved July 12, 2011, from http://sites.google.com/site/liakhovich/Index/chernobyl.

Lopez, S. J., Rose, S., Robinson, C., Marques, S. C., & Pais-Ribeiro, J. (2009). Measuring and promoting hope in schoolchildren. In R. Gilman, E. S. Huebner, & M. Furlong (Eds.), *Promoting wellness in children and youth: Handbook of Positive Psychology in the Schools* (pp. 37–51). Mahwah, NJ: Lawrence Erlbaum.

Lowry, J. (2005, September 4). *Citizen-soldiers distribute food, water, ice as Louisiana recovers.* Retrieved July 15, 2011, from U. http://www.defense.gov/news/newsarticle.aspx?id =51041.

Maccoll, M., Morgan, C. A., Hill, S., Fox, P., Kingham, P., & Southwick, S. M. (1999). Anniversary reaction in Gulf War veterans: A follow-up inquiry 6 years after the war. *American Journal of Psychiatry, 156*, 1075–1079.

Marples, D. (1993, September 1). *Chernobyl's lengthening shadow.* Retrieved July 26, 2011, from http://www.highbeam.com/doc/1G1-13257431.html.

McCarthy, B. (2010, April 22). Copper theft suspects identified by New Orleans police. *Times-Picayune.* Retrieved July 16, 2011, from http://www.nola.com/t-p/.

More than 2 million affected by earthquake, Chile's president says. (2010, February 27). Retrieved July 15, 2011, from http://articles.cnn.com/2010-02-27/world/chile .quake_1_magnitude-haiti-quake-chilean-president-michelle-bachelet?_s =PM:WORLD.

Murphy, K. (2011, May 23). *Tornado devastates Joplin, Missouri, 116 dead.* Retrieved July 12, 2011, from http://www.reuters.com/article/2011/05/23/us-usa-weather -tornadoes-idUSTRE74M08L20110523.

National Commission on the BP Deepwater Horizon Oil Spill and Offshore Drilling. (2011, January). *Deepwater: The Gulf oil disaster and the future of offshore drilling* (Report to the President). Retrieved June 16, 2011, from http://www.oilspillcommission .gov/final-report.

National Medical Association. (October 2005). NMA calls response to Hurricane Katrina a "national disgrace." *Journal of the National Medical Association, 97*(10), 1334–1335.

Nemeth, D. G. (2005, September). *Millennialism, terrorism, and the healing journey.* Paper presented at the 58th Annual United Nations Department of Public Information and Non-Governmental Organizations Conference, New York.

Nemeth, D. G. (2008, October). *The anatomy of a disaster: Streamlining the recovery process: Lessons learned.* Paper presented at the the 5th World Congress for Psychotherapy, Beijing, China.

Nemeth, D. G., Cameron, C., Creveling, C. C., Dreger, R. M., & Schexnayder, M. M. (2000, August). *Outcome of millennium 2000: Historical, technical, psychological, and research-based perspectives.* Paper presented at the 108th Annual Convention of the American Psychological Association, Washington, DC.

Nemeth, D. G., Kuriansky, J., Reeder, K. P., Lewis, A., Marceaux, K., Whittington, L. T., et al. (2012). *Addressing anniversary reactions of trauma through group process: The Hurricane Katrina anniversary wellness workshops.* International Journal of Group Psychotherapy, 62(1), 129–141.

Nemeth, D., Kuriansky, J., Olivier, T., Whittington, L. May, N., Hamilton., J., & Steger, A. (Spring 2011). Group interventions for disaster: Trauma anniversary reactions. *Global Horizons, 4*(1), 51–64.

NOAA Office of Response and Restoration. (2008, January 30). *Exxon Valdez Oil Spill.* Retrieved July 26, 2011, from http://response.restoration.noaa.gov.

Nolan, B. (2011, April 11). Hurricane relief groups are gutting, rebuilding homes found with Chinese drywall. *The Times Picayune.* Retrieved July 13, 2011 from, http://impact.nola.com/katrina.

Obama pays visit to damaged Joplin: President visits community for third time in a month. (2011, May 26). Retrieved July 13, 2011, from http://www.ktla.com/news/landing/ktla-obama-visits-joplin,0,5693934.story.

Onishi, Y., Voitsekhovich, O. V., & Zheleznyak, M. J. (2007). *Chernobyl: What have we learned? The successes and failures to mitigate water contamination over 20 years* (Vol. 12). Dordrecht, The Netherlands: Springer.

Osofsky, J. D., Osofsky, H. J., & Harris, W. W. (2007). Katrina's children: Social policy considerations for children in disasters. *Social Policy Report, 21*(1). Retrieved July 16, 2011, from http://www.srcd.org/index.php?option=com_content&task=view&id=232.

Prynn, R. (2010, March 20). *9/11 rescuers/responders: What price heroism?* Retrieved July 20, 2011, from http://www.familysecuritymatters.org/publications/id.5786/pub_detail.asp.

Reiss, B. (2010, March). Welcome to Barrow, Alaska: Ground zero for climate change. *Smithsonian,* 58–66.

Republic. (2011, April 28). From stockpiling to living off the grid, more Colo. residents preparing for disasters. Message July 15, 2011, posted by Simple Man to Backwoods Survival Blog: http://www.backwoodssurvivalblog.com/2011/04/from-stockpiling-to-living-off-grid.html.

Romero, S. (2010, January 13). Haiti lies in ruins; Grim search for untold dead. *New York Times.* Retrieved July 14, 2011, from http://www.nytimes.com.

Ross, B. (2005, September 7). *Katrina Internet charity scams try to dupe donors.* Retrieved July 14, 2011, from http://abcnews.go.com/Blotter/HurricaneKatrina/story?id=1106006&page=1.

Sattler, D. N., Preston, A. J., Kaiser, C. F., Olivera, V. E., Valdez, J., & Schlueter, S. (2002). Hurricane Georges: A cross-national study examining preparedness, resource loss, and psychological distress in the U.S. Virgin Islands, Puerto Rico, Dominican Republic, and the United States. *Journal of Traumatic Stress, 15*(5), 339–350.

Shoichet, C. E. (2011, February 27). *Chileans commemorate quake anniversary.* Retrieved July 15, 2011, from http://www.cnn.com/2011/WORLD/americas/02/27/chile.earthquake/index.html?iref=allsearch.

Simon, D., & Martin, A. (2010, May 6). *Alaska fisherman still struggling 21 years after Exxon spill.* Retrieved July 26, 2011, from http://articles.cnn.com/2010-05-06/us/exxon .valdez.alaska_1_cordova-fisherman-oil-spill-million-gallon-spill?_s=PM:US.

Somaiya, R. (2010, June 2). What not to say when your company is ruining the world. *Newsweek.* Retrieved July 16, 2011, from http://www.newsweek.com/2010/06/02/ what-not-to-say-when-your-company-is-ruining-the-world-.html.

Sorkin, A. (2009). *Too big to fail: The Inside story of How Wall Street and Washington Fought to Save the Financial System- and Themselves.* New York, NY: Penguin Group.

Spielberger, C. D. (1983). *State-trait anxiety inventory for adults.* Redwood City, CA: Mind Garden.

Strickler, L. (2010, March 9). *Watchdogs on alert for Haiti charity fraud.* Retrieved June 22, 2011, from http://www.cbsnews.com/stories/2010/01/13/cbsnews_investigates/ main6092813.shtml.

Structural damage, water, and power outages complicate evacuee return. (2005, September 3). Retrieved July 15, 2011, from http://www.salvationarmyusa.org/usn/www_usn_2.nsf/ vw-text-dynamic-arrays/3E3F0B4042322D75852574BA0050ECB4?openDocument.

Survivor stories: Escaping tornadoes' fury. (2011, April 29). Retrieved July 12, 2011, from http://www.cbsnews.com/stories/2011/04/29/national/main20058542.shtml.

Tabuchi, H., & Wald, M. L. (2011, May 12). Japanese reactor damage is worse than expected. *New York Times.* Retrieved July 20, 2011, from http://www.nytimes.com/ 2011/05/13/world/asia/13japan.html.

Tang, C. S. (2007). Trajectory of traumatic stress symptoms in the aftermath of extreme natural disaster: A study of Thai survivors of the 2004 Southeast Asian earthquake and tsunami. *Journal of Nervous and Mental Disease, 195*(1), 54–59.

Ted Kaczynski. (2011). Retrieved July 13, 2011, from http://www.biography.com. The Evacuations. (n.d.). Retrieved June 17, 2012, from http://www.chernobyl.org.UK/ evacuations.html

Thompson, G. (2010, March 6). Departing Chilean president defends government's actions after quake. *New York Times.* Retrieved July 15, 2011, from http://www .nytimes.com.

Thousands still without food, water in parts of quake-hit Chile. (2010, March 1). Retrieved July 15, 2011, from http://articles.cnn.com/2010-03-01/world/chile.earthquake_1 _concepcion-santiago-bio-bio?_s=PM:WORLD.

Trail of tears. (2010). Retrieved July 12, 2011, from http://www.cherokee-nc.com/index .php?page=62.

University of Alabama at Birmingham. (2008, September 2). *UAB's data mine on alert for Hurricane Gustav e-mail fraud.* Retrieved July 15, 2011, from http://main.uab.edu/ Sites/MediaRelations/articles/51430.

U.S. Coast Guard Pollution Reports. (1989). *Appendix A. Chronology.* (Appendices—2).

USSR & Chernobyl: One year anniversary. (1987, April 21). Retrieved July 26, 2011, from http://www.nader.org/index.php?/archives/585-USSR-Chernobyl-One-Year -Anniversary.html.

Vargas, R. A. (2010, April 21). Seven reported critically injured, 11 missing in oil rig explosion south of Venice. *Times Picayune.* Retrieved June 16, 2011, from http:// www.nola.com.

Verchick, R. R. M. (2010). *Facing catastrophe: Environmental action for a post-Katrina world.* Cambridge, MA: Harvard University Press.

Walker, J., & Heffner, F. (2010, Spring). Resilience is a critical factor in the workplace. *New Worker*. Retrieved from http://www.cecassoc.com/newsletters.htm.

Wallace, R. (2011, May 18). Fukushima nuclear plant shutdown on track. *Australian*. Retrieved July 15, 2011, from http://www.theaustralian.com.au/news/world/fukushima-nuclear-plant-shutdown-on-track/story-e6frg6so-1226057819843.

Wallie, P. (2005, October 13). Napoleon King: French Quarter painter. Retrieved July 10, 2011, from http://www.peeniewallie.com/2005/10/napoleon_king_-.html.

Williams, T. (2009, September 1). *Baton Rouge remembers Hurricane Gustav*. Retrieved July 26, 2011, from http://www.wafb.com.

Wolman, B. B. (Ed.). (1989). *Dictionary of behavioral science* (2nd ed.). San Diego, CA: Academic Press, Inc.

8

Our Communities: Healing after Environmental Disasters

Judy Kuriansky

Disaster has been defined in the context of community to signify stressful situations occurring relatively suddenly or unexpectedly in a geographic area that result in loss and interfere with the ongoing social life of the collective (Tierney, 1989). When disaster strikes, the resulting trauma affects not only individuals but their social context, disrupting the quality of life of the community and the fabric of society. The physical, emotional and social life of the citizens and social systems affected directly and indirectly undergo distress and disorganization as well as serious problems of displacement, social inequities and social injustice (American Psychological Association, 2010). Resulting disconnection among the members of the group can also lead to the dissolution of ties, which is referred to as debonding (Gordon, 2004). The process of recovery, however, can also lead to positive growth and stronger connections both within the community's intimate circle and within a broader social and global context. This phase, called posttraumatic growth (Tedeschi & Calhoun, 2004) or rebound (Gordon, 2004), can lead to social fusion and a new survival-oriented social system.

Since environmental traumas in this current age receive widespread media coverage, the impact is felt not only by those immediately exposed but by a broader social group. Healing therefore can take advantage of this wider context, providing a support system beyond the affected geographic area and even beyond borders to a global community.

This chapter addresses the nature of community psychological distress after environmental disasters and poses some strategies for community healing and recovery of the social fabric.

FACTORS AFFECTING COMMUNAL RESPONSE TO DISASTER

The ability of societies to adapt to environmental changes is determined in part by their ability to act collectively (Adger, 2003). Yet communities differ in their ability to rebound from disaster (Van den Eynde & Veno, 1999), depending on factors that include the severity and extent of damage. In addition, poorer and less-stable communities have fewer resources for recovery than more fiscally-sound societies with strong leadership. Already-fragile communities can further disintegrate and fragment under the pressure of limited resources. Despite limited resources, smaller and more tightly knit communities with strong traditions can fare better than more-dispersed communities with even stronger economic bases. Communities can also survive catastrophe when citizens are familiar with facing hardship (e.g., small villages affected by the 2004 Asian tsunami), have a characteristic strong spirit (e.g., Haitians hit by yet another disaster in the 2010 earthquake, after many floods), or exhibit traditional stoicism (e.g., those in Japan's northern region hit by the triple tragedy of the 2011 tsunami, earthquake, and nuclear disaster). Recovery can also be skewed by the style of coping, for example, needing to process emotions versus avoiding emotion or sublimating feelings into taking action (Kuriansky, 2005a).

Common contemporary practice refers to individuals enduring crisis as survivors instead of victims, whereby a person taking a stance as a victim would have a less-favorable prognosis for recovery than a self-definition of competency. In a similar approach applied to communities facing environmental disaster, victim-oriented communities are contrasted to competency communities, whereby the former are viewed as incapable of managing their problems and therefore are beholden to experts, while the latter are self-help–focused and use their own resources to manage problems (Van den Eynde & Veno, 1999). Consequently, interventions for victim communities require outside agencies to determine what is best to "fix" the community, in comparison to competency communities that build on their own strengths and get on with life in the best way that suits their individual constituency. For example, in the case of the tornadoes that ravaged the small American town of Joplin, Missouri, in 2011, religious and governmental leaders appealed to the community's ability to heal itself long after media and other agencies had withdrawn attention and aide. Such messages of self-healing delivered at public memorials resulted in enthusiastic responses in the audience, a social phenomenon in community healing explored more fully throughout this chapter.

A Resilient and Empowered Community

Similar to the process of personal recovery, a community can be more or less resilient when faced with crisis. A popular concept in contemporary psychological science, resilience refers to the ability to bounce back from a crisis, to engage in positive coping actions, to request and accept support, and to look toward a better future (American Psychological Association, 2010; Bonanno, 2004). In his address to the Missouri community after the traumatic tornado, Governor Jay Nixon said, "This storm—the likes of which we've never seen before—has brought forth a spirit of resilience the likes of which we've never seen." Similarly, memorials, after the 2011 Japan earthquake, resonated with the theme of resilience, with proclamations that "Japan will overcome" and that "the people of Japan are facing this tragedy with dignity and grace."

A concept related to resilience is empowerment, a term popular in contemporary psychology, to imply competency in the ability to take care of oneself and solve problems. I have applied this concept to group programs for youth in the United States and in Africa to build self-esteem and resist vulnerability to disease (Kuriansky & Berry, 2011; Kuriansky, Simonson, Varney, & Arias, 2009). This concept has been long identified as a central tenet of community psychology (Rappaport, 1987), whereby recovery requires a process of moving from the perception of self and community as powerless toward a resurrection of pride, deep rootedness, and attachment, as well as a renewed sense of mastery. This change leads to a commitment and mobilization to action, allowing for grassroots rehabilitation (Kiefer, 1984).

A resilient and empowered community is capable of what has been called post-traumatic growth, which refers to the process by which people develop emotionally-healthy and productive lives after a trauma. Tragic national disasters that create large-scale destruction offer a community and a nation a chance to create a new foundation, a stronger commitment to diversity, and a better life for all citizens. A disaster can further highlight the experience of interdependence among communities and a sense of "one world" that redefines social structures, government policies, and how resources are to be used and shared. Catastrophe can remind citizens of the universality of pain, suffering, grief, and loss as well as alert them to the need to learn about the forces and uses of nature, energy, and green conservation, and how to work within their family, community, nation, and the world.

Capacity Building

Facilitating a community's own resources to heal reinforces resiliency, a sense of empowerment, and post traumatic growth, which is considered best practice in psychology. A major method of capacity building is train the trainers programs, whereby local community members are trained to deliver necessary services. The psychological first aide training I organized immediately after the devastating earthquake in Haiti in 2010 involved training volunteer students in simple techniques that are easily learned and that follow the guidelines of both the Inter-agency Standing Committee and the American Psychological

Association, in being culturally sensitive, working in the local language, collaborating with local groups, and being sustainable (Kuriansky, 2010).

Importance of Social Support

While it has been pointed out that disaster can strain community bonds, "reducing community embeddedness, kin support and nonkin support" (Kaniasty & Norris, 1995), a large body of research points out that social support acts as a buffer against stress in the face of disaster; that people with a social support system cope better with crises (Norris & Kaniasty, 1996; Pierce et al., 1997); and that new social support systems can emerge out of traumatized societies. I know this firsthand from years of offering advice to the public over the radio, where callers feel comforted knowing that they are not the only one with a problem and that others care (Kuriansky, 2005c; Kuriansky & Pluhar, 2008). Community efforts after disasters have been shown to be effective when groups of people are brought together specifically for psychological healing (Nemeth, Kuriansky, Reeder, et al., 2012). Groups of people may also come together spontaneously for candle-lightings, memorial services, sing-alongs, walls of remembrance, and public rallies that unite members and provide mutual support to heal. Strangers can become immediate comrades when sharing grief and bond over shared experience and cooperative action (Kuriansky, 2003, 2008).

Sharing experiences can be even more important for community constituents expected to heal others, as was demonstrated by religious leaders coming together in a conference after the Haitian earthquake and forming a new organization: Centre de Spiritualité et de Santé Mentale (CESSA, Center for Spirituality and Mental Health, Jean-Charles, 2011a). Further healing is possible when community leaders publicly share their suffering, as was evident in the positive response of the audience I noted at a memorial when presidents of three Japanese prefectures affected by the tsunami and earthquake spoke about firsthand suffering from the loss of loved ones, homes, and livelihood; the threat from food shortage and radiation; and fears for the future. One gentleman even abandoned the traditional Japanese stoicism and allowed tears to flood his eyes, moving the audience to similar emotions and appreciation of his plight.

Social support creates a sense of solidarity, when people consider others as members of the same extended affiliation group, ensuring support on varied levels, including politically, economically, and emotionally (Ikeda, 2011). The more a community comes together to assist its members in reconstruction, rebuilding, and resilience, personally and collectively, the more effective and strong both the individual and the group can be. In the immediate aftermath of the Japanese tsunami and earthquake disaster, many individuals nobly helped others in their community, selflessly sharing their own meager resources and delivering water, rice balls, and toilets by alternate routes from disrupted roads (Ikeda, 2011). Some of these helpers were motivated by returning the assistance they had received from neighbors in other emergencies.

Social support, however, has been shown to be inequitable. One study showed that men, single and less educated people, African Americans, and older adults received less emotional support than women, Caucasians, and married, younger, and more educated people (Kaniasty & Norris, 1995). Of four types of identified social support, material support (e.g., money, goods, services, transportation, and shelter) was given most frequently, followed by informational support (e.g., facts, advice, emotional support, caring, and concern) and companionship (e.g., spending time and diversion). Emotional support, however, was given and received independent of direct experience of the disaster.

Sharing feelings about a natural disaster can be helpful in healing, to normalize reactions and offer reassurance of not being alone in the experience. While psychological best practice directs that not all people should be required to share emotions after a trauma, some people's coping style involves communicating distress. For them, expressing traumatic feelings releases emotional distress and eases physical symptoms (e.g., headaches, stomachaches, and even more serious disorders like heart attacks).

Dwelling on disaster is more likely when one is alone, in contrast to participation in group gatherings that reinforce a more positive outlook. Community memorials emphasize that a traumatic event is not just a personal tragedy but a shared experience. Public affirmations (e.g., "We will heal") encourage optimism. At a fundraising concert for the 2011 Japan relief effort, the audience was invited to "Stand with Japan in its hour of crisis" and to "Remind everyone in despair that they are not alone in their time of need." While isolation increases the distress of disaster, a sense of connectedness in community provides comforting and facilitates recovery. Speakers at the 2011 posttornado Joplin memorial emphasized the sense of togetherness. Reverend Aaron Brown addressed the audience as "Friends, neighbors, brothers and sisters" and used the word *us*, reminding the assembly to grieve together and "love thy neighbor."

Like affirmations and invitations to affiliation, appreciation—toward individuals, organizations, and other helping bodies—is an important expression in the wake of tragedies. At a memorial for the Japan disaster, the Japanese consul general's message emphasized that the Japanese government expressed gratitude for the "outpouring of kindness and support towards all the people."

Social support is further evident in volunteerism. The psychological and physical benefits of giving and helping others have been shown by research (Piliavin, 2003). After the Haiti earthquake, interviews with the student supporters that I trained revealed that helping increased their self-esteem. As one young male student said, "I feel overtaken by the spirit of my helping others." Helping others helped him get over the trauma of his own losses. Preliminary results of a survey a year after the 2010 Haiti earthquake showed that trained supporters' scores on the Impact of Helping scale indicated positive effects of helping. Another group of volunteer youth trained to help survivors in Haiti showed similar positive effects of participation in helping activities for children.

Visits by celebrities to disaster-torn communities brings media attention to a disaster zone and also has a healing effect in making a disempowered public feel energized and important. This was evident in the enthusiasm generated by a visit to the 2011 tornado-torn community of Joplin by hometown NASCAR racer Jaime McMurray and by a concert given by Yoko Ono at Columbia University Miller Theatre after the 2011 Japan disaster.

Community Meetings

After the earthquake in Haiti, community leaders met to identify needs of families and define strategies to help recovery. The community leaders represented various constituencies, including public services (electricity, waste, water), health (medical and psychological), and schools. These community meetings were eventually used to identify plans for preparation in the event of any future tragedies and to establish emergency procedures, including descriptions of roles of citizens, evacuation plans, practice drills, supplies, and contacts. Individual families were encouraged to develop such plans and safety kits (consisting of flashlights, water, first aid supplies, blankets, radios, clothing, photographs of family members, and copies of important documents).

Extent of Community Distress

Stress reactions resulting from an environmental crisis are experienced on a community level in similar ways to the personal level, for example, asking "Why did this happen to us?" is similar to questioning, "Why did this happen to me?" Collective emotions are wide-ranging, including mass shock, disbelief, numbness, vulnerability, hopelessness, helplessness, shame, guilt, anxiety, panic, anger, grief, depression, feeling overwhelmed and out of control, and disinterest in life, work, pleasures, and relationships (Kuriansky, 2002; Moser & Dilling, 2007). Reactions impacting interpersonal relations include distrust, conflict, withdrawal or over-dependency, and disruptions and problems at work, school, and family life. Extreme reactions result in domestic abuse and community violence (e.g., stealing, robbing, and personal attacks) (Houghton, 2010). Spiritual crises include disappointment, confusion, anger at others or at spiritual sources, withdrawal from worship or overly intense practices of rituals, and survivor's guilt that others suffer more heavily (Kalayjian & Eugene, 2010).

Disasters cause the breakdown of community infrastructure (e.g., delivery of essential services such as water, food delivery, and waste disposal, and impaired

functioning of schools and hospitals). Businesses are interrupted, cutting off people's income sources and creating a cycle of dysfunction in the social system.
Cars and public transportation are destroyed and roads are blocked, making it
impossible for many people to get to work, and those who do travel may become
fearful. For example, after the 1989 earthquake in San Francisco when major sections of the Oakland Bay Bridge collapsed, people feared commuting across the
bridge even when it was reconstructed. In another situation, a female caller to
a radio station where I was giving crisis advice after the 1989 earthquake in Newcastle, Australia, and who had been trapped in a supermarket during the 5.6
quake, told me she was afraid to go food shopping after her harrowing experience
(Kuriansky, 1990).

The Ripple Effect

The impact of a natural disaster on those directly exposed is evident, but the
circle of trauma extends beyond to wider societal stakeholders. The couple
whose home is washed away by a flood or the child whose parents died in a building collapse during an earthquake are obvious victims, but other sectors of society suffer more silently. These include first responders (e.g., firefighters and
police officers), government officials with limited resources to rebuild the community, journalists doing live reports in the midst of the downpours of hurricanes
or perilously stepping over earthquake rubble to get to the heart of a story, and
emergency workers (e.g., an electrical worker at a disaster site shared with me
his horror of having to drive his truck over body parts). Fortunately, an organization (www.dartsociety.org) raises awareness about journalists' plight, and a fund
supports mental health services among other health services for September 11
responders, but many groups have no assistance. Such groups need to seek out
services, and communities need to be more sensitive to their needs.

Vulnerable Community Groups

The physical damage that wildfires, floods, earthquakes, and tornadoes cause
to personal property, businesses, and forests is readily visible, but emotional
trauma is often overlooked, especially in at-risk groups.

The Vulnerability of Youth

According to a 2008 Save the Children's report, *In the Face of Disaster:
Children and Climate Change*, more than 50 percent of those affected by natural
disasters worldwide are children. More than adults, children are at risk due to diseases, inadequate sanitation facilities, anxieties related to separation from
parents, and exploitation due to lack of security and safety. Symptoms that can
emerge include nightmares, regression (e.g., bedwetting, crying out, wanting to

sleep with parents), physical complaints (e.g., stomachaches and headaches), overattachment to parents and fear of leaving home (e.g., school phobia), withdrawal from others, and acting out (e.g., aggression or delinquency). Younger children may not understand what is happening, and teens may engage in risky behaviors. An intervention by Save the Children in partnership with the American Red Cross, called Safe Spaces (Smith, 2008), provides children with structured activities like arts and crafts, while they are living in relocation centers, in order to re-establish needed stability in their lives. Another program, called Resilient and Ready, offers workshops for children to discuss their feelings about a particular crisis and encourages coping skills and lessons about what to do in emergency situations.

The Vulnerability of Older People

In a crisis, older adults often suffer more because of fewer resources to provide for basic needs (e.g., food, shelter, and health), limited ability to avoid falling buildings and debris, and challenges in transportation to evacuate an area. As a result, they are more dependent on others to care for them before, during, and after a disaster. In addition, feelings of vulnerability and fear escalate, leading to further disabilities. In a vicious cycle, older people fear leaving their residences and become housebound, leading to poor nutrition, isolation, and loneliness, which can escalate into depression and confusion. When hosting a radio call-in show after an Australian earthquake, I advised listeners to proactively visit elderly neighbors, bring supplies, and secure needed social services.

The Vulnerability of Women

Women are particularly vulnerable in natural disasters and more so in particular cultures. For example, women caught in the swirling waters of the 2004 Sri Lankan tsunami were less able to save themselves from drowning because they were not strong enough to grab onto trees, could not run fast enough to escape, or were dragged under the waters as their long saris got caught on debris. Also, after disasters, girls and women are subject to violence in relocation camps, and at home at the hand of male partners who are frustrated from an inability to fulfill male roles of providing for their family because of loss of work due to the disaster. This drastic situation is being addressed as much as possible by humanitarian organizations.

The Vulnerability of Men

While the deaths of fathers in disasters leaves families suffering and financially unstable, fathers who survive also suffer, yet their pain is all too often overlooked, especially in male-dominated societies where males are expected to cope stoically. This was the case in the fisherman communities of South Asia after the

2004 tsunami; yet, in the groups I led in a Sri Lankan village after the disaster, men were surprisingly eager to share painful feelings about survivor guilt and losing their wives and children (Kuriansky, 2005b). In several villages, up to 60 percent of men reportedly lost their wives in the waves, and even more lost one or more children. Widowers expressed feeling powerless over being unable to "save" their family members from the waves, and unprepared to raise children on their own. In a society with rigid gender roles, these men were further faced with struggles to rebuild their seaside industry without the help of their wives who had taken care of the home and helped with the marketing of fish or other goods. Support for these men is essential in order for the community to rebuild.

Importance of the Diaspora

Another group whose needs after a disaster are often overlooked is the diaspora. The word, derived from Greek, meaning "scattering, dispersion," refers to the extended relations of a particular group that has migrated, either forced or voluntarily, from their ancestral land but have common roots to those in the homeland. Such communities provide a powerful support system for survivors but can themselves be vicariously traumatized by trauma in their home country because of strong ties (e.g., to family, businesses or memories) or because they may harbor thoughts of return that are dramatically disrupted by the disaster. In the wake of the 2010 Haiti earthquake, communities in the United States with a high concentration of Haitians were gravely affected not only psychologically but also logistically, by relatives seeking to escape Haiti and come live with them. A complex of services in the community are needed for the diaspora and those newly relocating. One community center in Queens, New York, set up services to provide advice and guidance for legal and financial aid and housing, as well as psychological counseling, which was recognized as important by Haitian mental health professionals. At the request of these colleagues, I volunteered to join rotating teams sitting at a table with a simple sign on the wall advertising our availability to help.

Community Events: Memorials for Healing

As a psychologist who has helped at many disaster sites around the world, I know that people in crisis appreciate knowing that others care (Kuriansky, 2006). From a psychological point of view, when a crisis strikes one part of the world, global solidarity and support—both emotional and financial—are important in healing. These were extended to Japan in the wake of the 9.0 magnitude earthquake and subsequent devastating tsunami and nuclear plant disaster on March 11, 2011. The trauma claimed thousands of lives and left tens of thousands of people missing and displaced. Immediately after these tragedies hit Japan, health professionals and the interfaith community throughout the world mobilized special events, and international psychologists like myself began contacting Japanese mental health professionals and organizations locally and abroad (Kuriansky, 2011). One week after the triple tragedy (e.g., the tsunami, earthquake, and nuclear plant explosion), a prayer service and candlelight vigil for Japan was held at the Church Center for the United Nations in New York City, with an overflow audience. The solemn event involved rituals, which are effective in community healings, including incense offerings, meditation, musi- cal performances, prayers, and messages from government leaders and local com- munity leaders (e.g., the president of the Japanese American Association of New York and a former UN Ambassador). A sense of global community was evoked by a message on behalf of the Sri Lankan community in New York, expressing heartfelt sympathy since they "know the suffering caused by this even firsthand, since we also experienced a similar event." The subsequent candlelight vigil to a local community square allowed a gathering, also helpful in group healing, for people to offer personal testimonials and prayers. A volunteer community organizer told the assembled group that if we send love to the people of Japan, they will feel it. The gathering also provided an important way for people to net- work about ways to help.

Community Healing through Music

Much research (see, e.g., Campbell, 2001) has shown that music has power to heal, facilitating group cohesion and expression, especially in cultures that do not readily engage in group activities or verbal communication. It was impressive to me, for example, to see firsthand the extent to which singing pervaded and facilitated school children's coping with an earthquake in Yushu, China, in 2010 in workshops conducted by myself and others, and similarly, in the work- shops I implemented for school children on the anniversary of the 2011 Japan earthquake and tsunami (Kuriansky, 2012a). The Asian youngsters even responded enthusiastically to song and movement techniques adapted from interventions for African youth empowerment that were not designed specifi- cally for recovery from environmental trauma (Kuriansky & Berry, 2011). Messages that would be communicated in words in Western groups were sung out melodically, with traditional tunes, or improvisationally and spontaneously as a group. Hymns, like the popular "Amazing Grace," are mainstays at memori- als and events, as a testament to music as a universal language, bringing people together harmoniously. As such, concerts are useful at times of crisis to reach across cultures for healing on a diverse local and international level.

In a powerful example of music as a healing force, a concert was held at the United Nations in the impressive ECOSOC chamber on March 5, 2012, with the theme "Overcoming the Disaster: Gratitude from Japan to the World." Co-hosted by the Permanent Mission of Japan to the UN and by the Japan Foundation, it was titled, "The Great East Japan Earthquake Commemoration Concert: Global Solidarity for People Affected by Disasters and Conflicts" ("One Year On," 2012). The concert, which was dedicated to victims of disasters around the globe with prayers for peace, was a symbol of Japan's gratitude to the global community for their support and an affirmation of the country being headed towards recovery strengthened by a new Kizuna (bond of friendship) with the international community.

Music is consistently an important component in my healing interventions. In my Global Kids Connect Project (GKCP) described in more detail later in this chapter, children in Haiti who participated in a workshop immediately after the 2010 earthquake were taught an original healing song in their local Creole language, that also used phrases in Japanese, to connect them symbolically to children in Japan who are similarly recovering from a devastating natural disaster. The healing anthem was written by my co-lyricist Russell Daisey and myself, in collaboration with Haitian artists, poets and psychologists, to incorporate phrases commonly used in their culture (Jean-Charles, 2011c).

Six months later, my team held an event at a public school in New York City, where children learned and performed the same song in Creole. At a subsequent workshop in Haiti, the Haitian children sang the same song and were told about the New York children singing this anthem in the Creole language. The children expressed appreciation about this, and curiosity about their "new American friends."

In a subsequent phase of the GKCP held in the disaster zone in Japan in 2012, organized with Japanese partners, music played a similarly prominent role. Japanese pop star Shinji Harada and noted Japanese opera soprano Tomoko Shibata performed popular tunes and original healing music. Harada had previously done charity concerts for survivors, and Shibata had performed her signature "Songs for Hope" healing concert on the anniversary evening of the tsunami/earthquake. That concert includes her Japanese translation of the anthem my songwriting partner and I had written for healing after the 9/11 terrorist attack in New York. Now called "Souls Become Stars," the theme created a powerful connection among the two countries for trauma recovery and hope.

Using the Arts to Heal

Artistic projects of all kinds (e.g., literature, drawing, music, photography and video) allow a collective expression of experience in the face of extreme situations. Such approaches are particularly useful in communities where art is a major part of the culture but where such outlets of expression are vastly disrupted in the wake of disaster, as in the case of Haiti. Community efforts to rebuild these vital aspects of social life are notable—for example, the effort organized by the executive director of the Martin E. Segal Theatre Center at the Graduate Center of the City University of New York in "An Evening of Solidarity and Support," which brought together contemporary Haitian playwrights and performers to showcase indigenous talents and address recovery from the Haiti earthquake.

Having children draw pictures and tell a story about what they drew is a gold standard technique to help children recover from trauma. When training teachers after the 2010 earthquake in Yushu, China, I instructed them to have children draw the disaster on one side of a page, but then to draw a bridge in the middle of the page, and a scene that makes them feel happy on the other side of the page. This progression symbolizes movement from trauma to healing.

CREATING GLOBAL COMMUNITY HEALING AFTER NATURAL DISASTERS

Environmental disasters inevitably cause devastation and destruction. Yet the saving grace of such traumas is that they have increasingly brought peoples and countries together as "one world." First responders rushed to South Asian countries affected by the 2004 tsunami, and thousands of well-wishers around the world sent money or care packages to the thousands devastated by the earthquake in Haiti in 2010. People around the world sent prayers to the miners trapped in the collapsed mine in Chile and to heroic Japanese rescue workers at the Fukushima nuclear power plant after it exploded. Such intercultural and international connections and support facilitate tolerance of diverse religions, cultures and backgrounds.

INTERCULTURAL HEALING AND SUPPORT: THE CASE EXAMPLE OF THE GLOBAL KIDS CONNECT PROJECT

The value of such international connections, and sound psychological principles, form the foundation of my Global Kids Connect Project (GKCP) that connects kids in trauma from different parts of the world. This project emerged out of my ongoing work in Haiti and my deep connection to Japan from having spent 12 years traveling back and forth from New York to Japan doing many activities. These include teaching at a Japanese university-writing; advice columns for the popular Japanese magazine, *Hanako*; doing workshops; and hosting my live U.S.-based radio advice show occasionally from Tokyo (since the show also aired in Japan), as well as doing many symposia and "Global Harmony" peace charity concerts in collaboration with Japanese musician Shinji Harada with my Stand Up for Peace Project.

The project has connected children in Haiti with children in Japan, who are similarly dealing with the aftermath of devastating natural disasters. The circle of caring was also extended to children in the United States, who were coping with anniversary reactions of a disaster (the September 11, 2001 attacks on the

World Trade Center), deemed to be similarly traumatic even though it was human-made, rather than of natural causes.[1]

The content consists of two workshops. One workshop is for children. It has four components: (1) an exchange of an object (for play and comfort) with messages of caring; (2) psychological techniques for stress reduction; (3) a history lesson about the various countries; and (4) a cultural program (e.g., singing, movement, and dance indigenous to the participating countries) that constitutes cultural education and also celebration. For example, the Haitian children were taught some lyrics of the original Creole song in Japanese.

The second workshop trains youth volunteers to conduct the workshops to create sustainability. In Haiti in 2011, these youth were part of a local organization, The Haitian Action for the United Nations, a national non-profit organization dedicated to enhancing the education of Haitian youth and promoting both the UN and Haitian culture.

The project is based on several sound psychological principles: (1) People who have been through a trauma feel better knowing they are not alone, and that others—peers even far away—support and care about them. (2) Children need safety and comfort, which is facilitated by objects like dolls or teddy bears that constitute transitional objects that represent the parental/maternal nurturing figure (Winnicott, 1953) and offer "contact comfort" in the form of an object that can approximate a sense of security and caring (Harlow & Zimmermann, 1959). An exchange of teddy bears was prevalent following September 11, 2001, when the American Red Cross and other agencies distributed them to comfort children (interestingly, adults also asked to have a bear). The exchange allows children affected by disaster and trauma to experience support from peers in other parts of the world, uniting them in a global circle of caring; (3) Stress reduction techniques help children deal with trauma at all levels, whether related to the event or in other aspects of their personal life. (4) Children respond to recreational projects, including making the object to be exchanged, as well as engaging in singing, movements, dance and play. The cultural aspects of the program are further healing in that they connect the children to their roots as well as encourage their appreciation of other cultures.

Acknowledging the intercultural collaboration, Haitian priest, Father Wismick Jean-Charles, a partner in the project, observed, "The cooperation between Haiti, Japan and the U.S. truly gives a sense of hope that we live in a world community where all people care about each other" (Jean-Charles, 2011b). Such global connections make a powerful statement to a community and country enduring a disaster.

---

[1]Groups of children in New York included classes of school children and also youth from an outpatient service at a major New York hospital, included because of their interest in joining the project, their relevance in being "at risk," and the appeal of making connections with New York children.

As mentioned above in the section about music as a healing force, the next phase of the GKCP took place in Japan on the anniversary of the March 11, 2011, earthquake and tsunami. Workshops I designed were held at several schools in the affected disaster zone in northern Japan, made possible through a partnership with the Recovery Assistance Center of Miyagi, a local Japanese non-profit organization intended to provide services for survivors, including specifically for children, and focused on creative arts and psychological support (Kuriansky, 2012b). Interspersed with the musical performances, I led healing exercises, with some adapted from my toolbox of interventions (Kuriansky, 2008). The techniques were intended to reduce stress, re-establish a sense of control, facilitate empowerment, and affirm a sense of safety. They were simple, involved more movement than verbalizations (especially useful in a setting where participants speak a different language from the facilitator), and, importantly for children, they were fun.

Multistakeholder Partnerships for Community Healing

Recovery efforts can be more effective when resources are pooled. Multistakeholder partnerships refer to relationships formed by individuals, groups, or organizations with mutual interests who come together, as the result of a common interest or event, to address problems and achieve mutually-defined goals. Partners can include professional groups (e.g., medical, public health, and social welfare), media sources, the private sector (e.g., corporations), government agencies, community centers, and religious organizations. For a comprehensive community response, schools should always be included. The GKCP is an example of such a multistakeholder approach, bringing together several organizations, including the International Association of Applied Psychology (www.iaapsych.org), an NGO accredited at the United Nations, whose mission is to promote the science and practice of applied psychology around the world; my Stand Up for Peace Project that has created and performed at peace charity events around the world (www.towersoflightsong.com); and partners locally "on the ground" in the affected country. In Haiti, local partners included le Centre Bon Samaritan (the Good Samaritan Center), a ministry of hope involved in community social services; and the Haitian Action for the United Nations, a nonprofit NGO dedicated to enhancing the education of Haitian youth and facilitating more active participation and representation of Haiti in the United Nations. In Japan, the local partner was the Recovery Assistance Center of Miyagi, located in the zone where the tsunami/earthquake hit.

The Role of Religion, Rituals, and Spirituality in Community Healing

The tragic experience of disasters in certain parts of the world has highlighted the role played by religion as well as traditional healing and spiritual traditions. For example, experiences after the 2004 tsunami in Southeast Asia reinforced the importance of reconciling scientific knowledge with belief systems from the spiritual world. Understanding the meaning of life and death, and typical ways of coping with disaster and suffering in different cultures and for different religions (e.g., Christian, Jewish, Buddhist, Hindu, Muslim and others) in the affected countries is crucial when implementing trainings or interventions.

In certain cultures, religious beliefs play a crucial role in recovery. For example, in Hinduism—the predominant religion in the northern area of Sri Lanka which was affected by the 2004 tsunami—the Hindu god Shiva symbolizes both destruction and creation, meaning that even in destruction, something new is created. Mourning in Hinduism is threefold: grieving, praying, and celebrating the kindnesses of others.

In the religious community of Joplin, Missouri, in America, one week after the destructive tornado in 2011, the memorial service featured religious leaders. In his address, Reverend Aaron Brown told the gathered community that his words of comfort came from God, that "Death does not give the last word" and that "Death does not win, life wins," to the enthusiastic clapping of the gathered crowd. He reminded the congregation that "This life is not the only life." In efforts to help people explain the tragedy, he noted that "God did not do this to punish us" and that it "happened because life is unpredictable." Professing honesty, he addressed the question on many people's minds, "Why did God allow this?" His answer: Jesus never promised to protect us from the storms of life but promised to be with us, to listen to us, to guide us." He implored the audience to "let Him love you."

At that same service, Missouri Governor, Jay Nixon, similarly emphasized the role of faith in healing. In his address to the community, he noted the "destructive power of nature" in comparison to "the invincible power of faith." The tragedy has "given 'love thy neighbor' new meaning." He reassured the congregation "We will heal . . . and rebuild on the granite foundation of faith."

The value of such religious gatherings was patently evident to me when I was in Haiti a few days after the earthquake. Sleeping in a tent on the church grounds, I would awake every morning at 5 a.m. to the sounds of services being conducted. It was the first of several occasions during the day at which the community gathered. Preliminary results of a survey conducted by myself and Father Wismick Jean-Charles showed that such religious services and a persistent belief in God, despite the tragedy, were the most commonly reported ways of coping with the tragedy (Jean-Charles, 2011a).

Group mourning in religious ceremonies is also helpful and especially valuable in postdisaster situations where the physical bodies of loved ones are not recovered, as happened after the Haiti and Japan earthquakes, and the Asian tsunami, when so many people were lost in the sea or buried under rubble. The pain of Hindu Sri Lankan men, for example, was escalated even more after the tsunami by the destruction of temples that left no opportunity to properly perform mourning rituals. One particularly moving memorial organized by the Haiti Council Centers featured mass for the souls of the victims of the earthquake held at the Church of St. Francis of Assisi in New York City. The main celebrant, retired Archbishop François-Wolff Ligondé of Port-au-Prince (who had presided over the iconic Roman Catholic Notre Dame Cathedral in Port-au-Prince for years previous to Archbishop Joseph Serge Miot, who tragically perished in the earthquake) acknowledged the earthquake in his sermon as an act of nature and reaffirmed his belief in God, offered comfort to the mourners. He spoke with strength, despite his own trauma of losing everything in the quake.

Rituals are an important part of community life in many cultures and religions (D'Souza, 2009; Kalayjian & Eugene, 2010) and play a major role in disaster recovery. These become even more crucial in postdisaster situations requiring mourning. In one particularly moving ritual designed by Father Wismick Jean-Charles and myself for healing after the 2010 earthquake in Haiti, nuns placed rocks from the rubble on a potted plant, and then watered the plant; this was meant to be symbolic of life rising out of destruction.

Professional Mental Health Response

The American Psychological Association (APA) has developed a Disaster Response Network for training psychologists, maintaining a directory of psychologists able to react to a disaster, and drafting guidelines for recovery operations and reactions to the media. A UN accredited organization, the World Council of Psychotherapy, is developing a Disaster Training Certificate Program to train and identify gatekeepers. In addition, "The Guidelines on Mental Health and Psychosocial Support in Emergency Settings," drafted by the Inter-Agency Standing Committee (IASC, 2007), outlines four levels of intervention in a pyramid. At the base, primary attention is paid to basic services (e.g., food, water, and shelter) and security; the second level involves strengthening community and family supports (including activating social supports, communal traditional supports, and supportive child-friendly spaces). The third level of focused nonspecialized support includes basic mental-health care and basic emotional and practical support by community workers; and the apex involves mental health care by mental health specialists (including psychologists, psychiatrists, and psychiatric nurses). Key directives for communities in the IASC Advocacy package are to normalize strong reactions and feelings; take care of oneself and others, especially children and those who are marginalized; ask for help from others, including from professionals; avoid alcohol and drugs; re-establish daily routines; organize religious ceremonies, community meetings, sports, arts and related group activities; and clean up the community.

A considerable amount of psycho-educational materials about coping with natural disasters has been produced by psychological organizations. These are available from the American Psychological Association (www.apa.org) and from the Australian Psychological Society (http://www.psychology.org.au/). E-therapy programs have been developed by Swinburne University in Australia, addressing anxiety and posttraumatic stress disorder (www.anxietyonline .org.au).

Trainings have also been made available for mental health professionals. After the Haiti earthquake, a one-day session was held at Brooklyn College in New York to train mental health professionals in the IASC guidelines. Several academic institutions offer professional development, including a global post-disaster reconstruction and management certificate offered by the Center for Rebuilding Sustainable Communities after Disasters in collaboration with the University of Massachusetts in Boston, Massachusetts (www.rebuilding.umb .edu/).

Seminars and Presentations of Professionals

Events by mental health professionals help highlight the importance of community responses to disasters. For example, at Psychology Day at the United Nations in February 2010, the World Health Organization's Dr. Karen Sealey and I were among presenters discussing access to humanitarian aid, including in the aftermath of the earthquake in Haiti. Another panel and fundraiser (for Haiti), held at Columbia's School of International Affairs, brought together experts, including UN Assistant Secretary-General Robert Orr, whom I interviewed for a television report, who validated the importance of psychological first aid in the wake of such disasters. "In a dramatic and devastating situation like that faced in Haiti today, the mental health needs are extreme and massive, and spread throughout the population both to those affected and to those trying to help," Orr said. "We need to look at ways to reach those needs as well as the material needs: food, water, shelter, the basic needs. We're going to have to be very innovative to reach all the people who need those services." The panelists agreed about the necessity of organizations coordinating their efforts instead of overlapping their work, and about the need to involve Haitians to build back their communities and their country.

THE REASSURE MODEL: A USEFUL METHOD FOR PUBLIC HEALING

A model I have developed for healing in public arenas, that is appropriate for group healing, is the REASSURE model, whereby the word is an acronym for various interventions. Applying this model is possible not just for experienced mental-health professionals, but for lay helpers as well. The word REASSURE expresses the essence of healing: offering reassurance that things can return to normal (or rather a "new normal"), that any one person is not alone in suffering, and help is available. This approach evolved from years of my crisis counseling and radio call-in advice, and has been successfully applied in many settings, with varied populations and cultures.

The model has applicability for communities coping with environmental disaster (Kuriansky, 2009). "R" refers to offering reassurance to survivors that post-traumatic reactions are normal, for example, mothers normally worry about sending their children to school after a hurricane; survivors of floods can normally be uncomfortable running bathwater that can remind them of the rushing flood waters; and after an earthquake, employees' fears of entering tall buildings are normal. "E" stands for explanation about the disaster, for example, explaining what a tsunami is to villagers who fear its recurrence. "A" stands for asking questions, to clarify confusion about events. "S" stands for seeking and offering support, for example, establishing a social network. The second "S" stands for specific suggestions about coping, such as applying for social services or engaging in a relaxing, pleasurable activity. "U" stands for understanding at a deeper level, for example, how feeling helpless after a disaster can remind a survivor of early childhood experiences of powerlessness or abuse. "R" stands for referrals, for example, to organizations that offer help. "E" stands for encouragement, since research shows that people can more easily recover from crises when they have hope that their circumstances will improve (Groopman, 2004; Seligman & Csikszentmihalyi, 2000).

PROFESSIONAL ORGANIZING IN COMMUNITY SETTINGS

In the wake of environmental disaster, psychological professionals need to organize in order to present an integrated, rather than fragmented, response, merging mental health support with legal, health, insurance and home construction services. Lists of available resources and referral services need to be updated and documented. In response to floods in Santa Catarina, Brazil, that caused the deaths of 135 people and two billion dollars in damages, a Brazilian psychiatrist colleague and friend, José Thomé, MD, organized seven groups (each from a different damaged city) to educate community members about possible problems and social disorganization, and to offer brief counseling groups that focused on sharing feelings and facilitating resilience. Long-term plans also needed to be implemented, as one year later, 24,000 people still had not returned to their homes, neighborhoods were still collapsed, roads were blocked, the water supply was impaired, regions were isolated, and thousands were suffering emotionally. In his role as Brazil's representative to the Section on Catastrophes of the World Association of Psychiatry, Thomé mobilized the Brazilian Association of Psychiatry's Community Program and coordinated with the governor of the state of Santa Catarina to offer a two-year program of mental-health support that would further develop models for intervention by national and international institutions.

"The local authorities expected that their emergency efforts were enough and had not yet understood the extent of the mental health problem," Thomé told me. "Our proposal of intervention was explained and accepted. It mobilized complementary efforts to offer support for first responders, health professionals, and others exposed to the disruptive situation and consequently, to illness." His mental health group traveled to each affected area, not to offer direct psychiatric treatment, but to meet with local leadership to enable "key people" to develop resilience and, therefore, to bolster recovery of the communities. Staff of the department of education and first responders were apparently particularly responsive, attending group meetings with the mental health professionals, and seeking consultation and support to alleviate emotional suffering. People in one of the affected states with a higher socio-economic status (as measured by the Index of Human Development) were receptive to support offered, but conflicts arose over people who were homeless. This was similarly noted following Hurricane Katrina in the United States, when citizens of Baton Rouge resented the influx of refugees from the affected nearby community of New Orleans.

Emotional Preparedness of a Community

Consistent and persistent environmental disasters have proven that life is unpredictable and that unexpected events can happen at any time that changes life drastically forever. Therefore, being prepared for emergency is essential. This involves not only getting the facts about what an environmental disaster entails (e.g., after the Asian tsunami, groups were held to explain signs of an impending tsunami such as swelling and drastic receding of waters) but communities knowing what types of disaster can happen in their area and how to be prepared (e.g., people in the tornado alley of the Great Plains states, including Kansas and Oklahoma, and people on the fault line in San Francisco). Also, citizens need to be aware of the challenges that lie ahead in emergencies, as well as their strengths and weaknesses in dealing with those events. Further, they need to know about the dangers of negative coping mechanisms, like alcohol abuse, and the value of prosocial actions, like helping others.

The Psychological Role of Community Leaders

The presence and participation of authority figures and leaders in an emergency is crucial for community recovery, by drawing attention to the tragedy and potential aide to the area, and by offering a sense of vicarious power to those who feel powerless. Like spiritual leaders, they can be valuable to acknowledge suffering yet point out strengths and resilience, offer explanations, and reaffirm meaning. In his speech after the Midwest tornados in 2011, which was broadcast live on television, United States President Barack Obama said, "The question is 'Why?'" By saying this, he verbalized others' feelings and identified with the suffering. His answer: "We do not have the capacity to answer, it is beyond our power to control, but that does not mean we are powerless. How we respond is up to us, that's in our control." While apologizing for being abroad and not present with them at the time of the disaster (like a parent who feels guilty for not being present if a child has an accident), he offered reassurance by saying that he could feel their pain. "Let the people of Joplin know that we love them," he said.

Authority figures further help the community healing process by fostering and acknowledging community cohesion. This was evident by enthusiastic audience clapping in the tornado-stricken Biloxi community when President Obama noted that amid heartbreak and tragedy, "No one is a stranger, everyone is a brother, and everyone is a sister" and that the devastated community is not isolated but is part of a "national tragedy." Since collective hope is crucial for healing, in the midst of the populace feeling abandoned, threatened, helpless, and unprotected (whether by forces of nature or by God), pledges of support from authority figures perceived as powerful are valuable, even despite widespread skepticism about promises of help. The President promised the tornado-torn city that he (and the country) would continue to oversee the rebuilding. The gathered audience clapped again as the president promised, "We will stand together . . . I can promise you . . . the cameras may leave, but we will be with you every step of the way, we're not going anywhere."

Good Samaritans and Heroes

A mother shields her son from falling debris, a husband throws himself over his wife when winds rip through, a man reaches out to grab the hand of a drowning child in a flood. These stories of good Samaritans are inspirational after a natural disaster, letting people know that others, even strangers, are willing to help and protect. The effort is even more encouraging when a person puts his or her own life in danger. Such people, known as good Samaritans, voluntarily offer help to another person (or to an institution) in times of trouble or difficulty. Such benefactors lend a helping hand by financial aid or heroic actions, with the latter being powerful on a deep-emotional level due to their personal nature. Inspirational speakers at memorials commonly refer to these people and praise their actions.

Good Samaritans become heroes when they perform acts that are seemingly impossible or super-human, when put to the test in an emergency. These people rush into—rather than out of—a fire to save a trapped crying child or jump into raging waters to pull out someone drowning. Heroes can be everyday people or those in jobs where they pledge to help, like police, firefighters, and other emergency workers who go "beyond the call of duty" and endure and overcome obstacles to help others. CNN television honors such everyday heroes yearly in a campaign. The affirmation that heroes are all around us gives people hope that a savior can come out of the blue. Such fantasies of being rescued are embedded in childhood fairy tales, for example, Rapunzel trapped in a tower or a maiden strapped to railroad tracks. Stories of the arrival of a Prince Charming in the nick of time give children security that they will be protected; a need that persists well into adulthood.

Government Action

In January 2005, 168 governments associated with the United Nations adopted a 10-year plan called the Hyogo Framework for Action to make the world safer from natural hazards. This framework offers guidelines and priorities for action and practical means for achieving disaster resilience for vulnerable communities. Its goal is to substantially reduce disaster losses in lives, and in social, economic, and environmental assets, by 2015 (UNISDR, 2012). In 2007, I attended meetings at UN headquarters in Geneva to review progress of the UN member state governments in achieving the goals of disaster risk reduction, where it was clear that much more needed to be done to achieve these lofty goals. Many pamphlets are available about how all stakeholders can contribute to campaigns about disaster risk reduction, like Making Cities Resilient, including participation by citizens as well as local associations; national governments; international, regional, and civil organizations; businesses; schools; and hospitals.

Fundraising

Natural disasters can cause intense destruction that demands extensive funding for rebuilding. Fundraising efforts after such disasters can be launched at local community levels (e.g., clothing drives, food drives) or at international levels (e.g., through the Red Cross or similar international aid societies). Such efforts have been enhanced by media and particularly by the Internet, where donations can be made efficiently by logging on to sites. Fundraisers are an opportunity for communities to show their support by turning out in large numbers, giving awards to serve as valuable recognition, and bringing together various constituencies. For example, a fundraiser for Haiti by humanitarian Jim Luce's Orphans International Worldwide honored people as Global Citizens for Leadership in Helping Humanity, with plaques given to the UN Sri Lankan Ambassador Palitha Kohona, U.S Congresswoman Carolyn Maloney, myself and Father Wismick Jean-Charles, as well as to noted folksinger and peace activist Peter Yarrow. Events can benefit local organizations. For example, following the Japanese tsunami and earthquake, benefactors included an organization with direct ties to Japan (e.g., the Japan American Association); an organization on the ground (e.g., the American Baptist Church); and an organization with a longtime presence in the affected area (e.g., the New York Japanese-American

Lions Club). Benefactors were listed on a website (www.jaany.org) to make them easily accessible to those who wanted to make contributions.

Media as a Community Resource for Sharing

When a natural disaster occurs and people are cut off from others physically and emotionally, the media plays a key role. On evening news shows' coverage about disasters, psychologists like myself describe symptoms and coping techniques as well as affirm the importance of recognizing symptoms, expressing feelings when and where appropriate, and seeking and offering help.

As a personal medium, radio provides an excellent resource to communicate information and also to offer people an opportunity to share and receive help related to their suffering. Public sharing about trauma normalizes reactions and comforts people that they are not suffering alone. The value of radio in the aftermath of environmental disaster became eminently evident to me while traveling the coast of Australia when an earthquake struck the town of Newcastle, destroying many buildings and causing some deaths. Having considerable experience in disaster recovery, I went to the center of town and asked the police how I could help. Hearing my background, they ushered me into the local radio station and suspended regular programming. I found myself on the air taking phone calls from troubled listeners. People called the show, expressing their feelings and fears, including disbelief that such an event could happen, and their feelings of despair. Neighbors who feared for the safety of older people were encouraged to reach out, to visit and bring food. Parents who worried about their children's fears were alerted to the possibility of school phobia, leading to refusal to go to school. Radio is a valuable medium for communication, particularly in developing countries. When the broadcasting system in Haiti was decimated by the earthquake, the NGO Internews helped rebuild the communications infrastructure and emergency broadcasting resources, including providing health information. While not as accessible to survivors in tragedies, television can be a powerful communication medium to inform a broad global community about needs and issues. Although television traditionally focuses on dramatic footage of damage and controversies, some outlets are increasingly recognizing positive healing efforts. For example, CNN International, ABC News, and Global Connections Television on UN TV have interviewed me on my return from sites of environmental trauma, focusing on psychological first aid, and positive efforts in my trainings and psychological first aid missions.

Communities can urge media to present many educational programs to help citizens deal with the trauma associated with natural disasters. Mental health professionals, who are often hesitant to use the media to highlight their efforts, need to participate with media as a partner in such public education. This philosophy has been espoused by several APA presidential initiatives dating back to the 1950s with George Miller's motto "Giving Psychology Away." Following simple steps can help professionals present stories about the community in a way that facilitates healing and community resilience (Kuriansky, 2005a, 2009).

Writing press releases to alert news media about mental health efforts in a tragedy is a useful skill to aide community recovery and highlight the role of mental health professionals. When a colleague in Brazil (Dr. Thomé mentioned previously in the section about professional organizing) asked me to help raise awareness in the media about psychological issues in the aftermath of floods there, I drafted a press release for his local organization to send to the media. This release addressed issues that I knew, as a reporter myself, would appeal to producers in their coverage of an event, by focusing on stories of real people affected by the trauma rather than intellectual discussions of issues; highlighting the persistent enormity of the problem and practical solutions; and exposing corruption by the government and other organizations.

Social Networking

To reach communities around the world, social networking sites and other Internet resources can be valuable after a disaster. Through these contacts, activities can be organized, and people can connect in ways not available before the advent of computers and various handheld devices. Community members need to take advantage of these possibilities, using "text-messaging" Web-based video channels, podcasts, and other communication methods and devices to communicate about resources for recovery and prevention. In the wake of the Haiti earthquake, the internet site called HaitiXChange offered people unique access to information. Increasingly used social media resources include Twitter, which involves sharing short updates in messages limited to 140 characters that are posted and shared with everyone who is "following you"; Facebook, which is a social networking site featuring detailed profiles and advanced ways of sharing texts, photos, and videos; Myspace, which is a version of Facebook; LinkedIn, which is a site for networking and creating new business connections and maintaining or rebuilding past connections that can be helpful postdisaster to help rebuild professional connections; blogging, which involves reporting one's personal experience along with photo galleries and/or videos, like a diary that shares information and can publicize work; niche sites for communicating with people about specific subjects; photo sites like Picasa and Flickr where you can post pictures; and listservs for particular invited groups to communicate. An email listserv for a network about disaster risk reduction education is CYDNET-L@groups.preventionweb.net. Some mainstream media are now inviting the public to submit their own "news" via written stories or video reports, for example, CNN's "I report," where anyone can post commentary on an event or issue.

SUMMARY: CREATING A RENEWED SENSE OF COMMUNITY

As an increasing number of environmental disasters seem to be impacting many countries in recent times, people of diverse cultures and backgrounds are beginning to recognize their shared experience and increasingly reach out to provide communal assistance. Efforts for such community healing described earlier in the chapter embody the Haitian saying, "Where there is life, there is hope." Both folklore and psychological research support the principles of resilience and post-traumatic growth in the face of trauma that can be applied to social groups as well as to individuals. In essence, citizens of a local community facing disaster and of the broader global community, can heal more readily from the trauma when inspired by *rebati*, which is a Creole word meaning to "build back better." Efforts at rebuilding are universal in the face of environmental disaster; and recognition of this shared experience offers support necessary for healing for the suffering population as well as those in the extended social and world context. A catastrophe reminds people of the universality of pain and suffering but also of strength and hope, offering an opportunity to create new civilization (Homer-Dixon, 2006), to respect the forces of nature, and to learn new ways to harness those forces for the survival and flourishing of the individual community and the global community.

REFERENCES

Adger, W. N. (2003). Social capital, collective action and adaptation to climate change. *Economic Geography, 79*(4), 387–404.

American Psychological Association. (2010). *Psychology and global climate change: Addressing a multi-faceted phenomenon and set of challenges.* Report of the American Psychological Association Task Force on the Interface between Psychology and Global Climate Change. Members: Swim, J., Clayton, S., Doherty, T., Gifford, R., Howard, G., Reser, J., Stern, P., & Weber, E. Retrieved June 18, 2011, from http://www.apa.org/science/about/publications/climate-change-booklet.pdf.

Bonanno, G. (2004, January). Loss, trauma, and human resilience: Have we underestimated the human capacity to thrive after extremely aversive events? *American Psychologist, 59*(1), 20–28.

Campbell, D. (2001). *The Mozart effect: Tapping the power of music to heal the body, strengthen the mind, and unlock the creative spirit.* New York: Harper Collins.

D'Souza, R. E. (2009). Spirituality, religion and resilience promotion in disasters trauma. In J. T. Thomé, M. Benyakar, & I. H. Taralli. (Eds.), *Intervention in destabilizing situations: Crises and traumas* (pp. 233–258). Rio de Janeiro: Associação Brasileira de Psiquiatria.

Gordon, R. (2004). The social system as site of disaster impact and resource for recovery. *Australian Journal of Emergency Management, 19*(4), 16–22.

Graff, L. (1991). *Volunteer for the health of it.* Etobiocoke, Ontario: Volunteer Ontario.

Groopman, J. (2004). *The anatomy of hope.* New York: Random House.

Harlow, H. F., & Zimmermann, R. (1959). Affectional responses in the infant monkey. *Foundations of Animal Behavior: Classic Papers with Commentaries, 16*(843), 376–387.

Homer-Dixon, T. (2006). *The upside of down: Catastrophe, creativity and the renewal of civilization.* Washington, DC: Island Press.

Houghton, R. (2010). *Domestic violence and disasters: A fact sheet for agencies.* Retrieved July 22, 2011, from http://www.mmsi.org.nz/toolkit-pdfs/Newsletter/DVDisaster Factsheet.pdf.

Ikeda, D. (2011). *Japan: Responding creatively to crisis.* Retrieved August 3, 2011, from http://www.transnational.org/Resources_Treasures/2011/Ikeda_JapanCatastrophe.html.

Inter-Agency Standing Committee. (2007). *Guidelines on mental health and psychosocial support in emergency settings.* Retrieved July 1, 2011, from http://www.who.int/mental_health/emergencies/guidelines_iasc_mental_health_psychosocial_june_2007 .pdf.

Jean-Charles, W. (2011a). *Cross-National Service: Haiti, a review of projects.* Centre de Spiritualité et de Santé Mentale (CESSA): A ministry of transformation of Haiti. Presentation at the 23rd Greater New York Conference on Behavioral Research, Touro College, New York, November 20.

Jean-Charles, W. (2011b). Personal communication, Port-au-Prince, Haiti.

Jean-Charles, W. (2011c). Rebati: After the earthquake the IAAP team continues to remember Haiti. *The IAAP Bulletin of the International Association of Applied Psychology,* 23(1–2). Retrieved from http://www.new.iaapsy.org/uploads/newsletters/April2011 .pdf. pp. 32–34.

Kalayjian, A., & Eugene, D. (Eds.). (2010). *Mass trauma and emotional healing around the world: Rituals and practices for resilience and meaning-making.* Westport, CT: Praeger.

Kaniasty, K., & Norris, F. H. (1995). In search of altruistic community: Patterns of social support mobilization following Hurricane Hugo. *American Journal of Community Psychology,* 23, 447–478.

Kiefer, C. (1984). Citizen empowerment: A developmental perspective. *Prevention in Human Services,* 3, 9–36.

Kubler-Ross, E. (1969). *On death and dying.* New York: Simon and Schuster.

Kuriansky, J. (1990). Talk away your fears. Help also needed for victims of shock. *Daily Telegraph.* Sydney Australia. January 1.

Kuriansky, J. (2002). Emotional response and recovery. In E. Hand (Ed.), *Access: Emergency survival handbook* (pp. 14–20). White River Junction, VT: Nomad Press.

Kuriansky, J. (2003). The 9/11 Terrorist Attack on the World Trade Center: A New York Psychologist's Personal Experiences and Professional Perspective, *Psychotherapie-Forum* (Vol. 10(1), pp. 36–47). Blackwell.

Kuriansky, J. (2005a). *Healing in troubled regions and times of terrorism and trauma: Theory, techniques, and psychotherapy models.* Presented at the Convention of the World Council of Psychotherapy, Buenos Aires, Argentina, August 29.

Kuriansky, J. (2005b). *Psychological rebuilding in the tsunami aftermath.* Presented at the Asian Applied Psychology International -Regional Conference, Bangkok, Thailand, November 15.

Kuriansky, J. (2005c). Working effectively with the mass media in disaster mental health. In G. Reyes & G. A. Jacobs (Eds.), *Handbook of international disaster psychology* (Vol. 1, pp. 127–146). Westport, CT: Praeger.

Kuriansky, J. (2006). Making paper flowers bloom: Coping strategies to survive the Israeli-Palestinian conflict. In J. Kuriansky (Ed.). *Terror in the Holy Land: Inside the anguish of the Israeli-Palestinian conflict* (pp. 239–247). Westport, CT: Praeger.

Kuriansky, J. (2008). A clinical toolbox for cross-cultural counseling and training. In U. P. Gielen, J. G. Draguns, & J. M. Fish (Eds.), *Principles of multicultural counseling and therapy*. Philadelphia: Taylor and Francis/Routledge.

Kuriansky, J. (2009). Communication and media in mass trauma: How mental health professionals can help. In J. T. Thomé, M. Benyakar, & I. H. Taralli (Eds.), *Intervention in destabilizing situations: Crises and traumas* (pp. 195–232). Rio de Janeiro: Associação Brasileira de Psiquiatria.

Kuriansky, J. (2010). Haiti Pre and Post Earthquake: Tracing a personal and professional commitment. *International Psychology Bulletin*. Vol. 14, No. 2, pp. 29–37.

Kuriansky, J. (2011). Aftermath of the Japanese earthquake and tsunami: Immediate response and impacts of events as healing efforts. *International Psychology Bulletin*, 15(2), 67–70.

Kuriansky, J. (2012a). Recovery Efforts for Japan after the 3/11 devastating tsunami/earthquake. *IAAP Bulletin*, Issue 24, June.

Kuriansky, J. (2012b). *Soothing Sendai*. Retrieved June 9, 2012 from http://www.humnews.com/the-view-from-here/2012/3/22/soothing-sendai-report.html.

Kuriansky, J., & Berry, M. O. (2011). Advancing the UN MDGs by a Model Program for Girls Empowerment, HIV/AIDS Prevention and Entrepreneurship: IAAP Project in Lesotho Africa (pp. 36–39). Retrieved June 9, 2012 from http://www.new.iaapsy.org/uploads/newsletters/April2011.pdf.

Kuriansky, J., & Pluhar, E. (2009). Sexuality advice on the radio: Tuning in and turning out healthy. In E. Schroeder & J. Kuriansky (Eds.), *Sexuality education: past, present and future* (Vol. 4, pp. 146–171). Westport, CT: Praeger.

Kuriansky, J., Simonson, H., Varney, D., & Arias, J. (2009). Empower now: An innovative holistic workshop for empowerment in life skills and sexuality education for teens. In J. Schroeder & J. Kuriansky (Eds.), *Sexuality education: past, present, and future* (Vol. 3, pp. 129–162). Westport, CT: Praeger.

Moser, S. C. & Dilling, L. (Eds.). (2007). *Creating a climate for change*. New York: Cambridge University Press.

Nemeth, D. G., Kuriansky, J., Reeder, K. P., Lewis, A., Marceaux, K., Whittington, T., Olivier, T., May, N. E., & Safier, J. A. (2012). Addressing anniversary reactions of trauma through group process: The Hurricane Katrina Anniversary Wellness Workshops. *International Journal of Group Psychotherapy*, 62(1), 129–141.

Norris, F. H., & Kaniasty, K. (1996). Received and perceived social support in times of stress: A test of the social support deterioration deterrence model. *Journal of Personality and Social Psychology*, 71(3), 498–511.

One Year On, UN pays tribute to resilience of Japanese quake survivors. (2012, March 05). Retrieved June 9, 2012 from http://www.un.org/apps/news/story.asp?NewsID=41464.

Pierce, G. R., Lakey, B., Sarason, I. G., & Sarason, B. R. (Eds.). (1997). *Sourcebook of social support and personality*. New York: Plenum.

Piliavin, J. A. (2003). Doing well by doing good: Benefits for the benefactor. In C. L. M. Keyes & L. Haidt (Eds.), *Flourishing: The positive personality and the life well lived*. Washington, DC: American Psychological Association.

Rappaport, J. (1987). Terms of Empowerment/Exemplars of Prevention: Toward a Theory for Community Psychology. *The American Journal of Community Psychology*, 15(2) 121–148.

Rotter, J. (1966). Generalized expectancies for internal versus external control of reinforcements. *Psychological Monographs: General and Applied*, 80(1), 1–28.

Seligman, M. E. P., & Csikszentmihalyi, M. (2000). Positive Psychology: An introduction. *American Psychologist*, 55, 5–14.

Solomon, Z., Mikulincer, M., & Avitzur, E. (1988). Coping, locus of control, social support, and combat-related posttraumatic stress disorder: A prospective study. *Journal of Personality and Social Psychology*, 55(2), 279–285.

Smith, F. (2008). The smallest victims of California wildfires are often forgotten. *Institute for Crisis, Disaster, and Risk Management Crisis and Emergency Management Newsletter Website*, 14(1). Retrieved June 9, 2012, from www.seas.gwu.edu/%7Eemse232/february2008_7.html.

Tedeschi, R. G., & Calhoun, L. (2004, April 21). Posttraumatic growth: A new perspective on psychotraumatology. *Psychiatric Times*, 21(4). Retrieved July 10, 2012, from http://www.psychiatrictimes.com/ptsd/contract/article/10168/54661.

Tierney, K. J. (1989). The social and community contexts of disaster. In R. M. Gist & B. Lubin (Eds.), *Psychosocial aspects of disaster* (pp. 11–39). New York: John Wiley and Sons.

UNISDR. (2012). Retrieved June 9, 2012, from http://www.unisdr.org.

Van den Eynde, J., & Veno, A. (1999). Coping with disastrous events: An empowerment model of community healing. In R. Gist & B. Lubin (Eds.). *Response to disaster: Psychosocial, community and ecological approaches*. Philadelphia: Taylor & Francis.

Winnicott, D. W. (1953). Transitional objects and transitional phenomena. *International Journal of Psychoanalysis*, 34, 89–97.

9

Our Critical Issues in Coping with Environmental Changes: The Intersection of Nature, Psychology, and Spirituality

Susan Zelinski

While the implications of the socioeconomic environment on mental health have been abundantly demonstrated in psychological literature, the impact of the natural environment has received much less attention. Recently, however, interest in this relatively unexplored realm of psychology has burgeoned in step with the increase of concern about global climate change. Evidence is continually accumulating that the buildup of greenhouse gases and destruction of natural resources is eroding our planet's ability to sustain life as we know it. The scientific community at large concurs that this impending global crisis will widely impact humanity in the coming years, and, in fact, it already has in many regions. Most notably, this phenomenon is demonstrated by an increase in number and magnitude of natural disasters across the planet in recent years (Diaz, 2007).

The road to recovery from earthquakes, hurricanes, tsunamis, and other environmental calamities can devastate communities physically, psychologically, and economically. Conversely, survivors can rise to the challenge to develop meaning in the face of serious environmental, personal, and social degradation. This juncture offers a fruitful opportunity to explore both the influence of humans on the earth and the earth's influence on people's lives and well-being. What emerges from a study of those who thrive rather than deteriorate post-disaster can inform not only methods of prevention and coping with natural disasters, but also a holistic approach to psychological health in conjunction with the natural environment. Recent research increasingly shows that religious and spiritual practices can greatly encourage resilience in survivors of natural disasters. Thus, the role of spirituality factors heavily into a shift from pathology to posttraumatic growth, and provides researchers and survivors alike with a means to explore the value of the relationship between people and the earth.

Psychology has historically focused on relationships among people and their social environment. Little regard has been paid to the role of the ecological aspect of human interactions. Until recently, that is, when the rise in evidence of global warming galvanized a movement for conservation and a renewal of interest in the environment. The threat of climate change creates a variety of potential challenges, including jeopardized resources, decreased biodiversity, the displacement of populations, and many others (American Psychological Association, 2010), which invariably impact mental health. The field of psychology has responded by generating a number of subdisciplines that examine this relationship between human mental health and environmental health. Ecopsychology, for instance, works at the center of this connection and seeks to promote interaction with nature as a means of healing, as well as the human imperative to sustain life on our planet. Additionally, ecopsychology seeks to "place psyche (soul) back into the natural world," to repair the rift between the human spirit and the spirit of the earth (Fisher, 2002). Similarly, conservation psychology encourages the development of environmentally sustainable practices as a means to support mental health. It is rooted in the importance of place, as in the regional, environmental setting in which one lives, to personal and collective identity (Saunders, 2003). Most importantly, this field highlights the central role of collective action as a means to bolster social relationships in conjunction with environmental health.

This notion of a human-nature connection is supported by an ever-growing body of research testifying to the beneficial effects of exposure to nature on psychological health. Various studies have demonstrated that children with attention deficit hyperactivity disorder (ADHD) experience an improvement in cognitive functioning after brief exposure to a natural setting such as a park (Kuo & Faber-Taylor, 2004; Wells, 2000). In fact, simply viewing a green space through a window has been shown to relieve stress. A study of Alzheimer's patients found that those who had a view of a garden showed lower levels of aggression and violence than those who did not (Ulrich, 1993). Another study showed that a view of a natural setting through a hospital window helped patients to recover from surgery more quickly than those who did not have a view (Ulrich, 1984). Many other health benefits associated with contact with nature, including greater physical health and recovery from depression, have been demonstrated (Beauchemin & Hays, 1996; Hartig et al., 2003).

Such a positive relationship between human health and environmental exposure is grounded in the theory of biophilia, which means "love of life or living systems" (wiki). This hypothesis essentially states that humans, as conscious products of biological evolution, show an affinity for other forms of life and therefore, by extension, the natural world in general. Viewed from the lens of pathology, this explains the development of phobias such as a fear of snakes, as humans are biologically prepared to fear and avoid potentially harmful creatures and forces in their environment. *Biophobia* is the term given to such negative manifestations of the human-nature relationship. On the opposite end of the spectrum, biophilia accounts for the psychologically beneficial effect of nature and even suggests that a spiritual dimension exists in the relationship between people and their world (Ulrich, 1993). The implicit meaningfulness experienced through a personal connection with the natural environment, therefore, has seemingly been evolutionarily constructed and progressed through systems of biology and psychology.

Biophilia and a related concept, biodiversity, play significant roles in how people relate to their environments. Biodiversity is the variety and richness of species and the attributes they possess within a given defined geographical area. Both concepts contribute to an individual and collective "sense of place," a feeling of belonging to a particular geographical place that is supported by a familiarity with and fondness for the features and creatures of that place. Horwitz, Lindsay, and O'Connor (2002) emphasize that since humans are embedded in their local environment, the relationship among the various interacting systems within it constitutes a comprehensive model of health, in both human and environmental terms. They sagely cite how Australian populations have been affected by deteriorating conditions of inland waterways due to factors directly related to human activities, such as clearing of native vegetation, and indirectly, such as through climate change. Here a cycle is born, where human disregard for the environment leads to its degradation, leading to greater stress and disenchantment of individuals and communities, which may exacerbate the degradation process. Many scientists suspect that such a reciprocal relationship may account for the current shift in global climate patterns.

In psychological terms, such environmental disruption can generate serious consequences. Individual and community identities are often highly vested in their geographical setting, as it provides the framework for daily activities, historical events, and shared places and experiences. Simply stated,

> Environmental issues are important when they are rooted in people's interconnections with other people and with their natural environment. Just as a personal relationship can deepen, there is an argument that so too can our relationship with places and features of places. (Steel, 2000, pp. 796–816)

No more dramatic demonstration of the dire consequences for human populations as a result of environmental degradation exists than the aftermath of natural disasters. The importance of studying the impact of natural disasters lies not only in the need to develop robust preparation and response strategies but also because the increase in their prevalence in recent years is often cited as the most salient manifestation of climate change (Diaz, 2007). While this juncture incites great suffering and fear for many people, it is also ripe for developing a proactive, alternative approach to mending the rupture in the relationship between people and our planet.

Among the most immediate consequences of biometeorological events such as hurricanes, earthquakes, and tsunamis are loss of life and home. Even greater devastation often lies in the wake of such disasters: resource depletion, economic ruin, and extremely averse psychological reactions such as posttraumatic stress disorder (PTSD). Notably, a social justice issue presents itself in the midst of the difficulties of recovery: those of lower socioeconomic status are at much greater risk for pathological reactions, likely due to a lack of access to necessary resources. This was vividly illustrated during the aftermath of Hurricane Katrina (Gheytanchi et al., 2007).

Conversely, these catastrophes do produce highly resilient survivors who provide a model for optimal coping. On a personal level, self-efficacy forms the foundation for positive coping after a potentially traumatic event. Self-efficacy is best characterized as an individual's set of beliefs in his or her personal ability to "manage [his or her] own functioning and to exercise control over events that affect their lives" (Benight & Bandura, 2004). The pervasive influence of self-efficacy manifests in cognitive, motivational, and behavioral processes, and allows individuals to maintain a sense of self-reliance even in the most dire of circumstances. This facilitates decision making, lowers overall stress reactivity, and speeds recovery time. For these reasons, developing self-efficacy in individuals affected by natural disasters has been suggested as a target for intervention practices (Benight & Harper, 2002).

Not surprisingly, certain demographics appear to play a considerable role in whether an individual demonstrates resilience after a traumatic event. Bonanno and colleagues (2007) found that educated, white males of higher socioeconomic status tended to show greater resilience than their less privileged counterparts. Social support has also been implicated as a primary determinant of resilience after traumatic experiences (Bonanno & Mancini, 2006). Yet resilience remains a multifaceted phenomenon, the dynamics of which psychology is just beginning to uncover.

When an individual transcends recovery to discover a life that is enhanced by the meaning gleaned from the wreckage of a natural disaster, he or she is said to have achieved posttraumatic growth (Jang & LaMendola, 2007). Also called salutogenesis or positive adjustment, this seeming paradox of personal evolution arises from an individual's determination to appreciate life in the face of tremendous challenges such as those posed by the occurrence of a natural disaster. Central to posttraumatic growth is an abiding investment in religious or spiritual beliefs (Cadell, Regehr, & Hemsworth, 2010; Shaw, Joseph, & Linley, 2005). To date, a vast literature on the benefits of religion on mental health has been established (Miller & Thoresen, 2003). The development of posttraumatic growth in individuals who have survived the incredible destruction exacted by natural disasters further bears witness to the interconnectedness of spirituality and mental health, particularly in regard to the way in which people relate to their natural environment.

Definition of religion or spirituality prove elusive in qualitative terms, yet both concepts can provide a sense of meaning to those who subscribe to them (Daaleman & Frey, 2004). Also, such beliefs typically center on the existence of a higher power and encourage faith that ultimate outcomes are rooted in the benevolence or will of this higher power. Spiritual and religious traditions are often culturally rooted, and therefore intrinsically offer a means for social support and sharing of a traumatic experience, which may account for some of the salubrious effect of spirituality (Cadell et al., 2010). Additionally, many spiritual customs seek to buffer a harmonious relationship with the earth, as it is the provider of all life (Jang & LaMendola, 2007). Self-efficacy is also embedded in the notion of an active spirituality, as it is characterized by persistence and enduring faith in oneself regardless of the circumstances one encounters (Daaleman & Frey, 2004). Taken together, these features of spirituality make its practice an ideal foil for the extraordinary physical, emotional, and psychological demands imposed by the aftermath of natural disasters.

In the immediate fallout of a natural disaster, timely intervention in terms of material and psychosocial support is crucial for achieving positive outcomes. Hurricane Katrina provided a dramatic example of the consequences of neglecting the needs of survivors, as inefficient communication and coordination of local and federal aid services left many urban poor stranded, psychologically distressed, or dead (Gheytanchi et al., 2007). Conversely, the model of Psychological First Aid provides a simple and inexpensive intervention method that is quickly taking hold as the dominant means of disaster response (American Psychological Association, 2010). It focuses on fostering self-efficacy through contact and engagement, information on coping, practical assistance, stabilization, and connection with collaborative services (Gheytanchi et al., 2007). In this way, comprehensive psychosocial support can be immediately delivered, boosting the likelihood that survivors will be geared toward adaptive functioning.

Examining the outcomes of several recent disasters offers insight into the evolution of individual and community recovery, as well as the unique cultural context that colors each example. The methods of coping espoused are greatly determined by cultural preferences, as are the attributions of the causes of natural disasters. Overriding these differences, however, is the contribution of spirituality to the attainment of posttraumatic growth in survivors.

In September 1999, an earthquake with a magnitude of 7.6 on the Richter scale pummeled central Taiwan. Casualties amounted to more than 2,000 dead and 11,000 injured, and another 100,000 people were left homeless. The area affected by the quake was predominately rural, with a sparsely educated population. Estimates of the incidence of posttraumatic stress disorder ranged between 11 and 30 percent one year after the quake, which is considered relatively standard for such a large-scale disaster (Lai et al., 2004).

From the alternative perspective, Jang and LaMendola (2007) assessed post-traumatic growth in survivors by using the Posttraumatic Growth Inventory that was developed by Tedeschi and Calhoun (1996), as well as *continuous religious affiliation*, which the authors assessed as a result of participants' self-reports of whether they had identified with a religious tradition prior to, during, and after the earthquake. The researchers found *continuous religious affiliation* to be a significant predictor of survivors' posttraumatic growth. In qualitative analyses, several beliefs espoused by those who claimed continuous religious affiliation consistently emerged as central to their understanding of the meaning of the earthquake. These were the role of fate and destiny, ancestor worship, and lessons from the gods. These beliefs were highly shaped by the predominantly Buddhist affiliation of the region. In short, many believed that the earthquake was a lesson sent from the gods to admonish the people to properly honor their ancestors and restore a harmonious relationship with nature. In interviews, some survivors indicated that they felt that their healing depended on their religious rituals rather than any mental health services offered. For instance, "there were proper spiritual rituals for the deceased to ensure that they were at peace that brought great comfort to survivors" (Jang & LaMendola, 2007, 313).

In terms of reporting the greatest difficulty they faced, many participants in the Jang and LaMendola study noted delays in government providers distributing material aid, an issue replicated in both the tsunami of 2004 and Hurricane Katrina (as discussed later in the chapter). The authors emphasize that disaster response efforts should coordinate immediate physical and mental health needs in the manner of Psychological First Aid.

Similarly, preliminary interviews of survivors of the 2010 Haiti earthquake revealed that a high percentage of respondents mentioned religion as an explanation for the cause of the disaster and also as reassurance about their safer future. This is consistent with the religious nature of the culture. Another posttraumatic growth study was conducted in a sample of Haiti survivors (students) who were trained to be emergency comforters to patients at a hospital. The results showed that the respondents found positive effects of helping, specifically that helping others helped assuage their own suffering and made them feel useful.

Additionally, the helpers deployed in disaster response efforts should heed the dominant cultural narrative, which is the distinctive set of values and beliefs that govern the way of life of a people, as for many survivors it provided a direct means for achieving posttraumatic growth. By adhering to rituals and customs in the face of turmoil, survivors are able to find a way to cull meaning from what may otherwise seem like a hopeless situation. Such practices may include funeral rites and bereavement strategies and provide a dimension of explanation for tragedy as well as a means to move beyond it (Neimeyer, 2006). This is demonstrated in each case discussed here, as every culture studied in the aftermath of a natural disaster highlighted the importance of their unique traditions in the healing process.

Five years after the earthquake in Taiwan, in December 2004, a colossal tsunami struck the coast of southeastern India. Nearly 3 million people were killed and another 1million were left homeless. Near the epicenter of the tsunami's impact was the state of Tamil Nadu, one of India's most industrialized areas. Tamil Nadu swiftly became the focal point of posttsunami research because of its proximity to the heart of the tsunami and the rich economic state it had previously been. Studies evaluating affected communities for posttraumatic stress disorder PTSD found a prevalence rate of 12 to 40 percent up to one year after the tsunami (Kumar et al., 2007; Neuner et al., 2006).

In psychosocial care efforts, community cohesion was encouraged through group sessions aimed at emotional ventilation and normalization of the experience of survivors (Becker, 2007). Significantly, many cultural issues came to the forefront of these group discussions. One of the most commonly cited difficulties was loss of pride, often due to loss of livelihood. Fishing and farming were the two main occupations of residents prior to the tsunami and both were severely impacted in its wake. To address this loss of self-reliance through livelihood loss and to renew self-efficacy, Psychological First Aid became the preferred method of intervention. In addition, social and spiritual coping strategies proved to be of significant value. Gatherings took place in which community members were invited to honor deceased children by planting coconut saplings. Such a simple practice vividly demonstrates the spiritual renewal that is possible through a direct interaction with the natural environment.

In surveys conducted with survivors, 67 percent cited their religious beliefs as the single most important factor contributing to their resilience (Rajkumar, Premkumar, & Tharyan, 2008). Thus, integrating mental health services with community spiritual groups and other cultural organizations proves to be incalculable.

In the case of Hurricane Katrina in the United States in August 2005, about 1,600 people were killed, 100,000 were displaced from their homes, and another 1,000 remain missing. The highly publicized failure of the U.S. government to coordinate disaster response efforts in a quick fashion stunned the nation and left many in New Orleans in a state of desperation and chaos. Older and poor African Americans were grossly overrepresented among the dead for many reasons; one of which was that they presumably lacked the resources to evacuate in time (Henderson, Roberto, & Kamo, 2010).

The situation unfolded in stark contrast to the optimized framework of Psychological First Aid, in which survivors' physical and psychosocial needs are addressed in rapid succession (Gheytanchi et al., 2007). As such, it might be expected that greater psychopathology might be seen among survivors. In fact, estimates of PTSD prevalence hovered in the 12 to 30 percent range of those affected (Bonanno & Mancini, 2006; Kessler et al., 2008).

In surveys measuring posttraumatic growth in survivors of Hurricane Katrina, themes of increased self-efficacy and spiritual meaning emerged among the vast majority of participants. For example, one study found that 95.6 percent of participants developed greater faith in their personal abilities to rebuild their lives, 66.8 percent acknowledged becoming more spiritual or religious, and 75.2 percent affirmed that they had found greater meaning and purpose in life post-Katrina (Kessler et al., 2008). In studies of older African American adults displaced by Katrina (Henderson et al., 2010; Lawson & Thomas, 2007), active spiritual coping strategies, such as praying, attending Mass, and reading the Bible, were frequently observed. Thus, despite facing tremendous odds, many of those most seriously affected by Hurricane Katrina recovered and even evinced resilient outcomes, likely owing at least in part to their personal spiritual beliefs and practices.

After being devastated by natural disasters, perhaps the most telling element of the path to recovery comes from people's commitment to nature and spirituality, both of which are conducive to positive survival. One fisherman interviewed in Tamil Nadu after the tsunami stated:

> Sea water means mother's milk to us . . . we cannot retaliate against anything she does. This was the first time she became angry with us. We still value her love and care. No one will hate their mother if she shows her anger once. (Rajkumar et al., 2008, p. 847).

This man's words beautifully elicit the delicate balance between livelihood, community, natural environment, and spiritual well-being. His statement identifies with the collective, allying him with his fellow fishermen and community members. He speaks of love and forgiveness rather than anger concerning the tragedy of the tsunami, acknowledging the intimacy between the life of the community and the life of the ocean. A certain grace imbues his words and summons others to reconceptualize each element as part of a greater unified whole biosphere rather than disparate, competing parts.

CONCLUSION

That the influence of spirituality permeates not only the coping methods involved in achieving posttraumatic growth but also the relationship between people and their natural environment on the whole testifies to the need for a crucial reconfiguration of health frameworks. Not only is empirical evidence increasingly supporting this shift, the vast changes in global climate patterns demand it. If human life is to be sustained on earth, a deep, actively engaged appreciation for its resources and limitations must be cultivated across cultures and disciplines. Because of its descriptive power in explicating human behavior, psychology plays a vital role in this transformation. If a comprehensive understanding of what motivates people to live in harmony with their natural environment can be achieved, it could pave the way for a more sustainable future.

Studying the impact of natural disasters on human populations provides a crystallized representation of what happens when the rift between people and the earth exposes itself in a dramatic way. While an element of tragedy indubitably presents itself, in actuality the greater part of those who survive continue to flourish and derive meaning from their suffering. This pattern illustrates that the impressive potential for growth is always alive. To validate this concept, further research needs to explore the view of people as adaptable and resilient rather than disordered and dysfunctional in response to natural disasters. This requires a more holistic understanding of the human-nature connection.

REFERENCES

American Psychological Association. (2010). *Psychology and global climate change: Addressing a multi-faceted phenomenon and set of challenges.* Report of the American Psychological Association Task Force on the Interface between Psychology and Global Climate Change. Members: Swim, J., Clayton, S., Doherty, T., Gifford, R., Howard, G., Reser, J., Stern, P., & Weber, E. Retrieved June 18, 2011, from http://www.apa.org/science/about/publications/climate-change-booklet.pdf.

Beauchemin, K. M., & Hays, P. (1996). Sunny hospital rooms expedite recovery from severe and refractory depressions. *Journal of Affective Disorders, 40*(1–2), 49–51.

Becker, S. (2007). Psychosocial care for adult and child survivors of the tsunami disaster in India. *Journal of Child and Adolescent Psychiatric Nursing, 20*(3), 148–155.

Benight, C. C., & Bandura, A. (2004). Social-cognitive theory of posttraumatic recovery: The role of perceived self-efficacy. *Behaviour Research and Therapy, 42*(10), 1129–1148.

Benight, C. C., & Harper, M. L. (2002). Coping self-efficacy perceptions as a mediator between acute stress response and long-term distress following natural disasters. *Journal of Traumatic Stress, 15*(1), 177–186.

Bonanno, G. A., Galea, S., Bucciarelli, A., & Vlahov, D. (2007). What predicts psychological resilience after a disaster? The role of demographics, resources, and life stress. *Journal of Consulting and Clinical Psychology, 75*(5), 671–682.

Bonanno, G. A., & Mancini, A. D. (2006). Resilience in the face of potential trauma: Clinical practices and illustrations. *Journal of Clinical Psychology, 62*(8), 971–985.

Cadell, S., Regehr C., & Hemsworth, D. (2010). Factors contributing to posttraumatic growth: A proposed structural equation model. *American Journal of Orthopsychiatry, 73*(3), 279–287.

Daaleman, T. P., & Frey, B. B. (2004). The Spirituality Index of Well-Being: A new instrument for health-related quality of life research. *Annals of Family Medicine, 2* (5), 499–503.

Diaz, J. H. (2007). The influence of global warming on natural disasters and their public health outcomes. *American Journal of Disaster Medicine, 2*(1), 33–42.

Fisher, A. (2002). *Radical ecopsychology: Psychology in the service of life.* Albany, NY: SUNY Press.

Gheytanchi, A., Joseph, L., Gierlach, E., Kimpara, S., Houseley, J., Franco, Z. E., & Beutler, L. E. (2007). The dirty dozen: Twelve failures of the Hurricane Katrina response and how psychology can help. *American Psychologist, 62*(2), 118–130.

Hartig, T., Evans, G. W., Jamner, L. D., Davis, D. S., and Garling, T. (2003). Tracking restoration in natural and urban field settings. *Journal of Environmental Psychology, 23*, 109–123.

Henderson, T. L., Roberto, K. A., & Kamo, Y. (2010). Older adults' responses to Hurricane Katrina: Daily hassles and coping strategies. *Journal of Applied Gerontology*, 29(1), 48–69.

Horwitz, P., Lindsay, M., & O'Connor, M. (2002). Biodiversity, endemism, sense of place, and public health: Inter-relationships for Australian inland aquatic systems. *Ecosystem Health*, 7(4), 253–261.

Jang, L. J., & LaMendola, W. F. (2007). Social work in natural disasters: The case of spirituality and post traumatic growth. *Advances in Social Work*, 8(2), 305–316.

Kessler, R. C., Galea, S., Gruber, M. J., Sampson, N. A., Ursano, R. J., & Wessely, S. (2008). Trends in mental illness and suicidality after Hurricane Katrina. *Molecular Psychiatry*, 13, 374–384.

Kumar, M. S., Murhekat, M. V., Hutin, Y., Subramanian, T., Ramachandran, V., & Gupte, M. (2007). Prevalence of post-traumatic stress disorder in a coastal fishing village in Tamil Nadu, India, after the December 2004 tsunami. *American Journal of Public Health*, 97(1), 99–101.

Kuo, F. E., & Faber-Taylor, A. (2004). A potential natural treatment for attention-deficit/hyperactivity disorder: evidence from a national study. *American Journal of Public Health*, 94(9), 1580–1586.

Lai, T. J., Chang, C. M., Connor, K. M., Lee, L. C., & Davidson, J. R. T. (2004). Full and partial PTSD among earthquake survivors in rural Taiwan. *Journal of Psychiatric Research*, 38(3), 313–322.

Lawson, E. J., & Thomas, C. (2007). Wading in the waters: Spirituality and older black Katrina survivors. *Journal of Health Care for the Poor and Underserved*, 18(2), 341–354.

Miller, W. R., & Thoresen, C. E. (2003). Spirituality, religion, and health: An emerging field. *American Psychologist*, 58(1), 24–35.

Neimeyer, R. A., Baldwin, S. A., & Gilles, J. (2006) Continuing bonds and reconstructing-meaning: mitigating complications in bereavement. *Death Studies*, 30(8), 715–738.

Neuner, F., Schauer, E., Catani, C., Rauf, M., & Elbert, T. (2006). Post-tsunami stress: A study of posttraumatic stress disorder in children living in three severely affected regions in Sri Lanka. *Journal of Traumatic Stress*, 19(3), 339–347.

Rajkumar, A. P., Premkumar, T. S., & Tharyan, P. (2008). Coping with the Asian tsunami: Perspectives from Tamil Nadu, India on the determinants of resilience in the face of adversity. *Social Science and Medicine*, 67(5), 844–853.

Saunders, C. (2003). The emerging field of conservation psychology. *Human Ecology Review*, 10, 137–153.

Shaw, A., Joseph, S., & Linley, P. A. (2005). Religion, spirituality, and posttraumatic growth: A systematic review. *Mental Health, Religion & Culture*, 8(1), 1–11.

Steel, G. D. (2000). Polar bonds: Environmental relationships in the polar regions. *Environment and Behaviour*, 32(6), 796–816.

Tedeschi, R. G., & Calhoun, L. G. (1996). The Posttraumatic Growth Inventory: measuring the positive legacy of trauma. *Journal of Trauma and Stress*, 9(3), 455–471.

Ulrich, R. S. (1993). Biophilia, biophobia, and natural landscapes. In S. R. Kellert and E. O. Wilson (Eds.), *The Biophilia Hypothesis*. Washington, DC: Island Press, pp. 73–137.

Ulrich, R. S. (1984). View through a window may influence recovery from surgery. *Science*, 224(4647), 420–421.

Wells, N. M. (2000). At home with nature: Effects of "greenness" on children's cognitive functioning. *Environment and Behavior*, 32(6), 775–795.

10

Our Indigenous People: Healing Ourselves and Mother Earth

Gloria Alvernaz Mulcahy

> . . . we have stories
> as old as the great seas
> breaking through the chest
> flying out the mouth
> noisy tongues that once were silenced
> all the oceans we contain
> coming to light
> —Linda Hogan, from *To Light*

GREETINGS AND ACKNOWLEDGMENTS

Our tradition as indigenous people is to begin speaking by acknowledging who we are and where we come from, and to honor our relatives and ancestors as well as Mother Earth. This is based on the understanding that the world cannot be taken for granted. It is implicit that we must "align the minds and hearts of the people with Nature" (Stokes & Kanawahienton, 1993). This perspective offers the possibility of a healing pathway and provides a way of being in the world that becomes a "guiding principle of culture." The focus of this chapter is on healing ourselves as indigenous people and our Mother Earth in a world of increasing human and earth trauma (Mark, 2011; van der Kolk, 2006).

REACHING BACK

Through an enduring colonizing process, indigenous peoples as well as the earth have suffered from trauma. For indigenous people, the wounding has been pervasive on many levels, including environmental, physical, mental, social, cultural, educational, and economic (Anderson, 2000; Anderson & Lawrence, 2003). The trauma can be traced back in history and has an ongoing generational impact for many reasons, including sending youth to Residential Schools (Chris-john, Young, & Maraun, 1997). In Canada, for example, the government created a tool for "taking the Indian out of the child," which was part of a larger system of Canadian policy that included the Indian Act, child welfare, reservations, and the justice system (Chrisjohn, Young, & Maraun, 1997).

The century and a half of cultural dislocation and genocide caused by residen-tial schools began with the opening of the first school in 1838 in Alderville, Ontario, and officially terminated with the closing of Akaitcho Hall (a Catholic residential school in the Northwest Territories) late in the 1990s as part of the Yellow Knife Indian Residential School system. The atrocities of this historical period include the removal of children from their families, communities, nations, and their land as well as the disappearance of children and the physical and sexual abuse perpetrated in residential schools (Royal Commission on Aboriginal People, 1996). http://www.aadnc-aandc.gc.ca/eng/1100100014597.

This generational trauma for our indigenous people and our beautiful planet has also been sustained throughout time, with numerous deleterious outcomes that include energy resources are depleted; chemical spills pollute the water that seeks to nourish us; and the atmosphere has changed, resulting in the fact that the climate has altered. Consequently, Mother Earth is wounded, or to use psychological language, she is traumatized.

In keeping with indigenous traditional practices when speaking, it is our protocol to recognize our ancestors and the traditional land where we reside. With this in mind, I acknowledge my ancestral roots with the Cherokee Nation (Tsalagi/Aniyunwiya) and my Cherokee grandmother (*etsi*) and mother (*elisi*), whose family migrated from the eastern shore of what is now called the United States to the west coast. Presently, I am located in southwestern Ontario in the traditional area of the Haudenosaunee people of Six Nations (Onyota'a'ka, Mohawk, Onondaga, Cayuga, Seneca, and Tuscarora) as well as the Lënape and Anishinaabe—approximately 40,000 indigenous people, including those in urban areas, reserves, and settlements.

The fluid movement among indigenous people living on reserves and settle-ments and those in urban areas offer an important perspective concerning a migratory relationship between our outlying local communities and the more-diverse urban populations. Indigenous peoples continue to maintain a connec-tion to their sense of place—the land and community. The migratory movement occurs in response to both economic and social pressures. It is important to note that environmental conditions on reserves in this area as well as others compro-mise the well-being of our people and Mother Earth.

My academic training and experience is in clinical developmental psychology as a professor, researcher, and therapist. One of my areas of research has focused on the trauma of indigenous women who have experienced being uprooted and displaced, and those transitioning to mothering who identify as having experienced trauma (Berman et al., 2011). In addition, I was a researcher and participant in a three-year community project called Re-Kindling the Fire, that was carried out in southwestern Ontario and supported by the Aboriginal Healing Foundation (Alvernaz Mulcahy & Ritchie, 2005). I produced and directed a series of documentary films centered on violence in our local communities and the role of the residential school experience on family breakdown, parenting difficulties, as well as drug and alcohol abuse. The focus was on offering healing pathways to change through revitalizing traditional practices.

Moreover, in 2006 at the seventh annual World Indigenous Women & Wellness Conference, I reported (with Edna Brass) on a series of Vision Quest documentaries (2000, 2001, 2005). These documentaries depicted community gatherings held in the Down Town East Side (DTES), Vancouver, British Columbia. The events were adapted to meet the needs of an indigenous urban community with challenging social and economic concerns. For example, the Hastings and Main Street area in the DTES is the poorest postal code in Canada. It has high rates of violence, drug and alcohol abuse, and prostitution. The documentaries offer a unique glimpse of Vancouver's DTES and a community seeking to heal.

A Vision Quest gathering includes a five-day fasting period where a dream/vision may arrive that will help both the person as well as the community, although traditionally vision quests involve individuals seeking a vision for clarity and guidance. Historically, such experiences were transitions or turning points—*kairos*. They served as a source of discovery through dream, song, healing knowledge, and spiritual direction.

An annual community Fast and Vision Quest began in July of 1998 under the direction of indigenous activist Edna Brass (Cree/Ojibwa) and four other survivors of residential schools who fasted, sang, and slept on the small triangle of cement and earth called Pigeon Park—a gathering place for drug dealers, prostitutes, pimps, and homeless people. They were seeking a healing pathway out of their residential school experiences of violence, and loss of family and language. They were uprooted from loving relations that sustain the body, spirit, and mind. In 2000, I participated in the Vision Quest at Victory Square and returned in 2001 and again in 2005 to film at Oppenheimer Park, documenting the community focus on empowerment and action through traditional healing practices addressing poverty, racism, and genocide.

The 2005 Fast was held only a few months before Robert William "Willie" Pickton, a former pig farmer and serial killer, was indicted for the murders of 15 women in Vancouver based on evidence from DNA samples unearthed at his Port Coquitlam pig farm. Pickton's activities were well known in the DTES to activists such as Edna Brass and families of the missing women, who placed continual pressure on police, politicians, and media to investigate their concerns about missing loved ones. Making films about these events supports and documents reclaiming and reframing indigenous lives and communities.

I was asked by the Native Women's Association of Canada to document the opening of the *voir dire* phase of Robert Pickton's murder trial on January 30, 2006. Interviews at the courthouse captured the powerful Down Town East Side community voices of 10 women who highlighted facts about social conditions surrounding the murdered and missing women: that is, the intergenerational impact of residential school abuse, social oppression, racism, historical trauma, poverty, and substance abuse. The film, "Indigenous Women in Action: Voices from Vancouver" has been screened in various university contexts, art galleries, museums, and other public venues in North America in an effort to raise awareness about the social conditions that created the opportunity for Robert Pickton to become Canada's number one serial killer in an impoverished community within a city known for its beauty, ambience, and welcoming atmosphere.

The focus of the Vision Quest documentaries and the Pickton trial documentary is to increase social awareness concerning violence against aboriginal women and to create social change to deal with the racialized and sexualized violence that confronts indigenous women. The Vision Quest and Pickton documentaries capture the voices of our indigenous women and their allies and create a forum to address conditions that have generated the context for over 600 missing and murdered women across Canada (*Sisters in Spirit*, Native Women's Association of Canada, 2009).

Using social media to address violence against indigenous women is a powerful tool for social change. In the context of research, teaching, and practice, it offers the possibility to expand and deepen our understanding of healing pathways to social awareness and provides a way of being in the world and becomes a guiding principle of culture. The focus of this chapter is on understanding healing pathways for indigenous people and the importance of developing a perspective concerning the world of relations with Mother Earth within communities where violence is prevalent against women and the earth. Particular attention is centered on the Haudenosaunee people of Six Nations as well as the Tsalagi/Aniyunwiya, who are one of the five tribes that also include, the Chicksaw, Choctaw, Muscogee, and Seminoles. As well, the discussion in this chapter spans the urban context comprised of women living in the Down Town East Side, Vancouver, British Columbia. Reference to indigenous peoples of mother earth in forms this discourse and includes original people from around the world. It will become clear throughout this chapter that some practices regarding culture and relations with the earth have a universal dimension that connects original people from many divergent nations. This chapter centers on the environment from an indigenous perspective and will:

- Acknowledge the *Ohénton Karihwatéhkwen* (Thanksgiving Address) as a statement (prayer) of reconciliation with the universe that embodies the relationship between the Haudenosaunee people and Mother Earth

- Reveal, in a broader cultural context, indigenous ways of being in the world that sustain the environment by fostering a connection that creates harmony and balance based on principles of respect, responsibility, reciprocity, and reverence— *Kunolunkwa or love.*

On the east coast of the United States, in 1838, the Cherokee Nation experienced a tragic forced removal from their homeland. They were rounded up and put in stockades, where many died. Those who remained began the 1,000-mile walk that became known as the Trail of Tears that led to Oklahoma and the Mississippi River. About one-fourth of the tribe, or some 4,000 Cherokee people, died along the way (Gilbert, 1996). This historical example of the Cherokee people in the United States is not an isolated event, and it is well documented in the health and healing literature that intergenerational trauma shapes identity and impacts growth and development and the well being of individuals and groups (van der Kolk, et al., 2005).

In Canada, the legacy of residential schools has had a devastating impact on over 90,000 survivors—not including their children and grandchildren. The atrocities of this historical period include the removal of children from their families, communities, nations, and land as well as the disappearance of children, undocumented deaths, and physical and sexual abuses. The impact includes an inability or difficulty in parenting, establishing and maintaining relationships, and problems in showing love and affection. Also, alcohol and drug addiction is prevalent. The Aboriginal Healing Foundation has played a central role in providing funding for families and communities to address the impact of sustained trauma and to offer community-based healing programs (Alvernaz Mulcahy, 2002; 2005a).

Ceremonies, Language, and the Land

I was given my *Onyota' áka* or Oneida name, *Ya Ko ni Kuliyo*, by one of our traditional healers here in southwestern Ontario. It means "she is of a good mind." Naming in our indigenous communities presents responsibilities, shapes identity, and gives direction. This being of a good mind requires a lifetime of learning the teachings of our original people and transforms, for me, into understandings anchored in the Haudenosaunee and Tsalagi/Aniyunwiya way of being in the world, including participation in gatherings or ceremonies. The Haudenosaunee cycle of ceremonies include the Feast for the Dead, Midwinter Festival, Strawberry Festival and so forth (www.kahnawakelonghouse.com). This way of being in the world offers an indigenous perspective that is earth centered. Thus, I work with communities using a holistic framework toward healing that is embedded in our relationship to the earth.

It is through our *indigenous* ceremonies that we are reminded of our cultural responsibilities, or duties as human beings, to live in harmony and balance with all that supports us on Mother Earth. This includes interdependent energy forces, whether seen or unseen, heard or unheard, that sustain life on planet earth. Chickasaw writer, poet, and environmentalist Linda Hogan (1995) says that by the end of a ceremony, " . . . it is as if skin contains land and birds. The places within us have become filled. We who easily grow apart from the world are returned to the great store of life all around us, and there is the deepest sense of being at home here in this intimate kinship" (p. 41).

Hogan's evocative description of her experience of ceremony provides a good example of how ritual involvement connects us with Mother Earth who provides for us. Moreover, it is out of this experience of kinship that we are offered awareness of the mutuality between earth and humans, and of our responsibilities to maintain this life connection.

For our original people, words are sacred. Metis/Cree-Salish writer Lee Maracle tells us that the First People regard words as coming from original being—a sacred spiritual being. They represent the accumulated knowledge, cultural values, and vision of an entire people or peoples (Alvernaz Mulcahy, 1994). Aboriginal people understand how language matters, as it arises out of our ancestral land and in relation to all of earth's creatures (Armstrong, 1998; Gunn Allen, 1983; Marmon Silko, 1996).

Melissa Nelson (2002), from the Turtle Mountain Band of Chippewas, states that language "shapes identity and indicates our uniqueness and cultural background. It tells us who we are as a group and as individuals" (p. 4). She makes connections among "all our relations"—the land, plants, animals, winds, forests, waters, and all of the natural sounds (called soundscapes)—arising out of diverse earthscapes—bird songs, ocean waves, wolf howls, coyote yipping, and so forth. These soundscapes offer an ecocultural context for our indigenous languages. It is clear that the language of science offers important information about the earth, but often it has little to do with our relationship to the earth. Hogan (1995) says we need to develop a language that:

> speaks with reverence for life, searching for an ecology of mind. Without it, we have no home, have no place of our own within the creation. It is not only the vocabulary of science we desire. We want a language of that different yield. A yield rich as the harvests of earth, a yield that returns us to our own sacredness, to a self-love and respect that will carry out to others. (p. 60)

Writer and naturalist Leslie Marmon Silko (1996), who is Laguna Pueblo and Cherokee, says that "according to the elders, destruction of any part of the earth does immediate harm to all living things" (p. 131). She points out that this approach to the environment places emphasis on "balance and harmony" and that the Laguna Pueblo elders extend their relational approach or "system of cooperation and conciliation" to all living things, even plants and insects " . . . because none can survive unless all survive" (p. 130).

Language offers the power for indigenous peoples to reclaim or restore their rightful place in society. Meaning belongs to the language that names it, thus language or "the word" has the power to make something present (Melnyk, 2003, p. 28). In Canada, for example, Indian children were removed from their homes, not allowed to speak or write their original language, and given new English names—thus erasing their identities. The residential school legacy is described by Haudenosaunee author of *The Circle Game* (1997; Revised Edition 2006, with Young & Maraun) Dr. R. Chrisjohn as follows:

> Residential schools were one of many attempts at genocide of the Aboriginal Peoples inhabiting the area now commonly called Canada. Initially, the goal of obliterating these peoples was connected with stealing what they owned (the land, the sky, the waters, and their lives, and all that these encompassed); and although this connection persists, present-day acts and policies of genocide are also connected with the hypocritical, legal and self-delusion[al] need on the part of the perpetrators to conceal what they did and what they continue to do. (Chrisjohn, 1998)

Aboriginal identity has been pervasively undermined through a colonization process that includes abuse by church and state that has resulted in the loss of family, culture, and language (Anderson & Lawrence, 2003; Razack, 2002). The outcome is what indigenous people have identified as the loss of several generations of their people to poverty, drug and alcohol abuse, high rates of suicide for youth, and violence against women (Native Women's Association of Canada, 2010).

The importance of cultural practices such as remembering through our ceremonies and, for example, engaging with the *Thanksgiving Address* for opening traditional gatherings, presents as an effective measure for reclaiming traditional knowledge. Participating in community events reflects how it is possible to re-establish relations with family, ancestors, tribes, and indigenous nations around the world.

International involvement offers a world political framework for initiating cultural action. It is critical for families and communities to recognize the deep psychosocial trauma that has occurred through abuse as well as loss of family, relatives, and a sense of place and belonging on the land that births our identity. This is only one dimension of the residue left from the impact of being forced to leave one's family, forced to relinquish one's name and language, one's world view and all one's relations and to adopt a new worldview and a language that was/is alien culturally, spiritually, and socially.

Our stories go missing along with the lost language and so do the cultural ceremonies and understandings. Children were taken from families, forced to mute their own words, or to engage in songs or ceremonies. Most important, they lost their parents, siblings, aunties and uncles, the extended family, community, and nations. Also, the existence of physical and sexual trauma is well documented

(Chrisjohn, Young, & Maraun, 1997). Loss of identity, uprooting, and displacement along with physical and sexual abuse were part of the psychosocial physical trauma experienced by our beautiful people and our earth.

> The land takes care to embrace us
> With its nourishment,
> Speak to us in our language,
> Give us stories to educate us
> And listen to the songs of beauty
> We sing in its honor
> —Otis Parrish, Kashaya Pomo Elder
>   (Nelson, 2002)

Tsalagi Morning Song

Although I have begun this chapter by recognizing our mothers, grandmothers, our families, and ancestors who have taught us about the interconnectedness of all life and of our responsibilities, it is our practice, as well, when we gather together to open with a song.

Singing is an important part of ceremony. Our ceremonies serve two basic functions. On the one hand, they remind us of our duties and responsibilities and on the other, they embody the message through ritual and symbols. In this way, we engage our bodies, minds, and spirits. Our song pierces the sky, and the drum is understood to be the heartbeat of the nation.

I acknowledge the Tsalagi (Cherokee) Morning song passed down in the family of Rita Coolidge and shared with Robbie Robertson (Mohawk, Six Nations). This song connects the Tsalagi people with the Haudenosaunee—it is a song from the Aniyunwiya (the Principal People) to greet each new day giving thanks to the sun rising. With light and warmth from the sun, we birth another day with our song of welcome and thankfulness.

A song that asks the spirits of the earth and sky—Thus weave for us a garment of brightness that we may walk fittingly where the birds sing—

Haudenosaunee Thanksgiving Address: Reconciliation with the Universe

The Thanksgiving Address came to indigenous people from the Haudenosaunee. The address is a prayer of reconciliation with the universe in that it:

- Pays tribute to the multiple forms of life on Mother Earth, including the plants and animals, the natural elements, the four directions, and the four seasons
- Acknowledges, supports, and sustains human beings on earth (Stokes & Kanawahienton, 1993)

Tom Porter, an elder from the Six Nations, says that giving thanks is a way both to acknowledge all that exists and to honor all life forms on Mother Earth, including the stones we call our grandfathers that are used during the sweat lodge ceremony (Haudenosaunee. Retrieved from www.kahnawakelonghouse.com). The act of giving thanks includes recognizing energy forces that sustain life, although these forces may be both invisible and unheard.

Acknowledging and giving thanks in the aboriginal culture is a way of reminding the people of their duties and responsibilities to live in balance and harmony with all life. It both identifies and pays attention to the interdependency of life forms and the inherent need to be respectful of them.

Greetings to the Natural World

There is an ancient tradition still followed today by original people to acknowledge our ancestors and to offer our greetings to the natural world. For the Haundenosaunee of the Six Nations, this tradition dates back over 1,000 years to the formation of the Great Law of Peace created by a person called the Peacemaker. These words said before all else are part of the Thanksgiving Address that is spoken at the opening and closing of important gatherings held by the Six Nations people located in southwestern Ontario. These people include Haudenosaunee from upstate New York and Canada—Mohawk, Oneida, Cayuga, Onondaga, Seneca, and Tuscarora (Stokes & Kanawahienton, 1993).

Ohén:ton Karihwatéhkwen: Words before All Else

Ohén:ton Karihwatéhkwen—words before all else—is the Thanksgiving Address (Stokes & Kanawahienton, 1993). It begins by acknowledging The People (Onkwehshn'a) who have gathered together to recognize that the cycles of life continue and that we have been given the duty to live in balance and harmony with each other and all living things. So now we bring our minds together as one as we give greetings and thanks to each other as people. Now our minds are one.

It is important to note that this is the only place in the Thanksgiving Address where the people are recognized. The focus of the address is to ensure that the people remember to live in such a way that there is the needed balance and harmony in our relations with the earth that are critical for survival. It also ensures an understanding that human beings, the people, are only one small part of our vast universe. Original people understood over 1,000 years ago that the possibility for human survival was interwoven with the caretaking role of humans regarding the world around us. This is an important message about the long-standing connection between our indigenous peoples of the world and our capacity to sustain ourselves on Mother Earth.

Earth Mother: Iethi'nisténha Ohontsia

Next, the address acknowledges our Earth Mother—*Iethi'nisténha Ohontsia*—by giving thanks as " . . . she gives us all that we need for life. She supports our feet as we walk upon her. It gives us joy that she continues to care for us as she has from the beginning of time. To our Mother, we send greetings and thanks. Now our minds are one—'Ehtho niiohtónha'k ne onkwa'nikónra" (Stokes & Kanawahienton, 1993).

Environmentalist David Suzuki (Suzuki, McConnell, & Mason, 2002) says that "every bit of the nutrition that we consume to create our bodies and minds was once living and almost all of it came from the soil" (p. 23). This way of thinking offers the possibility of a deepened and immediate connection with Mother Earth. It is important to remember that we are the earth, as our indigenous people have suggested, and that what we call the environment is not separate from us nor is it simply a figure of speech. As in all things, we originated from the four sacred elements of water, air, fire, and earth (Suzuki, McConnell, & Mason, 2002, p. 22).

Indigenous people have what we call our Medicine Wheel Teachings that use the ancient symbol of the circle to signify the four directions, the four seasons, and the four elements (earth, water, air, fire). Renowned scientist and spokesperson for the elders, Suzuki, points out that we are fire because all of the energy required for growth comes from the sun through photosynthesis, and our nutrition comes from what we consume to grow, develop, and maintain our bodies and minds. Perhaps many people have framed the issue wrongly, that is, "there is no environment out there separate from us" (Suzuki, McConnell, & Mason, 2002). Perhaps aboriginal people are right—we are the Earth, created like everything else from the four elements of water, air fire, and earth. This capacity to shift the image and reconnect our bodies and minds allows for a deep Mother Earth relationship.

Sean Kane (1998) in his book *Wisdom of the Mythtellers* says:

> What the myth tellers and oral poets know is the truth cannot be captured in a solitary idea. It is alive and uncatchable. It tumbles about in the polyphonic stories told by the animals and birds and mountains and rivers and trees—not in some taxonomy of their separate taxonomies but in the play of exchanges among them, which is the only way we really know nature. . . . those stories are still there in the earth, to be heard by anyone who has the patience to listen. (p. 255)

One way of thinking about myths, to paraphrase Bringhurst (1999), is to imagine doorways between realms. The journey between worlds is one of the basic themes. Perhaps we move through doorways of the story just as listeners we move through worlds "beside, behind, within our own" (p. 407).

The story is the experience—it is a voyage into another realm. According to Stokes and Kanawahienton from the Tracking Project at Six Nations (1993), it was Mohawk Jake Swamp's original vision to develop an adaptation of the

Thanksgiving Address to make it accessible to a broader range of people. The text used in this chapter is the modified English version: John Stokes and Kanawahienton. It is here to remind us of the original oral account *Ohén:ton Karihwatéhkwen: Words before All Else*.

The Waters: Ohneka'shón á

These four elements—fire, air, water, earth—can be discussed using a Medicine Wheel approach based on ancient teachings of indigenous peoples and recognized in petroglyphs and pictographs. At the end of each statement of thanks and with one voice, we say, *"'Ehtho niiohtnha'k ne onkwa'nikónra"* or "now our minds are one."

What follows after acknowledging the people and Mother Earth is to remember the waters (*Ohneka'shón á*):

> ... Water is life. We know its power in many forms—waterfalls and rain, mists, and streams, rivers and oceans. With one mind, we send greetings and thanks to the spirit of Water. Now our minds are one. (Stokes & Kanawahienton, 1993)

Closing of the Thanksgiving Address

The *Thanksgiving Address* as the spoken word continues then to acknowledge and offer thanks to all that supports us. This includes the fish, plants, food plants, medicine herbs, animals, trees, birds, four winds, thunderers, sun, grandmother moon and stars, the enlightened teachers, and the Creator. The closing words are worth remembering precisely because they recognize at the end of the address or *Our Words before all Else*, the possibility of leaving something out. The address reminds us that if " ... something was forgotten, we leave it to each individual to send such greetings and thanks in their own way—And now our minds are one" (Stokes & Kanawahienton, 1993). These closing words ensure that all things are recognized through naming and acknowledging and that the people have a responsibility for remembering. It is this inclusivity that serves as a guiding social principle of Haudenosaunee culture. The address closes by suggesting that "of all the things we have named, it was not our intention to leave anything out." Moreover, we are reminded to do the remembering in our own way.

Linda Hogan (1995) suggests that ceremony is about mending the broken connection between us and all that supports us. Ceremony involves restructuring the mind so that we create a relationship not only with each other, the people, but also with the earth. For sunrise or moon ceremonies, for example, we offer medicine (tobacco) to the earth or the fire (one of the four elements that includes earth, water, air, fire). Hogan says that this reorganization is accomplished by making a kind of inner map, "a geography of the human spirit and the rest of the world ... we bring together the fragments of our lives in a sacred act of renewal, and we re-establish our connections with others" and the Earth (p. 40).

Sakarihwahóton/ *Closing Words*

We have now arrived at the place where we end our words. Of all the things we have named, it was not our intention to leave anything out. If something was forgotten, we leave it to each individual to send such greetings and thanks in their own way.

—John Stokes and Kanawahienton (1993)

Ehtho niiohtónha'k ne onkwa'nikónra~~~Now our minds are one.

These words are based on the idea that our world, or Mother Earth, is apart of us and cannot be taken for granted. This connection with her is not only with our minds or intellects. We join together in ceremony to align our hearts and minds as one and to open the connection between our words and our lived experience with Mother Earth. It is a way of saying that as a collective " . . . our minds are one." This suggests that at the closing of the *Thanksgiving Address*, we have acknowledged all the gifts that are life sustaining.

This statement of thanks is a reminder of our sacred trust with the earth and all of creation. It, of necessity, includes human feelings and emotions as well as a recognition of our fragile yet resilient human bodies. The Thanksgiving Address acknowledges a relationship that supports all life on earth and in the most basic sense, this is a sacred trust.

INTERNATIONAL ISSUES: MOTHER EARTH HAS THE RIGHT TO EXIST

At an international level for indigenous people, there are parallel concerns about Mother Earth and worldviews that are harmonious with the Haudenosaunee Thanksgiving Address. Also there have been recent developments that are encouraging about a major shift in interest at the global level concerning our relationship with Mother Earth. For example, Ecuador has one of the highest indigenous populations in South America (20%), most of whom are Quichua, and in 2008 Ecuador became the first nation to constitutionally recognize nature's rights to "exist, flourish and evolve" (Mark, 2011a, p. 11). Thus, it codified a new system of environmental protection based on indigenous values and a deep ecological understanding of our relationship with the earth. It is important to recognize that this political move by Ecuador reflects beliefs and traditions of the people of Ecuador and that it was ignored by media in the United States (Mychalejko, 2008).

Two years after Ecuador declared nature's constitutional right to exist, the Plurinational State of Bolivia (which recently elected its first indigenous president) gathered 35,000 people in the city of Cochabamba to recognize Mother Earth's rights. They developed a Peoples Agreement on Climate Change and the Rights of Mother Earth, affirming Rights and Practices of Living Well. This was part of an international move to acknowledge the earth as a living entity—giving her the same status as humans in an effort to restore harmony with nature and respect for life. For example, the preamble to the document on the rights of Mother Earth document states that:

- ... we are all part of Mother Earth, an indivisible, living community of interrelated and interdependent beings with a common destiny
- ... gratefully acknowledging that Mother Earth is the source of life, nourishment and learning and provides everything we need to live well
- ... convinced that in an interdependent living community it is not possible to recognize the rights of only human beings without causing an imbalance within Mother Earth
- affirming that to guarantee human rights it is necessary to recognize and defend the rights of Mother Earth and all beings in her and that there are existing cultures, practices and laws that do so ...

Although the UN climate change negotiations in Bonn, Germany on June 13, 2011, failed to close the gap between how much climate pollution we need to reduce and how much countries are committed to reducing, there was hope for change at the UN Security Council meetings that followed in New York beginning July 20, 2011. What appears encouraging is a move to acknowledge and enshrine in agreements at an international level that nature as well as humans have inherent rights. This attempt to ensure rights for Mother Earth guarantees the potential for a balanced and healthy relationship between humans and Mother Earth. The document shares similar basic understandings that are at the core of the 1,000-year-old Thanksgiving address that is, it acknowledges Mother Earth as a living being with whom we have a spiritual, complementary, and interdependent relationship.

The *World People's Conference on Climate Change and the Rights of Mother Earth* forged the "*People's Agreement* in April 2010 that talks about the wounding of our Mother Earth and the need to restore harmony with nature and among human beings. It also speaks to a concern about the parallel between the issue of equality among human beings, and the need to be in harmony with nature. They discuss the idea of living well, recognizing "Mother Earth as a living being with whom we have an indivisible, interdependent, complementary and spiritual relationship." (World People's Conference on Climate Change and the Rights of Mother Earth, 2010, p. 2) In their comments on climate change, they suggest the need to recognize Mother Earth as "a living being" and as the source of life and to forge a new system based on principles of (1) harmony and balance among all and with all things; (2) interdependent, complementary, and spiritual relationships, based on solidarity and equality; and (3) people in harmony with nature.

According to the Elder, destruction of any part of the earth
does immediate harm to all living things—
none can survive unless all survive
                                    —Marmon Silko, 1996, p. 131

An interesting item and ultimately a turning point in our understanding is located in an historically distant reflection reported by Spencer (1959) from an earlier colonial period. It reveals the interface between our Inuit peoples of the north and the colonizing forces that arrived from Europe. The newcomers arrived with an antithetical worldview and a mindset on making North America their land—*owning the Earth*. This worldview is based on a different cultural story than that of our original people. We see the collision between the colonial imposition of the Biblical account of creation based on a system of discourse where writing was the privileged vehicle for understanding (the Bible), whereas the local Inuit people were immersed in an oral tradition where images and stories offer understandings. In this cosmology, the earth (the land) is alive and the animals are our relatives:

> It was related that the first missionaries at Barrow told of the creation according to the Biblical account. Many people, it was said, refused to accept this and were reported as having said "Very well, God made the world, but Raven made it first."
>
> —Spencer, 1959

We all have our stories that define who we are, where we come from, and how we see ourselves as people of the earth. We experience Mother Earth from different frames of reference—some are based on sustaining and nourishing the world around us, and others are not. These understandings are embedded in guiding principles for a way of being in the world, or as the German word suggests from the ecology literature, it becomes a *weltanschauung*, or a worldview. Our worldview is related to human values and attitudes toward relations among the people at local, tribal, community, nation, world, and metaphysical levels (Alfred, 1995). One level of identity is nested within the other. It all arises out of place—the land or Mother Earth. A particular way of being in the world emerges for indigenous people from around the world that challenges the West today to live in peace and harmony with Mother Earth and to have her come alive in our lived experience as a reflection of our worldview—one that supports our web of relations. It is a way of being in the world that seeks harmony and balance in life, and recognizes that the world or Mother Earth is a living organism. Environmentalist David Suzuki (Suzuki, McConnell, & Mason, 2002) says, "If we grasp that we are the world we depend on, then we will find where we truly belong and get on with seeking a way to live in harmony within a rich, vibrant community of living things" (p. 2).

The *Thanksgiving Address* is predicated on the idea that "the world cannot be taken for granted, that a spiritual communication of thankfulness and acknowledgement of all living things must be given to align the minds and hearts of the people with Nature" (Stokes & Kanawahienton, 1993). This Haudenosaunee perspective serves as the foundation for this chapter and offers an indigenous environmental weltanschauung or worldview. Tsalagi writer Thomas King (2003) argues that Native literature has a sort of magic. As with other literatures, it is not in the themes of the stories—identity, isolation, loss, ceremony, community, maturation, home—it is in the way meaning is refracted by cosmology, the way understanding is shaped by cultural paradigms (2003).

Some years the desert receives abundant rain, other years there is too little rain, and
    sometimes there is so much rain that floods cause destruction.
But rain itself is neither innocent nor guilty.
The rain is simply itself
                                                    —Leslie Marmon Silko, 1996, p. 64

CONCLUSION: RESPECT, RESPONSIBILITY, RECIPROCITY, AND REVERENCE: *KUNOLUNKWA*

To be sure, *Kunolunkwa*, or *love*, is a root word for this chapter about indigenous ways of being in the world that sustain the environment by fostering a connection with Mother Earth and creating harmony and balance based on principles of respect, responsibility, reciprocity, and reverence (Alvernaz Mulcahy, 2001; Archibald, 2008). (See Figure 10. 1, *Kunolunkwa*.) The figure represents a Medicine Wheel, which is a significant symbol that arises in the ancient teaching of indigenous people and can be found in petroglyphs and pictographs—drawings and stone circles. Teachings of the sacred circle are central to many tribal groups in the Americas and denote a lifetime of learning about ways of being. The circle represents the cycle of all life. (Alvernaz Mulcahy, 2001). It connotes a deep sense of connection with the land along with the development of caring and responsible relationships that ensure an ongoing state of well-being (life sustaining ways of being with the earth) regarding the air, water, land and all of our creatures and plants that maintain a balanced state of being that supports life on planet earth. These relations are implied in the Thanksgiving Address when we acknowledge all that nourishes and supports life—the people, earth mother, the waters, fish, plants, food plants, medicine herbs, the animals, the trees, birds, four winds, the thunderers, the sun and grandmother moon, the stars, the enlightened teachers, the creator.

Figure 10.1

Kunolunkwa means *love* in *Onyota': a'ka (Oneida, Haudenosaunee). The Haudenosaunee People* (Six Nations including Oneida, Mohawk, etc.) hold the notion that our relations with Mother Earth and each other are *sacred*. This implies a set of qualities or *ways of being in the world* (relational ones) that embody the notion of *love* i.e., *respect, responsibility, reciprocity, and reverence.* The figure (Medicine Wheel) represents "all my relations" or a set of qualities (embedded in appropriate actions) that are *ways of being* that reflect *love* and foster a connection with mother earth that creates harmony and balance.

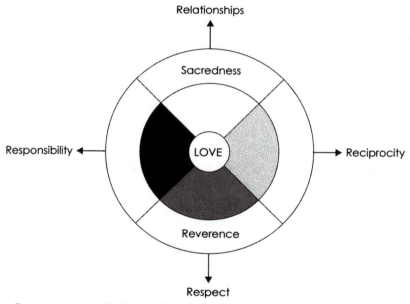

ALL MY RELATIONS: *Kunolunkwa*

Relationships

Sacredness

Responsibility   LOVE   Reciprocity

Reverence

Respect

Note: From printer materials, Kirkness, Verna J., Barnhardt, Ray. *First Nations and higher education: The four R's: respect, relevance, reciprocity, responsibility. Adapted by Gloria Alvernaz Mulcahy. King's College. The University of Western Ontario and Alannah Young. First Nations House of Learning, The University of British Columbia.* May 2000. © mm 2000

CLOSING WORDS: *SAKARIHWAHOTON*

We have now arrived at the place where we end our words.
Of all the things we have named it was not our intention to leave
    anything out.
If something was forgotten, we leave it to each individual to send
    such greetings
and thanks in their own way.
Ehtho niiohtónha'k ne onkwa'nikónra.

~~~~~~~~~~~~~~~~~~~~~~~~~~~~~~~~~~

*We are looking for a tongue that speaks with reverence for life,
searching for an ecology of mind. It is not only the vocabulary of
science we desire. We want a language of that different yield.
A yield rich as the harvests of earth*

—Linda Hogan, 1995

REFERENCES

Aboriginal Affairs and Nothern Development Canada. (1996). *Highlights from the Report of the Royal Commission on Aborginal Peoples.* Retrieved from http://www.aadnc-aandc.gc.ca/eng/1100100014597.

Aboriginal Healing Foundation. (2003). *Directory of residential schools in Canada.* Ottawa: Aboriginal Healing Foundation.

Aboriginal Healing Foundation. (2004). *Aboriginal domestic violence in Canada.* Ottawa: Aboriginal Healing Foundation.

Alfred, G. (1995). *Heeding the voices of the ancestors: Kahnawake Mohawk politics and the rise of Native nationalism.* Don Mills, Ontario: Oxford University Press.

Alfred, T. G. (1999). *Peace, power, righteousness: An indigenous manifesto.* Toronto: Oxford University Press Canada.

Alvernaz Mulcahy, G. (2001). Medicine wheel teachings: A language of healing as rich as the harvests of earth. In P. Prina, C. Shelley, & C. Thompson (Eds.), Society *of the United Kingdom and the Institute for Individual Psychology YearBook: 2001* (pp. 88–103). Chippenham, Wiltshire, Great Britain: Antony Rowe.

Alvernaz Mulcahy, G. (2002). From healing wounds to creating celebrations: Traditional pathways Canada's Original Peoples. In A. Pritz (Ed.), *Globalized psychotherapy* (pp. 735–760). Vienna, Austria: Facultas Universitatsverlag.

Alvernaz Mulcahy, G. (2005a). The role of aboriginal identity in a holistic approach to healing. In P. Baguma, S. Madu, & A. Pritz (Eds.), *Cross-cultural dialogue on psychotherapy in Africa* (pp. 55–68). World Council for Psychotherapy. Sovenga, South Africa: The University of the North.

Alvernaz Mulcahy, G. (2005b). Traditional healing: Pathways of orality, conversivity, survivance and sovenance. In N. S. Madu (Ed.), *Mental health and psychotherapy in Africa* (pp. 480–509). Polokwane (Pietersburg), South Africa: University of Limpopo Press of the University of Limpopo for the World Council for Psychotherapy, Sovenga, South Africa.

Alvernaz Mulcahy, G. (2007). *Indigenous women in action: Voices from Vancouver.* Documentary film: Community Interviews Robert Pickton Trial. G. Alvernaz Mulcahy, Director/Producer; Camera; S. Kaplun Editors, Balance Productions, London ON.

Alvernaz Mulcahy, G. (2008). *Symposium on trauma and disaster.* Fifth World Congress for Psychotherapy, Beijing China.

Alvernaz Mulcahy, G. (2009). *Song-lines.* Borderlands & bloodlines. Cape Croker, Canada: Kegedonce Press.

Alvernaz Mulcahy, G. (2010). *Oppression rocks the cradle: Violence against indigenous women.* Honolulu, HI: Healing our Spirits Worldwide.

Alvernaz Mulcahy, G., & Brass, E. (2006). *Vision Quest 2005: Healing our communities.* Seventh World Indigenous Women & Wellness Conference. The University of British Columbia, Vancouver.

Alvernaz Mulcahy, G., & Rtichie, D. (2005). *Traditional knowledge and aboriginal healing practices: Reaching forward.* World Conference on Psychotherapy. Prevention of Family Violence, Banff Alberta, Canada.

Anderson, E. N. (Ed.). (1996). Bird of paradox: The unpublished writings of Wilson Duff. Surrey, BC: Hancock House Publishers.

Anderson, K. (2000). *A recognition of being: Reconstructing Native womanhood.* Toronto: Sumach Press.

Anderson, K., & Lawrence, B., (2003). *Strong women stories: Native vision and community survival.* Toronto: Sumach Press.

Anonymous. (2006). A song that asks the spirits of the earth and sky. (poem). As cited in "The Cherokee Song." In Sacred Songs & Chants Lyrics. Michael Drake. http://www.lulu.com/items/volume_64/5228000/5228996/1/preview/Sacred_Songs__Chants_Lyrics.pdf. Retrieved on June 7, 2012.

Archibald, J. (2008). *Indigenous story work: Educating the heart, mind, body and spirit.* Vancouver: UBC Press.

Armstrong, J. (1998). The disempowerment of first North American native people and empowerment through their writing. In T. Goldies & D. Moses (Eds.), *An anthology of Canadian native literature in English* (pp. 239–242). Don Mills, ON: Oxford University Press.

Berman, H., Alvernaz Mulcahy, G., Forchuk, C., Edmunds, K., Haldendy, A., & Lopez, R. (2011). Uprooted and displaced: A critical narrative study of homeless, aboriginal, and newcomer girls in Canada. In C. Forchuk, Csiernik, R., & E. Jensen (Eds.), *Homelessness, housing, and mental health: Finding truths: Creating change.* Toronto: Canadian Scholars' Press.

Bringhurst, R. (1999). A story as sharp as a knife: *The classical Haida mythtellers and their world.* Vancouver: Douglas & McIntyre.

Chrisjohn, R. D. (1998). Speech by Dr. Roland Chrisjohn delivered in Edmonton, Alberta. http://sisis.nativeweb.org/resschool/chrisjohn.html. Retrieved on June 7, 2012.

Chrisjohn, R. D., Young, S., & Maraun, M. (1997). *The circle game: Shadows and substance in the Indian residential school experience in Canada.* Penticton, BC: Theytus Press.

Chrisjohn, R. D., Young, S., & Maraun, M. (2006). *The circle game: Shadows and substance in the Indian residential school experience in Canada.* Revised edition. Penticton, BC: Theytus Press.

Gilbert, J. (1996). *The Trail of Tears across Missouri.* Columbia, Missouri: University of Missouri Press.

Gunn Allen, P. (1983). *The woman who owned the shadows.* San Francisco: Aunt Lute.

Haudenosaunee. (website). http://www.kahnawakelonghouse.com. Reviewed on June 7, 2012.

Hogan, L. (1995). *Dwellings: A spiritual history of the world.* New York: W. W. Norton Company.

Jensen, D. (2011, May/June). To Live or Not to Live: The danger of the tragic hero mindset. Retrieved August 10, 2011 from Orion Magazine Website: www.orionmagazine.org/index/php/article/6266/.

Kane, S. (1998). *Wisdom of the mythtellers.* Peterborough, ON: Broadview Press.

King, T. (2003). *The truth about stories: A Native narrative.* Toronto: House of Anansi Press.

Mark, J. (2011a). South America: Bolivia decrees rights for Mother Nature. *Earth Island Journal, 26*(2), 10–12.

Mark, J. (2011b). We are all endangered now. *Earth Island Journal, 26*(2), 2.

Melnyk, G. (2003). *Poetics of naming.* Edmonton, Alberta: University of Alberta Press.

Mychalejko, C. (2008). Ecuador's constitution gives rights to nature. *Upside Down World,* September 25, 2008.

Native Women's Association of Canada. (2010a). *Voices of our sisters inspirit: A report to families and communities* (2nd ed.).

Nelson, M. (2002). Language and the earth. *Re-Vision: A Journal of Consciousness & Transformation.* Retrieved from http://www.heldref.org.

Razack, S. (Ed.). (2002). *Race, space, and the law: Unmapping a white settler society.* Toronto: Between the Lines.

Silko, L. M. (1996). *Yellow woman and a beauty of the spirit.* New York: Simon & Schuster.

Spencer, R. F. (1959). *The North Alaskan Eskimo. A study in ecology and society.* Bureau of American Ethnology. Bulletin 171. Washington, DC: Smithsonian Institution.

Stokes, J., & Kanawahienton. (1993). *Thanksgiving address: Greetings to the natural world: Ohén: ton Karihwaténhkwen: Words before all else.* Corrales, NM: Native Self-Sufficiency Center, Six Nations Indian Museum, Tracking Project: Tree of Peace Society.

Suzuki, D., McConnell, A., & Mason, A. (2002). *The sacred balance: Rediscovering our place in Nature.* Vancouver: Greystone Books.

van der Kolk, B. A. (2006). *Clinical implications of neuroscience research in PTSD.* New York: Academy of Science.

van der Kolk, B. A., Roth S., Pelcovitz D., & Spinazzola, J. (2005). Disorders of extreme stress: The empirical foundation of a complex adaptation to trauma. *Journal of Trauma and Stress, 18*(5), 389–399.

World People's Conference on Climate Change and the Rights of Mother Earth. (April 22, 2010). Peoples Agreement. http://pwccc.wordpress.com/programa/ Retrieved on June 7, 2012.

11

Our Information: Availability, Communication, and Perception

Anna T. Onishi and Alexander P. Steger

We live in a world in which we are bombarded with information. From ticker tapes to advertisements to Facebook, information has fundamentally changed the way we interact with others and how we perceive ourselves. Corporations and political entities already effectively use communications and information to influence perceptions, create demand for goods and services, and generate goodwill. Recent estimates are that the average American is exposed to 5,000 advertisements daily (Johnson & Walker-Smith, 2009), and global advertisement spending will only continue to grow, perhaps exponentially. But there is a positive side to this massive influx of data and hyperconnectivity—new media can facilitate emotional support during times of crisis. We can take advantage of the near-instant speed and global reach of communications to connect with loved ones and ease their anxieties. This can be especially helpful during rapidly developing events such as the Fukushima nuclear meltdown and the BP oil spill.

The Internet, and news media in particular, are part of a communications revolution analogous to Gutenberg's printing press. People use these outlets frequently, even daily in many cases. Usage fulfills curiosity and provides comfort. Hardly casual tools, these means of communication are an instant way to contact others, a way to conduct many-to-many relationships in real time. These new forms of communication may only supplement existing channels (Eisner, 2011), but more importantly, they connect us and make us better able to respond to others and provide emotional support. In contrast to the quickly adapting general public, well-established organizations such as governments and large corporations have been slower in adapting to the new age of instantaneous, mass-scale communication. This could be, in part, due to a lack of understanding about how interpersonal communication styles have adapted to technological advancement.

There are two effective tools to manage negative events: positioning and technology. When these two tools are used in concert, messages can be strong and pervasive. One example of movement in this direction is Dell Computer. Dell has recognized the power of new media and its impact on growth and profitability, and it has invested in a customer advocacy SWAT (special weapons and tactics) team. This team scours new media such as Twitter, YouTube, blogs, Facebook, and RSS feeds with an eye to quickly identify and respond to customer discontent. Feedback and answers to customer service questions are instant (as fast as 15 minutes), which assuages many concerns. For concerns that are not resolved, Dell has created a new infrastructure. This customer advocacy SWAT team is the nerve center and is directly connected to all of the product groups, marketing, and public relations centers to alert, respond to, and resolve potential and real problems. Dell's vision to control, triage, and enhance customer contentment and ultimately profitability is at the forefront of industry.

In managing communication following environmental disasters, however, companies are less successful. The most notable recent example is how BP mishandled the oil spill along the Gulf Coast of the United States. This is a case study on how miscalculations in perceptions of urgency, culture, and lack of brand control can worsen already sensitive situations. In a painful example of these gaps, BP former chief executive officer (CEO) Tony Hayward went yachting while chairman Carl-Henric Svanberg promised the public that the company cared for "the small people" (Gross, 2010). Yachting was clearly not consistent with their message of caring for the small people. Public relations efforts to repair BP's damaged reputation will take years, but the negative impact to their image could have been reduced through proper use of empathy and benevolence, both critical emotional factors. BP could have embraced new media and acted quickly to stymie brand damage online that bled out into more traditional forms such as TV and newspapers.

Many people have (unknowingly or knowingly) embraced the emotional transparency of real-time exchanges through social media (e.g., Facebook and Twitter). New media has become interwoven with everyday life and can provide interpersonal connectedness despite geographic disconnectedness. When a rapidly changing catastrophic event occurs, such as the Fukushima meltdown, technology and communication have an important role in influencing both public perception and emotional well-being. However, to take advantage of the promise of new technology, we need to understand the specific ways we might communicate using that technology in different contexts.

INTERNET SURVEY

To better understand contemporary interpersonal communication styles, we developed an online survey that we administered to 315 participants using the

Amazon.com Mechanical Turk Web site. Participants rated how often they used different forms of communication[1] on a scale of 1 to 5, from least often to most often. The forms of communication were:

1. Social networking Web sites (Facebook, MySpace, etc.)
2. Twitter and similar Web sites, instant messaging (AOL Instant Messenger, MSN Messenger, Gmail Chat, etc.)
3. YouTube or similar Web sites
4. Blogs
5. Internet message boards and forums
6. Face-to-face conversations
7. E-mail
8. Telephone conversations
9. Radio
10. Television
11. Handwritten letters

Principal Components Analysis

A Principal Components Analysis (PCA) of the 315 responses indicated that these communication methods could be simplified into four broader groups.

Instant Media

Facebook, Twitter, instant messaging, text messaging, and YouTube are modern forms of communication characterized by instantaneous transmission— you have probably seen "viral" videos on YouTube, which receive millions of views in just a few days, or have heard of celebrities with tens of thousands of Twitter subscribers who receive an update whenever the star goes shopping. Interestingly, the PCA included cellphone text messaging and instant messaging in this group, which are generally person-to-person forms of communication, rather than the broad audiences seen in Facebook, Twitter, and YouTube.

Blogging and Internet Message Boards

Reading and updating a blog and participating in Internet message boards and message groups comprise the second type of communication asked about in this survey. Blogs and message boards are generally slower in transmission than Facebook and Twitter because conversations, called threads, can evolve over days, months, or even years. Blog and message board content ranges from niche

---

[1] In this study, we were primarily interested in two-way forms of communication, so media such as newspapers and magazines were omitted. Television and radio, however, were included to contrast with these forms of interpersonal communication styles. As we expected, television and radio usage were relatively homogenous across the board, with one exception (the Info Junkies).

special-interest groups to mainstream news, and authors range from personal acquaintances to corporate bloggers. They can have very small or very wide audiences and are participatory in nature. Anyone can read and communicate in the form of comments or posts, although the percentage of people commenting or posting feedback remains small in comparison to the total number of readers.

Personal Communication

Personal forms of communication include e-mail, telephone conversations, and face-to-face conversations. These are the methods with which we are most familiar. Transmission of information by these channels tends to be generally slower than other methods because each person has only a limited amount of "face time."

Traditional Media

Radio, television, and written letters are all traditional methods of communication and, except for written letters, are not participatory. While some radio programs and television shows feature call-in segments, these are utilized by only a small percentage of total viewers and listeners. Thus, television and radio are one-to-many forms of communication in which one source broadcasts information without the opportunity for feedback. Information received via the visual and auditory channels of television and radio can be emotionally compelling.

Cluster Analysis

Within this framework of four broad types of communication, we next performed a two-step cluster analysis that categorized each survey participant into four main communication styles, each with a different emphasis on different communication mediums. Because the sample was based on the Amazon.com Mechanical Turk population, there is a potential for sampling bias, that is, the participants may not be a representative sample of our population as a whole, thus possibly skewing the results. However, results do show that, within this population, these different communication styles definitely exist and so provide a starting point for the discussion.

Now Generation

These participants had a strong preference for instantaneous communication via Internet and cellphone technologies. They actively participated in social networking Web sites, instant messaging, and text messaging (category one), and they read significantly fewer blogs and internet message boards than did other participants (category two). They utilized traditional media of television and radio (category four) about the same as other participants did. Although new media generally includes all of categories one and two, the Now Generation group clearly preferred "now media"—instant, broad-reaching, and collaborative communication.

Bloggers

Participants in this category had a strong preference for blogs and message boards (category two) compared to other participants. In contrast to the Now Generation, they had a significantly lower usage of television, radio, and personal letters (category four) but had about the same usage of social networks and instant messaging technologies.

Info Junkies

These respondents had the highest preference for television, radio, and personal letters (category four). They also used blogs and message boards significantly more than other participants (category two), and used instant messaging and social networks somewhat more than other participants (category one). Overall, these participants are well-connected, rapid, and voracious consumers of information (they are not primary producers), as indicated by their usage of television and radio, with its one-to-many content and one-way communication.

Introverts

These participants simply communicated less than all other groups in all categories.

Category three media (telephone, e-mail, and conversation) were about the same in all groups of participants.

Follow-Up

Next, we posed a hypothetical scenario involving a nuclear meltdown and asked participants how likely they would be to use each form of communication in each of four cases: the day of the event, one day after, one week after, and one month after. Incidentally, this survey was administered roughly two weeks after the Fukushima nuclear meltdown in Japan. Across all communication styles, participants tended to prefer category one media to send and receive communication closer to the event. Why is this? We speculate that because media in categories one and two directly connect people with each other, it can provide the most immediate emotional connection for relief and empathy during traumatic experiences. The availability of near instant, many-to-many communication is especially important today when many people have significant personal relationships with family and friends who live thousands of miles away.

Communication and access to information during times of disaster is crucial for survivors, aid workers, and survivors' loved ones. Access to this essential information can improve post-disaster trauma effects, disease, and public safety (Hamilton, 2008). The Disaster Information Management Research Center (DIMRC) was created by the National Library of Medicine (NLM) to collect, organize, and disseminate information to aid in the management of trauma following natural, accidental, or deliberate disasters.

In 2005, after Hurricane Katrina, the public used library databases and networks to access health information, obtain information on recovery efforts, perform rehabilitation efforts, and aid in tracking displaced persons. Working in conjunction with responder networks and collaborating on various tasks and training efforts, these resources will become an essential mechanism for communication during disasters. The NLM, through the DIMRC has committed to this mission, as evidenced by the creation of a long-range plan through 2016.

With a growing desire for connectedness, fueled by the availability of cellular and computer technology, we are increasingly less dependent on traditional one-way media such as newspapers, television, and radio. We are often savvy enough to recognize propaganda for what it is, and the intense negative public reaction following the BP disaster exemplifies this. Public outrage conflagrated through the instant channels of new media resulted in global dissent as mistakes by the embattled BP grew exponentially, and their public image spun out of control.

To better understand the psychological impact of this disaster, the authors developed a 62-item survey via SurveyMonkey.com that was taken by over 300 respondents. Factor analysis revealed two small but significant groups of respondents.

Prepared Militants

Respondents in this category indicated that they were stockpiling reserves of food, ammunition, and money in preparation for the aftermath of the oil spill. They believed that they had to "fight for their rights" and that a military struggle was likely to occur because of the spill.

Religious Fundamentalists

These participants indicated that they believed that the aftermath of the oil spill was a period of upheaval of religious significance. Most felt that "God's plan would be revealed," and some even believed that the Messiah would come during this time.

Although two significant factors accounted for 18 percent of the responses, these were similar in tone to two of the six primary factors in a similar survey about reactions to global climate change (Lamar et al., 2008). In that study, the factors included: general population, prepared militants, religious fundamentalists, psychoid leaders, disturbed followers, and corporate sociopaths.

The emergence of these two factors, however small, provides meaningful information about the long-term psychological impact of the BP oil spill. In addition to the physical effects of the disaster, the outrage of these participants could fuel their paranoid beliefs or religious fervor and worsen psychological distress in a population already vulnerable to mental health difficulties. By failing to leverage new media during the weeks following the spill, BP's communication was limited to the one-way, receive-only transmissions of television, radio, and news outlets. The organization did not realize the significant psychological impact of the disaster. Without a reciprocal channel of communication, the two-way communication necessary for healing and support left the victims feeling isolated, disconnected, unheard, unimportant, and without control—a downward emotional spiral. The only emotional outlet people had was through mutual support, but to effectively heal, everyone must contribute—including BP. Without the organization's participation in the communicative process, victims can only assume the worst—that BP does not care about them at all. That is not a comforting thought.

The psychological impacts of living in the new media age are palpable. Instantaneous communications are opening up the faucet of interaction, intentionally and unintentionally, and we can often get information directly from its source. A new, grittier reality is readily accessible and can be broadcast unfiltered to the world. Although its impact can be psychologically overwhelming, the influx of new data and viewpoints has the potential to ease anxieties.

LIMITATIONS

It should be noted that participants were not selected randomly, but rather, through a convenience sample of available workers at mturk.com. Therefore, each participant had Internet access and a computer, over-representing this segment of the population and related forms of communication.

CONCLUSION

We live in a rapidly changing world and we are surrounded by media and advertising. Internet resources allow us the opportunity to gather significant information both quickly and over time. New social-networking channels also provide us with the chance to connect with others and share information and feelings. There is also the potential to be more closely connected with others. According to Turkle (2011), in her recent book *Alone Together*, these connections are, however, not always meaningful and frequently result in increased loneliness. Yet, humanity, compassion, and all innate emotions will always find their way through innovation to keep us bonded with others and true to our human spirit and core.

Technology is neutral. It is the application and audience that can transform it for greater purpose or toxicity. Our new interconnectedness can augment the footprint of groups like the prepared militants and the religious fundamentalists. People and companies are coming to grips with both how to react to and how to apply these new forms of communication.

It is imperative to have a free exchange of ideas through an open information environment. There will be significant economic, sociological, political, and cultural ramifications if we pursue a closed-content model. In times of rapid change, like during the Fukushima nuclear meltdown, easy access to information, public trust of leaders, and multidisciplinary and specialist experts are needed to build a solution. This trifecta of free exchanges, trust, and experts is needed to build a multilayer engagement model. This new model can interact with diverse facets of society, respond to brand deterioration and new media torrents, and comfort those who are impacted. With this open information accessibility model, we can provide content, analysis, and eventually create solutions to human-made and natural disasters while emotionally fulfilling our most basic human needs.

REFERENCES

Eisner, M. D. (2011, March). From Gutenberg to Zuckerberg. Omniture Summit 2011. Salt Lake City, UT.

Gross, D. (2010, June 22). Skip the yacht race: The three rules about conspicuous consumption for embattled CEOs. *Slate*. Retrieved from http://www.slate.com.

Hamilton, J. W. (2008, October). Accessibility to information resources in managing post-disaster trauma. Paper presented at the fifth World Congress for Psychotherapy. Beijing, China.

Johnson, C. A., & Walker-Smith, J. (2009, February 11). *Cutting through advertising clutter*. Retrieved from http://www.cbsnews.com.

Lamar, C., Nemeth, D. G., Gilliland, V., Whittington, L. T., & Reeder, K. (2008, October). Climate change questionnaire. Presented at Climate Change, Social Trauma and Lifestyle Modification Symposium at the Fifth World Congress for Psychotherapy. Beijing, China.

Turkle, S. (2011). *Alone together: Why we expect more from technology and less from each other*. New York: Basic Books.

Part III

Our Visionary Resources: Respect, Resilience, and Resolution

With an understanding of the science of natural events presented in Part 1 and coping models from psychological perspectives presented in Part 2, this part brings together those disciplines into a holistic view. The underlying principle prevails: that change is inevitable and we must adapt. These naturally occurring environmental traumas are out of control but humankind can either exacerbate or ameliorate the situation. While people typically live for less than 100 years; the Earth is over 4 billion years old, requiring that humans have perspective about how the environment is changing. The purpose of the concluding chapter in this part of the book is to offer a view of how to face the challenges posed by our ever-changing world. Armed with facts and the ability to cope with feelings, we can begin to heal ourselves and our planet.

12

Our Ever-Changing World: An Overview and a Look toward the Future

Robert B. Hamilton, Darlyne G. Nemeth, and Judy Kuriansky

Living in a dramatically shifting and environmentally-traumatized world is taking its toll on our citizens, communities, countries, and continents. Given humankind's inability to completely control the environment, as well as the growing abuse of natural resources, our planet is now "at risk." Natural changes in the environment that have led to trauma have been exacerbated by our actions, leading to incidences of debilitated habitats and even loss of life. This book has taken us through a journey of looking at our traumatized world through the lenses of natural science and psychology, providing a holistic view so we can better understand our world and better plan for healing ourselves and our planet. This chapter presents a brief overview and a look ahead.

It is worthwhile, in reviewing the nature of this book in this chapter, to look at the specific case of Hurricane Katrina, the strong winds that devastated the southern coast towns of the United States in 2005. That case provides a good example of the themes in this book by demonstrating the interactions of natural processes and human mistakes that led to an environmental tragedy, what should have been done to prevent the problem, lessons learned, and what is needed for prevention and recovery.

The tragedy of Hurricane Katrina is an example of the combustion of traumatic natural events and people's behaviors. Flooding was unpreventable, given the breaches of poorly constructed levees, yet as in the case of other such events, the tragic outcomes might have been avoided. History gives some insight into this. From its founding in 1718 by the French along a precarious crescent-shaped natural levee at the mouth of the Mississippi River, New Orleans has been a disaster waiting to happen (Kelman, 2007). Basically, when human beings choose to live in precarious places, they must be prepared. So, why do people insist on building in such precarious places without being prepared? In the case of New Orleans, as early as 1852, a civil engineer, Charles Ellet, offered a visionary, multitiered approach to protect the city. His plan included levee improvements, spillways, reservoirs, and wetlands (Kelman, 2007). Ambitions and politics, however, prevailed over holistic planning. Historical efforts at levee stabilization, which persisted over time, became based on "for profit" rather than "for people" motives.

One critical lesson from this tragedy is that we often ignore knowledge and select simple solutions to complex problems that maintain the illusion of safety but do not offer safety. Another lesson from the Hurricane Katrina tragedy is that we go about our daily lives without perspective, allowing self-serving leaders and corporations, driven by motives of power, control, and greed, to dominate our collective decision-making. Like New Orleanians, we go about life without paying attention to potential dangers.

To survive on our planet, especially with threats of environmental disasters, we must be alert to all aspects of our environment, and also pay attention to lessons learned, now available from many instances of global environmental tragedies. At this point in history, we need to face the reality that some events that are impossible to control, can be better managed. Better management includes preventing misguided efforts to control and reshape nature. As in the case of the hurricanes devastating New Orleans, humans' shortsighted decisions are resulting in physical illness, emotional trauma, and even death.

Psychologically, as a result of environmental trauma, we have become disoriented, displaced, discouraged, and distraught. Without resolution, these feelings dissolve into depression. Our minds become toxic, unable to think creatively and to solve problems. When we can rekindle our inner strength via hope, we can begin to heal. When our minds heal, our bodies can heal, and we can make healthy decisions to take care of ourselves and our planet.

Healing requires a spirit of universality, thinking of the global community rather than just our provincial selves. As long as we remain provincial, territorial, and/or imperialistic, our spirit and our environmental resources will continue to dissipate. Prosocial behavior, that is, thinking of the good of the whole, on the other hand, will rekindle our spirit.

With prosocial behavior, and proactive thinking (planning ahead), a healthy future is possible. This requires multitiered efforts, including a consideration of all points of view and all peoples, all levels and all scales. We must seek truth and avoid the political spin that manipulates us. In the past, bad choices have made us ill. Good choices can allow us to heal and to move on, even from environmental trauma.

This book is about our ever-changing world and how we as humans must wake up to these changes and better adapt lest we become extinct. Such a statement sounds stark, but it is necessary as a wake-up call. In recent times, environmental events have subjected many countries to natural disasters, threatening our survival and testing our strength. A recent onslaught of hurricanes, floods, tornadoes, oil spills and nuclear power plant explosions has killed thousands of people, devastated lands, and drained resources. While such events are often beyond the control of humans, there are ways we can prepare and even prevent the extent of damage such hazards cause. The chapters in this book have outlined those threats and suggested constructive actions we can take. In this chapter, we summarize those points.

Rather than just doomsaying, this book presents hope. While pointing out clear and present dangers to our air, waters, forests, livelihood and lives, we also emphasize that we are not totally helpless at the mercy of raging waters in floods, twisting winds in tornadoes, or shaking earth in quakes. We can take action to protect and prepare.

This book is reassurance that we can indeed have some control. A favorite concept in social psychology is one of locus on control. The Locus of Control Scale measures the degree to which you feel on the one hand that your life is controlled by destiny and fate, or on the opposite end that you are the master of your fate and that you can control whatever happens. The scale is a continuum so that you can rate yourself somewhere in-between. The most logical assessment is that we are not fully in control of everything that happens, but that we can control our actions and our reactions to what happens to us, particularly regarding those things over which we are not in control (like others' behavior and events in the universe). Culture and traditions also play a role in our ratings on the scale, namely that eastern peoples are more prone to believe in fate and destiny, while westerners tend to think they have more control over events and take more personal responsibility for what happens.

Even if you believe that you are not in control of what happens, the authors of these chapters alert us that we must take responsibility for what is happening to our universe and our natural resources. These chapters point out the value of our natural resources and how disregard can lead to disaster, as has happened in cases described in these chapters about the tragic oil spill, nuclear power plant explosion, and other events. The authors call for appreciation of nature. They also acknowledge appreciation for ourselves since some positive outcomes about humankind have emerged from the traumas. People have proved their ability to bounce back (called resilience, as referred to in these chapters), and peoples of the world who have been divergent (in race, culture, religion, or otherwise) have found more common ground in compassion for others in the face of natural disasters. Throughout this book, the chapter authors urge awareness of our natural resources, our personal strengths, our interpersonal support systems and the need to work together to protect ourselves and our environment.

In doing so, the message is not one of doom, but of hope. To boost that hope, this chapter reviews the issues and the way forward.

GAINING PERSPECTIVE

Inevitable changes caused by natural laws and the influences of humans and other components of our environment have created the world that we have today. It is not uniform, but varies from place to place. It is changing, so it varies in time. We know what it was in the past, but we cannot know the future precisely. We try to affect the future—and humans are very successful at doing so—but the results are not always what we planned or anticipated. This book has highlighted the importance of using lessons of the past to help us manage the future. We an behave proactively.

Our present world is not without problems, despite our attempts to prevent, manage or ameliorate them. As the numbers of people increase it will become more and more difficult to solve our problems. These problems include that we are dependent on energy and materials, and competition for them naturally increases as the number of people increases and our way of living changes, Just as we explored the tragedy of Hurricane Katrina, it is worthwhile to explore the issue of energy, as an example of the theme of this book in terms of coping with our environment, using a lens of natural science and psychology. Emotions run high when it comes to considering the issue of energy and climate change. We must be aware of all these emotions, and also of the conflicting factual perspectives. For example, in the United States today there is profound disagreement about the sources of our needed energy, both in the short term and in the long term. Each option has its pluses and minuses and is championed by specific constituencies. All potential sources have advantages and disadvantages and decisions are not easy. Availability is a major problem as is consequences of use. Our knowledge of availability changes as we discover new sources or new means of extracting old sources like fracking of subterranean deposits. A major complication to the issue is the effects of releasing carbon dioxide (CO_2), a greenhouse gas, into the atmosphere. While our CO_2 levels now are increasing, they are much lower than they have been in the past at times when humans had not yet evolved. However, many interest groups believe that CO_2 and other greenhouse gases are causing global warming. Some alarmists may appear to have an agenda, using fear to promote changes for personal profit. Recently, in the United States the EPA (Environmental Protection Agency) declared CO_2 a pollutant, despite the fact that it is a product of respiration that is essential for life. The concern about CO_2 release is greatly affecting energy use, seriously threatening the coal industry, and leading to our search for alternative energy supplies. While this issue is not resolved, it is crucial for all of us to be as educated as possible about the facts and the feelings surrounding there, in the search for solutions. Some suggested alternatives to use of oil and coal are to emphasis ethanol and other biofuels and to build farms of energy producing windmills and solar panels. These alternatives and others are promoted by many environmental groups, whose focus is on reducing reliance on oil and promoting alternatives. The use of these methods increases competition for land. Many who actively seek to reduce or eliminate habitat clearing and increase conservation efforts for endangered and rare species are supporters of the use of these lands for development of energy sources. The impact on the surface of drilling is much less than the impact from these alternative sources. It is clear that the two uses are somewhat incompatible.

The use of nuclear power is very appealing from the aspect of long-term energy production, yet the potential danger can be severe. Those planning such development did not adequately anticipate problems concerning safety and disposal of spent fuel. In this case, again, we did not think holistically enough. The problems in time and space were much larger than anticipated. The nuclear disasters discussed in this book have resulted in much suffering and ongoing problems. Once again, planning was not holistic enough. We must learn to deal with these types of problems, as they are universal and will increase as the world gets more crowded and in need of more energy and materials.

A theme that has been emphasized in this book is that change is inevitable. It is also not a mystery, even though at times we perceive it as such. In fact, change is the result of physical laws that are explicable and can be understood. Changes that occur can be explained and understood once we adequately know initial conditions and the nature of the available material and energy. As available material and energy are used up or depleted, conditions change, which in turn can result in some material or energy becoming unavailable. Thus, a cycle of events is created whereby changes engender other changes. As this cycle progresses, future changes may be different than earlier ones. In this way, nature is not static. Because change is universal, it is not surprising that many academic disciplines deal extensively with change, for example, anthropology, archeology, embryology, paleontology, evolution, genetics, and history. Change is also an important and unifying component of other disciplines, like biology, where most differences can be explained through an evolutionary analysis. Certainly the field of psychology is attentive to changes as a person goes through stages in life.

THE FUTURE

The outlook for the future depends on prosocial behavior and the Golden Rule. There are almost 7 billion people on earth now, and an additional 2 billion are expected by 2040. Our world already is crowded, with many people not being adequately nourished and lacking basic amenities. The correct path for the future is based on a hierarchical approach that involves all the levels of organization. With respect to human social relations, the bottom level in the levels of organization is comprised of the individual; followed by the family or the clan; followed by the city, state, and country; and then the biosphere, or earth level.

Each level affects us. We all seek to ensure our survival, at the individual level, with as much assistance from the higher levels as possible. With increasing complexity in the world and our dependence on distant resources, survival increasingly depends on higher levels and the actions of others. As a result, we must all help each other and follow the Golden Rule: "Do unto others as you would have them to do unto you." That rule is most easily applied to family, friends, and neighbors, but it should also apply to people at all levels. What is also needed is more prosocial behavior, meaning altruistic actions that benefit others more than oneself. The more we avoid selfishness and act in a prosocial way at all levels, the more likely we are to survive.

As we look to the future, we need to anticipate environmental change and plan to manage it. To minimize unexpected consequences, our approach must be holistic. We must realize the extent of our dependence on the environment and understand the relevant factors influencing what is around us. We must evaluate plans at all levels, and all appropriate spatial and temporal scales. Most of all, we must maintain the flexibility to back off plans that are not working, especially those that seriously modify the environment in unexpected ways.

We must remember the holistic principles espoused in this book. Each person is responsible for oneself and the greater good. In this way, the goals of a sustainable future in our natural habitat should, and can, be established by the people. The levels of organization within a country goes upward from the individual through the levels mentioned previously, that is. to the family, through to the city level, the state and then the national government and the international community. Governments should represent and support the people in their goals for a preserved environment and an ensured survival.

As noted above, attention must be paid to the dangers of special interest groups that actively promote their own agenda but are narrowly based and do not advance the common good. These groups may be passionate about their cause and work to thwart policies that have been democratically determined. People in the general public may be swayed to support the agendas of these special interest groups, which may not be in their own best interests or for the good of the greater whole. Awareness and education must be available to put the agendas of those with power, money, and influence in perspective so the needs of the people can be heard and heeded.

RESPECT, RESILIENCE, AND RESOLUTION

Coping with environmental change is the responsibility of all of the world's people, on all levels. In this regard, much can be learned from our Indigenous Peoples, as has been pointed out in this book. Clearly, Indigenous People respect the land, which they call "Mother Earth," a title that in itself implies respect.

They pass on this respect for the land to each new generation via their stories, songs, and poems. In her chapter on indigenous people, Dr. Gloria Mulcahy shares that her indigenous name means "she is of a good mind" and that achieving this state requires a lifetime of learning, transforming, and understanding as well as a holistic framework for addressing our environmental, interpersonal and intrapersonal issues. In stark contrast to others' behaviors that are self-serving and for-profit, indigenous people typically look at issues holistically for the good of all, strive to respect Mother Earth, and to honor their traditions and communities. For indigenous people, words are sacred, whereas in many other cultures, words are readily available for persuasion, half-truths, and hidden agendas. Balance and harmony have always been a part of indigenous peoples' approaches to the land and all living things. It would be wise for all of us to adopt this more relational approach to nature and fellow humans, an approach based on a system of cooperation and conciliation.

Indigenous peoples are also committed to respect and living in harmony, values that should be applied to every personal and environmental relationship. Actions contrary to this lesson have been replete throughout history, based on motives like power, control, greed, and religious and cultural domination, conversion and mainstreaming. For example, others who have dominated indigenous peoples have tried to break their connection to Mother Earth and have used, abused, and ravaged these people and their land. As a result, indigenous peoples in countries all over the world have suffered displacement, physical and sexual trauma, and destruction of families, as in the example of Africans who were transported across the Atlantic Ocean to become slaves in the southern states of America and elsewhere. In this way, the exploitation of indigenous peoples is as tragic as the decimation of natural resources pointed out earlier in this chapter and throughout this book. In the long run, imposing one group's will on another group is not constructive for our survival or the survival of our environment. All peoples must be respected in their natural habitats just as much as the water, air, and earth must be respected, as has been pointed out in chapters in this book.

It can take centuries—more than days, weeks, or months—to heal from such abuses of the land or of peoples. Yet hope resides in the fact that healing is possible. For example, despite abuses, many indigenous peoples have endured, clinging to their interdependence and never losing sight of their respect for the land. Even as those with more westernized ideas gained power, control, and wealth, the indigenous people did not lose sight of the land and all of the living things provided by Mother Earth. In this way, the chapter in this book about indigenous people serves as a good example of how we all need to preserve our traditions in order to survive.

While humans have often been unkind to humans, at times nature has not been kind to humans as well. Nature-induced hazards have resulted in severe emotional trauma and environmental damage. Persistent and pervasive emotional response to natural disasters like hurricanes, floods, tornadoes, tsunamis, and earthquakes have necessitated that people develop psychological resilience to mitigate the negative emotional aftermath. As pointed out in this book, people can thrive when given opportunities to face their feelings and fears. Programs and techniques have been developed by mental health professionals to give people the support and tools they need to muster their inner strengths. These have been pointed out in many chapters in this book.

As people are naturally interdependent, they thrive from receiving acknowledgement and affirmation from others about their experiences and losses. They must unfreeze themselves emotionally and begin to solve the challenges and problems caused by natural disasters. They must reassess and reprioritize their needs, and they must commit themselves to implementing positive recovery plans individually and collectively. These plans must be holistic, benefiting themselves, their families, their communities and their environment.

Chapters in this book highlight the role of resilience in survival. Resilience allows people to hope and cope. Resilient people are active, not passive. They are survivors, not victims. They recover from trauma and tap into their personal strengths and support systems to rebuild. That ability to bounce back was evident in Haiti after the devastating earthquake there, where the theme of the people is one of *rebati*, which means to "build back better." The robust experiences of people was also evident after the tragedy of Hurricane Katrina in the United States.

Recovery, rebuilding, and resolution of emotional and physical disruption are what all people, all living things, and Mother Earth seek in the aftermath of environmental disaster. Whether the disaster is induced by nature, by humans or a combination of both, recovery is a process that is universal. Yet, this process is not easy nor necessarily a linear experience. It can be a process of forward movement, then regression and then forward movement again. As pointed out in a chapter in this book, six stages can be anticipated: shock, survival mode, basic needs, awareness of loss, susceptibility to spin and fraud, and resolution. During these stages, memories and pains can return on anniversary dates of the trauma when cues bring unresolved feelings and fears to the surface. When these are brought into awareness and processed, post-traumatic growth, healing and forward movement can happen.

Healing with forward movement is a personal process as well as a group process that has to happen on a community level. Just as individuals must move forward and not allow themselves to be victimized, so must communities. Communities must empower themselves, build on resilience, and use the tragedy as an opportunity for growth and social cohesion. Social support is needed to brace communities for collective emotional complications and to create new connections to foster cooperation and strength. Group gatherings and programs can foster healing and build stronger community support. Environmental trauma brings havoc to communities in the form of physical destruction (e.g., of homes and places of business and worship), which is compounded by collective emotional distress. Adding to the drama of this mix in the aftermath of environmental damage is the potential for the emergence of violence, evidenced in looting, pillaging and personal attacks. When community infrastructure is destroyed by disasters, personal values disintegrate, relationships become strained, and people lose control.

But this situation is not hopeless. Communities can develop plans of action for catastrophic events. Special attention and services must be made available to vulnerable groups such as children, older adults, and even men, traditionally expected to be stoic. Assistance must be made available for traumatized citizens, as well as for the diaspora, which also suffers. Memorials, music, art, spiritual events, and rituals can valuably be included in recovery plans. In the aftermath of environmental disaster, people need government action, but they also need people-to-people action. Caring should be personalized. In addition, authority figures should be on-site to offer support and reassurance, Communities must reach out to other traumatized communities to feel the connectedness and reassurance of others. Fortunately, some positive outcomes balance these exceptionally negative after-effects. Public sharing and collective community interventions can help ameliorate traumatic symptoms. Community helpers can aid and facilitate healing. Professional mental health services can also mitigate the suffering of survivors.

Another dimension of our relationship to our environment, and to healing, is spirituality. It is increasingly important in the recovery process. Connection to spirit can bring hope to the hopeless and turn victims into survivors in the face of environmental trauma. A recommitment to nature through spirituality greatly enhances opportunities for a positive outcome.

The overall theme of this book calls for a human–nature connection. This notion of a human–nature connection is now being reaffirmed as a basic aspect of psychological health. Fields like ecopsychology seek to promote interaction with nature not only as a part of the healing journey but also as a requirement of sustainability. A tenet in the theory of biophilia (the bond between human beings and other living systems), that is now becoming mainstream, encourages love of life and living systems. By the opposite token, biophobia focuses on fear and avoidance of living things and Mother Earth, whereby biophobics have negative relationships with the land and therefore disregard its importance.

When extreme meteorological or other traumatic events occur, social injustice issues may arise and further complicate the recovery process. This was vividly illustrated during the aftermath of Hurricane Katrina, whereby the poor and socially disadvantaged people were herded into the New Orleans Superdome (a sports arena) as a shelter; yet their basic needs—for safety, food, and water—went unmet, in what became an over-crowded, unsanitary, and unholy environment.

In our current technological world, new methods of communication can be harnessed for healing from environmental disaster. Information presents another opportunity to increase a positive outcome in the aftermath of environmental trauma. Social networking and new media can greatly assist in community awareness and healing. The availability of Internet and social networking resources allows people to connect, to seek or receive good information as quickly as possible, and to evaluate and avoid spin from governments, corporations, or special interest groups. Media can be so helpful in the aftermath of disaster, through both traditional forms (e.g., radio, TV) and new forms (e.g., blogging, Internet message boards). The nature of peoples' characterological response styles of responding to trauma, as has been tracked by Internet surveys, must also be understood. As a result, technologies can be applied appropriately to people with those different styles in order to help them rebuild after crises. For example, the Now Generation prefers Internet and cellphone technologies to radio and television communication. Studies have shown that only certain styles of people sought to better understand the psychological aftermath of the BP oil spill. In addition, better and more timely information in the days, weeks, and months following the environmental tragedy, allowing for individual voices to be heard, would have lessened the negative psychological impact on individual and community levels. The lesson from this environmental tragedy is that technology is neutral but how we use it is not. Technology can either assist in resolution, or, as in the case of the BP oil spill, it can hinder recovery.

A UNIQUE VIEW

To our knowledge, this book is unique in that it brings the natural sciences together with the social and psychological sciences. This multilevel collaboration has allowed a holistic view of human and natural resource management to emerge. While some critics may say that these disciplines do not overlap, the authors in this book prove otherwise. The author of our chapter on living waters, Dr. Yasuo Onishi, an international expert on environmental risk assessment, has recognized the important role of psychology in citizen recovery. His consultation was requested in both the Fukushima and Chernobyl nuclear disasters, and with colleagues, Oleg V. Voitsekhovich and Mark J. Zheleznyak, he co-authored the 2007 book *Chernobyl: What Have We Learned?* These natural scientists concluded that the largest public health effect of the Chernobyl accident was psychological and that, 20 years later, the two most critical remaining issues have been mental health and socioeconomic problems. For his contributions to the assessment and remediation efforts for the Fukushima disaster and the BP oil spill, Dr. Onishi received two awards from the U.S. Department of Energy.

We must all work together to heal ourselves and our supporting planet. This requires a multilevel approach to thinking, planning, experiencing and solving problems. No one discipline has all of the answers. To survive, and indeed to flourish, in our psychological and physical environments, we must follow these guiding principles:

- Understand our changing environments
- Be alert to environmental dangers
- Learn from history
- Be responsible citizens
- Resolve emotional trauma
- Behave proactively
- Act prosocially, for the good of all
- Embrace the inevitability of change
- Live in peace and harmony within ourselves and with the world

REFERENCES

Kelman, A. (2007). Boundary issues: Clarifying New Orleans's murky edges. *Journal of American History, 94,* 695–703. Retrieved July 23, 2011from http://www .journalofamericanhistory.org/projects/katrina/Kelman.html.

Onishi, Y., Voitsekhovich, O. V., & Zheleznyak, M. J. (2007). *Chernobyl: What have we learned? The successes and failures to mitigate water contamination over 20 years* (vol. 12). Dordrecht, The Netherlands: Springer.

Epilogue

Judy Kuriansky

In the aftermath of the 2004 Asian tsunami, psychologists facilitating groups for recovery found that a predominant question of survivors was, "Will this happen again?" Many were not only worried about a recurrence but confused about what actually happened. Additionally, while the people were impressively getting on with their lives despite the direst circumstances, beneath the surface they were struggling emotionally. Faced with the extensive loss of loved ones, homes, and livelihood from living near the water, they were suffering from deep depression and hopelessness.

This sad situation is testimony to the importance of the approach of this book. Survivors were perplexed by the actions of nature. They needed to know what caused the terrorizing floods. Why did it happen? When would it happen again? Such anxiety caused by lack of information about the natural environment compounds psychological devastation caused by extensive losses.

Thus, what was helpful in the healing process was a multidimensional approach. This means providing survivors with knowledge about nature; for example, specific information about what a tsunami is, what causes it, and the conditions under which it could happen again. Knowledge included the not-so-welcome news that another occurrence cannot be definitively predicted, and the more optimistic news that a better emergency alert system and preventive measures can help people be more prepared to prevent extensive multilevel damage. The survivors of the tsunami who participated in the groups were relieved and reassured to have this knowledge. Essentially it gave them more control over their environment and therefore their lives.

Another equally important service was to help the survivors cope emotionally. Even in cultures where talking about troubles is not traditional, having a safe place to discuss the trauma, and even just the knowledge about "normal" and expected emotional responses, offered added relief and reassurance.

This multilevel approach that proved helpful to survivors in the aftermath of an environmental trauma is the essence and intent of this book. The chapters offer an understanding of one's outer world and one's inner world, as the most effective way to cope with the disasters that we continually faced today.

The authors, as psychologists and natural scientists, and as researchers and practitioners, are hopeful that this holistic approach can better arm us for the present and future. Also, as nongovernmental organization (NGO) representatives at the United Nations, we are also encouraged that governments, academia, businesses, and citizens and all levels of civil society are paying attention to the environment and to psychology's role in fostering development.

This holistic view was evident, for example, at a recent high-level meeting at the United Nations about the future of world development that brought together experts from all disciplines, including government leaders, the UN Secretary General, Nobel Prize–winning economists, natural scientists and, notably, psychologists. This meeting focused on including a measure of development focused on the level of people's happiness, satisfaction with life and quality of life, rather than just on monetary gains. The Royal Government of Bhutan is leading the way in this movement, as is evident in their Gross National Happiness Index. Another index, the Happy Planet Index, measures a country's accomplishments in terms of a green economy as well as citizens' life satisfaction. Notably, the "father of positive psychology," Martin Seligman, was an invited speaker at the Bhutan-convened conference, and psychologists from all over the world, including this author continue to participate in the ongoing development of the initiative.

The importance of attending to our environment by all disciplines is also evident by the intense attention given to the UN Conference on Sustainable Development, where world leaders, academicians, and representatives from civil societies' interest groups of all kinds came together to adopt practical measures on how to solve the world's environmental problems, like conserving energy; ensuring a green economy; clean energy; reducing poverty; and assuring social equity, decent jobs, environmental protection, food security and sustainable agriculture; clean water and oceans in our increasingly crowded and endangered planet. Importantly, supporting the theme of this book, the topic of disaster readiness is also on the agenda. This meeting is referred to as "Rio +20," named for its being the twentieth anniversary of the first meetings of its kind held in Rio de Janeiro, Brazil. Also consistent with this book's theme; bridging natural sciences and psychology, the coalition of psychological associations accredited at the United Nations advocated on behalf of the contributions of psychology to the achievement of sustainable development and preservation of the environment. The coalition presented a statement at the conference emphasizing psychosocial well-being, empowerment, mental health care and social protection, and human rights, social equality and social justice for all.

To readers of this book, the co-editors thank you, as you clearly care about healing ourselves and our planet. You clearly agree with us that we must move away from ravaging the environment to instead respecting our environment, and living in harmony with our surroundings. This approach is essential for a healthy mind, body, and spirit.

As natural scientists, we understand the importance of knowing the facts, and as psychologists we know the value of processing feelings. This dual approach, inherent in this book, is the most effective way to deal with our environmentally traumatized self and planet. Psychologically, as a result of environmental trauma, we become disoriented, displaced, discouraged, and distraught. With understanding and processing the natural stages of recovery, we do not have to dissolve into depression and a state of feeling powerless, but can think and act creatively, solve problems, rekindle our inner strength and embrace hope. While we cannot control all aspects of what happens in a changeable world—while we cannot stop an earthquake, tornado or tsunami—we can understand what these events are, and prepare logistically and emotionally for their occurrence and aftermath. We can be survivors instead of victims. And we can preserve our emotions and our planet to ensure sustainable safety and healing.

About the Editors and Contributors

THE EDITORS

DARLYNE G. NEMETH, Ph.D., M.P., M.P.A.P., C.G.P., an accomplished clinical, medical, and neuropsychologist, has a broad-spectrum practice at the Neuropsychology Center of Louisiana (NCLA). She is also Director of Neuropsychology at Sage Rehabilitation Hospital Outpatient Services. Dr. Nemeth was among the first medical psychologists in Louisiana to obtain prescriptive authority. She is a fellow of the American Psychological Association (APA) and she has served as World Council of Psychotherapy (WCP) United Nations (UN) nongovernmental organization (NGO) Delegate and Vice President for the U.S. chapter. As an expert in group dynamics, Dr. Nemeth has been nationally and internationally recognized for her Hurricane Anniversary Wellness Workshops, which were offered to the victims/survivors of Hurricanes Katrina and Rita in the summer of 2006. Her website is www.louisiananeuropsych.com.

ROBERT B. HAMILTON, Ph.D., is currently Vice President of Envirosphere Consulting, LLC. He served for 35 years on the faculty of the School of Forestry, Wildlife and Fisheries (now School of Renewable Natural Resources) at Louisiana State University. Dr. Hamilton's main research interest is wildlife habitat management, especially with regard to birds in bottomland hardwood forests. He is particularly interested in how levels of organization affect our views of the world. Much conflict is caused by various groups focusing on different levels, but goals, methods, and areas of interest all vary among levels. Dr. Hamilton believes the ecosystem and biosphere levels are especially important when dealing with management issues. His website is www.envirosphereconsulting.com

JUDY KURIANSKY, Ph.D., is a licensed clinical psychologist at Columbia University Teachers College and Honorary Professor at Peking University Health Sciences Center in China. UN NGO representative for the International Association of Applied Psychology and the WCP, Director of Psychosocial Programs for U.S. Doctors for Africa, and founder of the Global Kids Connect Project and the Stand Up for Peace Project; she conducts trainings and workshops worldwide on psychological first aid. The author of many articles and books, including *Beyond Bullets and Bombs: Grassroots Peace Building between Palestinians and Israelis*, she is also an award-winning journalist who appears on media worldwide. Her website is www.DrJudy.com.

THE CONTRIBUTORS

The architect JOÃO LUCILIO RUEGGER DE ALBUQUERQUE, born in Sao Paulo, Brazil, has more than 30 years of experience in the environmental area. He was the Director of the Evaluation of Environmental Impact Department of the Environment Secretariat of Sao Paulo State for four years. In this office, he was responsible for environmental impact assessments, including highways, mining plans, and hydroelectric power stations in the Mata Atlântica Region. Being a master in Environmental Impact Assessment, he was appointed to serve a season in the Environment Ministry of France. João Albuquerque has worked for the last 20 years in the Mata Atlântica Biosphere Reserve, where he has coordinated important programs and projects.

GLORIA ALVERNAZ MULCAHY, Ph.D., CPsych., comes from the Monterrey Bay area of California and is of Tsalagi/Aniyunwiya ancestry. She is an academic, psychologist, researcher, mixed media artist, musician, poet, and member of the League of Canadian Poets. She is Professor Emerita at the University of Western Ontario, Canada; Academic Research Associate, Centre for Research and Education on Violence against Women and Children; and Adjunct Professor Faculty of Education there. She has authored numerous publications and produced several documentary films focusing on indigenous social issues, the environment, and mental health. Dr. Mulcahy serves as WCP Vice President for the Canadian chapter and as a WCP NGO representative to the United Nations.

ROBERT A. MULLER, Ph.D., is a professor emeritus in the Department of Geography and Anthropology at Louisiana State University (LSU). He came to LSU in 1969 after appointments at the University of California at Berkeley and Rutgers University. At LSU, Dr. Muller and his graduate students utilized climatic water-budget components for analyses of environmental impacts across the South, pioneered the development of weather types for environmental analyses, and, with Dr. Barry Kelm, co-authored a book on the long-term climatology of hurricane strikes around the Gulf of Mexico and the Atlantic Coast. Dr. Muller also founded the Southern Regional Climate Center at LSU with federal funding.

DONALD F. NEMETH, Ph.D., has worked in the academic, research, and corporate worlds. He taught geology at Citrus College in Azusa, California, and at

California State University in Los Angeles, California. His dissertation research, conducted on the North Slope of Alaska, concentrated on landforms near the apex of the Colville River Delta. He was a member of the Research Staff at the Institute for Environmental Studies at Louisiana State University, Baton Rouge, Louisiana, where he studied salt domes in northern Louisiana. Dr. Nemeth also worked as a Developmental Geologist for Marathon Oil Company in Lafayette, Louisiana. Dr. Nemeth is currently President of Envirosphere Consulting, LLC, in Baton Rouge, Louisiana. His website is www.envirosphereconsulting.com.

ANNA T. ONISHI, CFA, is an expert in Internet intelligence and marketing strategy. Ms. Onishi has extensive experience managing award-winning marketing and analytical workstreams for companies such as General Motors, AT&T, Procter & Gamble, Bayer, and Liberty Mutual Insurance. Her work has included creating and implementing multichannel analytical foundations for marketing and sales, advising senior management on exploring new business ventures, and developing and implementing corporate strategy for sales growth and profitability, operational efficiency, and brand health. She serves on an advisory board to Adobe. Ms. Onishi was formerly a bond analyst at Fidelity Investments, conducting in-depth research for over $80 billion in portfolio holdings and at the Federal Reserve Bank of Boston.

YASUO ONISHI, Ph.D., an Adjunct Full Professor at Washington State University, is a U.S. pioneer on environmental and risk assessments. He received two 2011 Secretary Awards, the highest nonmonetary award of the U.S. Department of Energy for his contributions to responses to the 2011 Fukushima Nuclear Plant accident and the BP 2010 oil spill accident in the Gulf of Mexico. He has extensively worked on water and waste issues, nuclear plants, carbon dioxide disposal, oil spills, and environmental/risk assessment/remediation. His computer models have been the most advanced contaminant transport codes for surface waters for three decades. He was the U.S. Government Coordinator of Chernobyl water and soil environmental program. He is an adjunct member of the National Council of Radiation Protection and Measurements, and was a member of the National Academy of Sciences' committee on oil spill. He has been a technical advisor to the International Atomic Energy Agency. He was a delegation of the National Academy of Sciences to 2009 workshop and 2010 international conference on climate change.

ALEXANDER P. STEGER received his B.S. in Mathematics from Louisiana State University and is pursuing his Ph.D. in Clinical Psychology at Palo Alto University. He has been a Research Associate at the Neuropsychology Center of Louisiana (NCLA) and at Vanderbilt University in the Department of Psychology and Human Development. Through his affiliation with NCLA,

Mr. Steger has co-authored numerous presentations for meetings of the American Psychological Association, the Louisiana Psychological Association, the National Academy of Neuropsychology, and the International Neuropsychological Society. He has had 15 years of software development experience. He enjoys playing chess competitively, and, in 2008, Mr. Steger won the Louisiana State Chess Championship.

L. TAIGHLOR WHITTINGTON graduated from Louisiana State University with a B.A. in Psychology and intends to pursue a doctorate in Clinical Neuropsychology. She is a Clinical Assistant for Darlyne G. Nemeth, Ph.D., M.P., M.P.A.P., C.G.P., at both the Neuropsychology Center of Louisiana (NCLA) and at Sage Rehabilitation Hospital Outpatient Services. Ms. Whittington has co-authored several presentations for meetings of the American Psychological Association, the Louisiana Psychological Association, the National Academy of Neuropsychology, the International Neuropsychological Society, and the Louisiana Group Psychotherapy Society. In 2010, Ms. Whittington received the award for Best Undergraduate Research Poster at the sixty-second Annual Convention of the Louisiana Psychological Association.

SUSAN ZELINSKI, B.A. is a graduate student in the Department of Clinical Psychology, Columbia University Teachers College, working toward her master's degree. She graduated from Lehigh University in 2008 with a double major in Psychology and English, and plans to pursue a Ph.D. in Clinical Psychology, with a goal of integrating the fields of psychology, nature, and spirituality to help people heal through the use of humanistic therapies.

Index

Note: Page numbers in *italics* indicate an in-depth discussion. Page numbers followed by an *f* refer to figures. Page numbers followed by a *t* refer to tables.